"Unwrapping"
the
Common
Core

"Unwrapping" the Common Core

A Practical Process to Manage Rigorous Standards

► LARRY AINSWORTH ◄

LEAD+
LEARN
PRESS

ENGLEWOOD, COLORADO

The Leadership and Learning Center
5680 Greenwood Plaza Boulevard, Suite 550
Greenwood Village, Colorado 80111
Phone 1.866.399.6019 | Fax 303.504.9417
www.leadandlearn.com

Published by Lead + Learn Press.

Cataloging-in-Publication Data

    Ainsworth, Larry.
      "Unwrapping" the common core : a practical process to manage rigorous standards /
    Larry Ainsworth.
         pages   cm
      Includes bibliographical references and index.
      ISBN 978-1-935588-51-1
        1. Education—Curricula—Standards—United States—States.   I. Title.
    LB3060.83.A36 2014   375'.0010973
                                                 QBI14-600181

ISBN 978-1-935588-51-1

Printed in the United States of America

01 02 03 04 05 06   19 18 17 16 15 14
4500515898   A B C D E F G

CONTENTS

LIST OF FIGURES

ABOUT THE AUTHOR

 **Larry Ainsworth** is the author or coauthor of 14 books, including this volume— *"Unwrapping" the Common Core* (2014), *Prioritizing the Common Core* (2013), *Rigorous Curriculum Design* (2010), *Common Formative Assessments* (2006), *"Unwrapping" the Standards* (2003), *Power Standards* (2003), *Five Easy Steps to a Balanced Math Program* (2000 and 2006), *Student Generated Rubrics* (1998), and his coauthored collection of Rigorous Curriculum Design success stories, *Getting Started with Rigorous Curriculum Design: How School Districts Are Successfully Redesigning Their Curricula for the Common Core* (2013).

Larry served as the Executive Director of Professional Development at The Leadership and Learning Center in Englewood, Colorado, from 1999 to 2013. He traveled nationally and internationally to assist school systems in implementing best practices related to standards, assessment, curriculum, and instruction across all grades and content areas. Throughout his career as a professional developer, Larry has delivered keynote addresses and breakout sessions across North America and in Latin America and regularly worked on-site in school systems to assist leaders and educators in understanding and implementing powerful standards-based practices: prioritizing and "unwrapping" state standards and Common Core standards, developing common formative assessments, designing authentic performance tasks, and creating rigorous curricular units of study in all content areas, pre-kindergarten through grade 12.

Drawing upon 24 years of experience as an upper elementary and middle school classroom teacher in demographically diverse schools, Larry brings a varied background and wide range of professional experiences to each of his presentations.

ACKNOWLEDGMENTS

I am grateful to the following four school districts that generously contributed kindergarten through high school examples of "unwrapped" Common Core State Standards in English language arts and literacy and in mathematics for inclusion in this edition:

- San Diego Unified School District, San Diego, California
- McMinnville School District, McMinnville, Oregon
- Bloomfield Public Schools, Bloomfield, Connecticut
- West Hartford Public Schools, West Hartford, Connecticut

It was my sincere honor and privilege to work on-site in these school districts, guiding hundreds of K–12 educators through my curriculum framework, Rigorous Curriculum Design (RCD), in their collaborative efforts to create new curricular units of study to meet the instruction and assessment demands of the Common Core. Even though it is not possible to acknowledge here the names of each and every educator who gave of their time to be away from their classrooms throughout this process, I want each of you to know how much I respect and value the contributions you made to this body of work. Thank you for all you do for your students.

My special thanks extend to the following key individuals in each of these four school systems who invested so much of their time, thought, and energy to overseeing the development of these "unwrapping" examples before, during, and after each of our professional development sessions:

San Diego Unified School District: Debbie Higdon, K–12 Program Manager for English Language Arts, and her valued ELA colleagues: Rosemary Staley, Program Manager for Secondary Literacy, Jennifer O'Connor, and Alexis Conerty; Sherry Lawson, K–12 Program Manager for Mathematics, and her equally valued secondary and elementary mathematics colleagues: Carol Treglio and Miko Uhuru. I also wish to thank Linda Trousdale, Program Manager Office of Teaching and Learning, and Karen Gomez, kindergarten classroom educator, for their ongoing assistance throughout all three cohorts of the RCD curricular unit design sessions. Being able to work closely with Debbie, Sherry, their assistants, and nearly 400 San Diego educators and instructional specialists throughout the 2012/13 school year was one of the brightest highlights of my professional development career.

McMinnville School District: Kyra Donovan, Director of Elementary and

Federal Programs, who has facilitated and guided the full implementation of the Rigorous Curriculum Design process in all district schools for several years. Even in her role as district administrator, Kyra is a teacher's teacher. Her deep commitment to implementing and sustaining educational best practices in order to help every educator and student succeed is exemplary. I would also like to extend a special thank you to Superintendent Dr. Maryalice Russell who has for years fully supported the important work of implementing and sustaining standards-based best practices to improve learning and achievement for all McMinnville students. In addition, the entire McMinnville School District education community should be recognized for their hard work and dedication to improving student outcomes.

Bloomfield Public Schools: Dr. Ellen Stolz, Chief Academic Officer, who saw the value of the "unwrapping" process as critical to educators deeply understanding the learning expectations of the Common Core and its role in redesigning district curricula using the RCD model. Thank you for being the champion of this work to benefit all Bloomfield students and teachers. Thanks also to Dr. James Thompson, Superintendent, and to the school leaders and educators who so generously gave of their time and energy to create their Rigorous Curriculum Design units, in which the "unwrapping" process sections were a key part.

West Hartford Public Schools: Dr. Sally Alubicki, former Director of Teaching and Assessment, who has continued to lead, mentor, and guide district educators through the RCD process, even into her retirement. Sally, thank you for your unflagging support and enthusiasm, and for always being willing to go "above and beyond," not only for students and educators, but also to accommodate my frequent requests for West Hartford examples to include in my books. I would also like to especially thank Dr. Eileen Howley, former Assistant Superintendent for Instruction and Curriculum, who, along with Sally, was instrumental in bringing me to West Hartford to lead district educators and leaders through the RCD process over a period of several months. Lastly, to Paul W. Vicinus, Jr., Director of Secondary Education, Jennifer Parsons, English Language Arts Curriculum Specialist, and Christine Newman, Mathematics Curriculum Specialist, my sincere appreciation for your ongoing assistance in facilitating the "production days" with your content-area groups.

I would also like to extend a sincere thank you to my former colleagues from The Leadership and Learning Center: Lori Cook, Lisa Cebelak, Aimee Corrigan, and Kara Vandas. Each shared with me examples of "unwrapped" Common Core State Standards in mathematics and English language arts and literacy developed in their seminar work with educators and leaders.

INTRODUCTION

"Unwrapping," from the Beginning to Now

In 2003, I wrote *"Unwrapping" the Standards: A Simple Process to Make Standards Manageable.* It contains more than 85 examples of "unwrapped" standards, with topical Big Ideas and Essential Questions specific to all four grade spans (primary, upper elementary, middle school, and high school) across various content areas.

Since that time thousands of educators all over the United States and Canada have applied that relatively simple process to their state and provincial standards, respectively. The reason it is used so widely is that it works! It is a practical and highly effective way to determine—in advance of curriculum, instruction, and assessment planning—exactly what the wording of the standards requires students to know and be able to do. From the beginning, educators liked "unwrapping" because it provided a simple way to make sense of the standards—it made them *manageable,* as educators in Lawrence Township, Indianapolis, Indiana, told me in 2002 when I asked them what value they saw in the process.

Many educators are "singletons." This has nothing to do with their marital status, of course: it means they happen to be the only one who teaches a particular grade or course and must do all of their instructional planning and teaching alone, without benefit of collaboration with other colleagues. One of the great benefits of the "unwrapping" process is that any educator in any content area and any grade, Pre-K through 12, can apply it immediately and on one's own. It does not require discussion and agreement with colleagues, although grade-level and course-specific teams find tremendous benefit in working through the process together. This is particularly apparent during key parts of the process, such as determining the level of thinking rigor for each skill-concept matchup and deciding the Big Ideas and Essential Questions. This collaboration not only provides professional support to one another; it also leads to a shared and consistent understanding of instructional targets and related assessment questions.

Even though "unwrapping" quickly became a popular tool for working with the standards, it remained somewhat of an isolated professional practice. Educators saw its value but not its relevancy or connection to other professional practices. To reveal how tremendously useful it could be, I realized it needed to be paired with assessment and instruction, in that order. As a result, three years later I coauthored, with Donald Viegut, *Common Formative Assessments: How to Connect Standards-Based Instruction and Assessment* (2006). In this book we presented the important connections between "unwrapping" and the *assessment* of those standards. By intentionally matching the assessment questions to the "unwrapped" concepts and skills, educators could then "backwards plan" their instruction to enable students to demonstrate proficiency on the assessment and thus demonstrate to what degree they had actually learned the standards in focus.

In my 2010 book, *Rigorous Curriculum Design: How to Create Curricular Units of Study that Align Standards, Instruction, and Assessment,* I extended these connections even further by placing "unwrapping," creation of the assessment, and related instructional planning within the context of *units of study.* Guided by the RCD framework, educators would follow these sequential steps:

- Select a specific unit of study

- Identify the standards (priority and supporting) to match that unit focus

- "Unwrap" the unit's Priority Standards (those to receive the greatest emphasis)

- Plan the end-of-unit assessment to directly align with those "unwrapped" standards

- Design the instructional pathways to enable students to learn those targeted concepts and skills and prepare for the unit assessment.

Even though the "unwrapping" process is clearly explained in *Rigorous Curriculum Design,* in 2012 I authored an additional chapter, "Connecting Common Core State Standards with Common Formative Assessments," in *Book Four, Navigating Assessment and Collaboration with the Common Core State Standards.* This chapter focused only on how to create the unit assessment in 10 sequential steps. But it underscored again the importance of "unwrapping" the standards for that unit *first.* Applicable to all grades K–12 in English language arts and math, the chapter shows the direct connections between the actual unit assessment questions and the concepts, skills, and taxonomy levels of the unit's "unwrapped" Priority Common Core Standards.

"Unwrapping" the Common Core:
A Practical Process to Manage Rigorous Standards

I wanted this present volume to serve as a stand-alone, how-to guide for busy educators who need a straightforward, practical, and proven way to work with the new standards. In it, I have explained each part of the "unwrapping" process in more detail than was possible in previous publications and also provided 60 illustrative examples of "unwrapped" Common Core standards in both English language arts and mathematics in all four grade spans: primary, upper elementary, middle school, and high school.

It is important to note up front that the "unwrapping" process remains universal in its application; it can be successfully used by *all* educators in *all* grades and *all* content areas, pre-kindergarten through grade 12. I have successfully taught this process to educators in visual and performing arts, physical education, early childhood education, and career and technical education throughout the United States and Canada. Even though the focus of this present volume is its application to the Common Core, "unwrapping" remains an effective way to deconstruct *all* state standards and provincial learning outcomes. Readers in states and provinces not implementing the Common Core will find new insights and helpful clarifications added since the original edition was published in 2003 that will prove applicable to their own standards and learning outcomes.

Over the last three years, while assisting educators across the country in the design of rigorous curricular units of study based upon the Common Core, I have had the opportunity to further refine the "unwrapping" process and help educators see its critical role in designing meaningful assessment, curriculum, and instruction. I have continued to incorporate the valued suggestions and insights I have received from educators all over the United States. One of the reasons this process continues to be embraced so enthusiastically by everyone is because it truly reflects the "collective wisdom" of all those K–12 educators with whom I have had the great fortune to collaborate. I am eager to share in these pages new insights and connections from my professional development experiences working with educators across the K–12 spectrum in both content areas of the Common Core.

What's New?

Even though the process of "unwrapping" has remained fundamentally the same since the beginning, two specific changes have occurred. First, there has been a shift away from educators picking and choosing random standards to "unwrap" for an isolated instructional topic or context. Now educators, working collaboratively in grade-level and course-level teams, will "unwrap" standards that have first been assigned to a specific *unit of study.*

> A **unit of study** is defined as a series of specific lessons, learning experiences, and related assessments based on designated Priority Standards—standards to emphasize the most—along with related supporting standards, for an instructional focus that may last anywhere from two to six weeks depending on the number and rigor of standards for that unit.

For this to work most effectively, *all* of the standards for a particular grade level or course must first be prioritized and then assigned to specific units of study. As presented in *Rigorous Curriculum Design,* these are the foundational steps for unit construction, a foundation that begins with prioritizing the Common Core for each grade and "naming" the specific units for that grade or course. Educators then "unwrap" the designated standards for that unit, one unit at a time. (Chapter 9 provides a synopsis of each of the steps of the Rigorous Curriculum Design model.)

Let me interject here an important note about the need to prioritize the Common Core *first,* in advance of "unwrapping," assessment creation, and curriculum design. Today educators often learn how to prioritize and "unwrap" the Common Core State Standards (CCSS) in close succession. These two widespread practices work closely together to provide the focus and the specificity educators need to design effective assessment, curriculum, and instruction, in that order. The challenge in "unwrapping" and prioritizing the standards *all at the same time* is that it can become an overwhelming and exceedingly time-consuming endeavor. Each practice is quite involved. A quicker, easier, and more manageable approach is to "unwrap" the already identified Priority Standards *within units of study after those identified standards have been assigned to the* units (this is explained further in Chapter 1).

The second important change in this book addresses the need to closely reference, during the "unwrapping" process, respected educational taxonomies of cognitive skills, such as the revised Bloom's Taxonomy (Anderson and Krathwohl, 2001)
and Webb's Depth of Knowledge (Webb, 1997). Doing so will enable educators to
pinpoint the level of rigor of each "unwrapped" skill. In this way, educators can then
more closely write assessment questions and plan related instruction to reflect that
same level of rigor. I will describe this in greater detail in Chapter 2: "Create the
Graphic Organizer."

Overview of the "Unwrapping" Process

Each part of the process will be fully described and illustrated in its own chapter. For
now, here is a quick overview:

1. **"Unwrap" the Unit Priority Standards.** Analyze the assigned Priority
   Standards within each individual unit of study to determine the
   specific, teachable concepts and skills (what students need to know
   and be able to do).

2. **Create a Graphic Organizer.** Next prepare a graphic organizer
   (outline, bulleted list, concept map, or chart) as a visual display of
   the "unwrapped" concepts and skills. Determine each skill's
   approximate levels of Bloom's Taxonomy and Webb's Depth of
   Knowledge. This will reveal each skill's level of rigor.

3. **Decide the Big Ideas.** Referring to the "unwrapped" concepts, now
   decide the Big Ideas (key understandings, student "aha's") you want
   the students to discover on their own by the end of the unit of
   study.

4. **Write the Essential Questions.** Referring to the Big Ideas, write
   open-ended Essential Questions that will engage students to
   discover for themselves the related Big Ideas and be able to state
   them in their own words by the end of the unit.

Even though the entire "unwrapping" process was developed in response to the
need for a more effective way to manage the standards, essentially this is about *good
teaching.* Experienced educators have told me that this technique formalizes what
they have been doing informally throughout their careers: deciding what is impor-

tant for students to learn in a particular content area ("unwrapping"), helping students make connections to other areas of study and utilize higher-level thinking skills (Big Ideas), and engaging students in the material to be studied by setting a purpose for learning (Essential Questions). Take away the standards and all high-stakes accountability tests, and educators would still utilize these methods because they are practical and because they work.

Organization of the Book

The book is organized in three parts.

Part One: The Process

Part One describes the complete "unwrapping" process in four chapters. Examples in both English language arts and literacy and mathematics illustrate each part. I recommend reading through *all* of the examples and accompanying commentary, even if your primary interest is in one content area or the other. Key points relevant to both content areas are interspersed throughout the text and will likely answer many of the questions that are sure to arise as you work through the process later on your own. To prevent the explanatory chapters from becoming too weighty, I selected just one elementary school example and two examples at the middle school level as illustrations. These representative examples in the Pre-K–12 spectrum of grade levels will hopefully suffice to explain the four-part procedure of "unwrapping." In Part Two, you will find grade-specific examples, ranging from kindergarten through high school.

Intellectual understanding ripens into experiential understanding whenever there is the opportunity to immediately *apply* new ideas. Toward this end, I have included at the end of each Part One chapter a "Your Turn" section to assist you in "unwrapping" your own self-selected standards as you work through the process. To make that process as meaningful and relevant to you as possible, I suggest you identify an upcoming unit of study that you intend to teach, and then apply the process to the standards within that unit. In this way, by the time you have finished reading the book you will have a work product ready to use in your own instructional program.

Part Two: The Examples

Part Two contains four chapters of 60 "unwrapped" Common Core English language arts and math examples, each specific to one of the four grade spans: primary

(K–2), upper elementary (3–5), middle school (6–8), and high school (9–12). To assist you as you work through the process, here is where you may wish to refer only to the specific chapter that is closest to your area of interest. I think you will find especially helpful the numerous examples of Big Ideas and Essential Questions in *both* English language arts and math as you strive to write your own.

Part Three: The Big Picture Connections

In Part Three you will see where "unwrapping" fits in the big picture of an integrated standards-assessment-curriculum-instruction system. It plays a pivotal role in the collaborative design of grade-specific rigorous curricular units of study necessary to meet the instructional shifts and assessment demands of the CCSS. Understood and applied rightly, the "unwrapping" process can do much to prepare students for success on the new national assessments developed by the Smarter Balanced Assessment Consortium (SBAC) and the Partnership for Assessment of Readiness for College and Careers (PARCC).

Summing up, the process of "unwrapping" is a powerful technique or tool for effectively deconstructing the Common Core standards. In seeking to familiarize educators with this process, the goal is not to standardize individuals' teaching styles and techniques; the goal is to *effectively teach students the standards*. Educators may collectively "unwrap" the same standards in the same way, but they must always be encouraged to draw upon their own individual talents, creativity, experience, and expertise in helping their students gain a deeper understanding of the concepts and skills within those "unwrapped" standards.

"Unwrapping" the Common Core will benefit classroom educators, school and district administrators, curriculum coordinators, and instructional specialists in all grade levels and content areas. It will assist you in improving achievement for *all* students by focusing on the concepts, skills, and levels of cognitive rigor that students need for success. The straightforward and easy-to-read format of the book, along with the wealth of grade-specific examples of "unwrapped" standards, will enable you to understand and then confidently apply this simple, proven technique for making the rigorous new standards *manageable*.

PART ONE

The Process

CHAPTER 1

"Unwrap" the Common Core

Definitions

For years I've heard educators in my workshops and seminars use the terms "unwrapping" and "unpacking" standards interchangeably to describe the method of taking a standard apart in order to zero in on its essential elements. Educators tend to use whichever term they were introduced to first. But in essence, the purpose of "unwrapping" or "unpacking" is the same: to identify the specifics of what students are to know and be able to do with regard to a particular standard.

My own introduction to the term "unwrapping" the standards came from educators and leaders in Merrill, Wisconsin, during my first professional development presentation there in 2000. Since then, my former colleagues at The Leadership and Learning Center and I have consistently used that specific designation in all publications, professional development seminars, and work in the field. Because it is a unique use of a common word (e.g., unwrapping a gift, unwrapping a package, unwrapping a mystery, and so on), I always place the term in quotation marks to signify its distinction in the standards-based context.

Here is the official definition of "unwrapping" the standards, a definition still applicable to state standards and provincial learning outcomes and now applicable and relevant to the Common Core.

 "Unwrapping" means analyzing and deconstructing the wording of grade-level and course-specific standards within each unit of study to determine exactly what students need to know (teachable concepts) and be able to do (specific skills).

"Concept" is an abstract word often used to represent a teachable idea (e.g., summary, interpretation, hypothesis, theme) or the name of a content-area term (e.g., volume, mass, temperature, angle, size, weight). The easier way to grasp what it means is to just think of the concepts as being *the important nouns and noun phrases* in the standards, and the skills as being *the verbs and verb phrases.* When educators "unwrap" standards, they are looking for the specific words that represent what students need to know and be able to do.

Whenever I introduce the term to a new group of educators and leaders, I first present the official definition and then add an easier way of describing it: when you "unwrap" the standards, you simply underline the important nouns and noun phrases and circle or CAPITALIZE the verbs. I show them quick examples, such as these random three "unwrapped" English language arts state standards that would be taught within the same unit of study:

- RECOGNIZE main ideas presented in texts and PROVIDE evidence that supports those ideas.

- DRAW inferences, conclusions, or generalizations about text and SUPPORT them with textual evidence and prior knowledge.

- CONTRAST facts, supported inferences, and opinions in text.

For a second illustration, I show these two "unwrapped" state math standards:

- SELECT and APPLY appropriate standard units and tools to MEASURE length, area, volume, weight, time, temperature, and the size of angles.

- KNOW common estimates of Pi (3.14, 22/7) and USE these values to ESTIMATE and CALCULATE the circumference and the area of circles. COMPARE with actual measurements.

Notice that in both examples, several of the underlined concepts are stand-alone terms: main ideas, inferences, conclusions, generalizations, length, area, volume, circumference, and so on. Others are noun *phrases,* such as "evidence that supports" and "common estimates of Pi." Still others include adjectives that are important to include because they add specificity to the meaning of the noun they modify: "*appropriate* standard units and tools"; "*actual* measurements"; "*supported* inferences."

This last example—supported inference—listed in the third bullet of the ELA "unwrapped" standard, is an important one to call out because it reveals a key instructional benefit of the "unwrapping" process. I often ask audiences which is more difficult for a student to be able to do: know what an inference *is* or be able to *support* an inference with evidence from the text. Always their response is the latter.

The "unwrapping" process shines a bright light on each and every concept (single word or longer phrase) within a standard. When educators "unwrap" *prior to* any instructional planning or assessment writing, they clearly understand the specific learning targets their students need to learn. This is an important point, especially supported by the research on *learning intentions* and their impact on both instruction and assessment:

> "Learning intentions describe what it is that we want students to learn and their clarity is at the heart of formative assessment. Unless teachers are clear about what they want students to learn (and what the outcome of this learning looks like), they are hardly likely to develop good assessment of that learning." (Hattie, 2012, p. 47)

"Unwrapping" the Common Core

The Common Core State Standards (CCSS) for English Language Arts and Literacy and the Common Core State Standards for Mathematics (CCSSM) are currently the singular standards focus of American education in the vast majority of U.S. states and territories.

The Common Core standards specify *what* K–12 students are expected to know and be able to do at each grade level by the end of the school year. Because these standards have been vertically "spiraled" from one grade to the next, with learning progressions carefully built into their design, the expectation is that all students will (must) learn them by the end of each school year to be prepared for the standards at the *next* grade level or course. This means that the prior grade's standards will become *prerequisites* for students to be successful at the next level of learning.

New national assessments have been created by two assessment consortia of member states—the Smarter Balanced Assessment Consortium (SBAC) and the Partnership for Assessment of Readiness for College and Careers (PARCC). These new exams for students (PARCC in grades 3–11 and SBAC in grades 3–10) will be officially administered for the first time in 2014/15. Since these new assessments will be directly aligned to the Common Core, these standards have naturally become the critical focal point for achieving the results that our educators (and their students) will be expected to produce.

The Common Core State Standards, internationally benchmarked to educational standards in high-performing nations around the world, are by and large more cognitively demanding than the vast majority of state standards. A 2010 report from the Thomas Fordham Institute stated that the CCSS are "clearer and more rigorous than the English language arts standards in 37 states and the math standards in 39 states" (Carmichael, Martino, Porter-Magee, and Wilson, 2010). In Common Core-adopting states around the country, the "unwrapping" process has proven to be a practical and effective technique for helping educators "get to know" and fully understand the rigor and complexity of these standards.

Here are three sets of "unwrapped" Common Core examples, the first in Grade 6 English language arts, the second in Grade 2 math, and the third in Grade 8 math. Note in the Grade 2 math example the capitalization of the root form of the verb "using" so that it appears as "USE." This is done to emphasize the active skill that students are to demonstrate.

From the Reading Informational Text and Writing strands of the Common Core literacy standards for history:

- **RI.6.2:** DETERMINE a central idea of a text and how it is conveyed through particular details; PROVIDE a summary of the text distinct from personal opinions or judgments.

- **RI.6.6:** DETERMINE an author's point of view or purpose in a text and EXPLAIN how it is conveyed in the text.

- **RH.6–8.8:** DISTINGUISH among fact, opinion, and reasoned judgment in a text.

- **W.6.2:** WRITE informative/explanatory texts to EXAMINE a topic and CONVEY ideas, concepts, and information through the selection, organization, and analysis of relevant content.

From the domain of Number and Operations in Base Ten:

- **2.NBT.7:** ADD and SUBTRACT within 1000, US(E)ing concrete models or drawings and strategies based on place value, properties of operations, and/or the relationship between addition and subtraction; RELATE the strategy to a written method. UNDERSTAND that in adding or subtracting three-digit numbers, one adds or subtracts hundreds and hundreds, tens and tens, ones and ones; and sometimes it is necessary to COMPOSE or DECOMPOSE tens or hundreds.

- **2.NBT.9**: EXPLAIN WHY <u>addition and subtraction strategies work</u>, US(E)ing <u>place value and the properties of operations</u>.

From the domain of Statistics and Probability:

- **8.SP.1:** CONSTRUCT and INTERPRET <u>scatter plots for bivariate measurement data</u> to INVESTIGATE <u>patterns of association between two quantities</u>. DESCRIBE <u>patterns</u> such as <u>clustering, outliers, positive or negative association, linear association</u>, and <u>nonlinear association</u>.

Notice in both sets of math examples the *length* of several underlined noun phrases. Educators will often comment when "unwrapping" standards such as these, "But we're underlining practically every word in the entire standard!" This is because the Common Core standards are dense, packed with information, with very few extraneous words. Yet the beauty of "unwrapping" lies in this up-close examination of the standard. Educators are analyzing each and every word and phrase and fully grasping what they mean.

Many times educators will admit to not understanding a certain concept at all and ask their colleagues seated nearby, "That's a term I haven't seen in state standards. What exactly does that mean?" This honest admission brings them to a sobering conclusion: "If *I* don't understand it, how can I teach it to my students?" And it motivates them to find out what it does mean. If they are able, through collaboration, to arrive at a consensus of understanding, everyone involved benefits from the discussion.

Again and again I have observed educators who may not see much value in the process initially ("All you do is underline the nouns and circle or capitalize the verbs…") suddenly realize how extremely helpful and important "unwrapping" is. The power of the practice reveals itself in the *physical doing* of it. By studying the wording of the standard to determine precisely what students need to know and be able to do, educators become acutely aware of what it is they are to teach and what they will later need to assess (again, clarity of learning intentions).

Which Common Core Standards Should Be "Unwrapped"?

Prior to the widespread adoption of the Common Core standards that began in the second half of 2010, educators would point out to me the different (and often confusing) categories or classifications of standards unique to their own state (i.e., main standards, benchmarks, indicators, essential standards, curricular outcome statements, and so on) and ask which specific standards they should be "unwrapping." This was an important question, applicable to all K–12 educators in all content areas since state standards were often voluminous in number and included generally worded and specifically worded statements. Many states had grade-span standards (K–2, 3–5, 6–8, and/or 9–12) that were often verbatim for each grade in the grade span.

To their question, I would reply: "Find those standards that are *grade-specific* or *course-specific*. These are usually the ones that are the most detailed, not the more general statements that may be identically worded from grade to grade." This guideline holds true with regard to the Common Core. I have observed that educators are not as interested in a generally worded grade-span standard as they are in the specific wording of it at the *particular grade level* they teach.

Therefore, the standards to "unwrap" are the *grade-specific* standards in English language arts and literacy and in mathematics. Before doing so, however, all of the K–12 standards should first be *prioritized*.

Priority and Supporting Standards

Here are two definitions to explain the difference between Priority Standards and supporting standards:

> **Priority Standards** are a carefully selected subset of the total list of the grade-specific and course-specific standards within each content area that students must know and be able to do by the end of each school year in order to be prepared for the standards in the next grade level or course. Priority Standards represent the *assured student competencies* that each teacher needs to help every student learn, and demonstrate proficiency in, prior to leaving the current grade or course.

> **Supporting Standards**. All other standards (with a few exceptions) are referred to as *supporting* standards—those standards that support, connect to, or enhance the Priority Standards. They are taught within the context of the Priority Standards, but do not receive the same degree of instruction and assessment emphasis as do the Priority Standards. The supporting standards often become the *instructional scaffolds* to help students understand and attain the more rigorous and comprehensive Priority Standards.

When the Priority Standards are carefully selected through school and/or district consensus, educators teach these particular standards for depth of student understanding using curriculum developed toward that end. Students demonstrate what they have learned on meaningful assessments—classroom, common, and district benchmarks—intentionally aligned to the Priority Standards. Educators systematically collect, examine, and use this formative student data to diagnose student learning needs and then to differentiate their instruction for individual students prior to summative assessments. Collectively, these assessments *for* learning (formative, in-process), when closely aligned to assessments *of* learning (summative end-of-course, end-of-year), provide the evidence of the degree of student attainment of the Priority Standards.

This intentional alignment between formative and summative assessments needs to extend to the Smarter Balanced Assessment Consortium (SBAC) and Partnership for Assessment of Readiness for College and Careers (PARCC) assessments as well. Educators should align their in-school formative assessments to the *formats and rigor* of the summative SBAC and PARCC prototype test questions so that students will be able to "make the transfer" of what they know and can do to these new and as yet unfamiliar national assessments (Ainsworth, 2013).

After prioritization and vertical alignment are completed, the Priority Standards need to be assigned to units of study at each grade level. These highly emphasized standards must appear in *multiple units* of study throughout the year so that students have repeated opportunities to acquire both "surface and deep" understanding of the concepts and skills within them that often scaffold in difficulty. The Priority Standards are then "unwrapped" *within the context of each unit.* By completing these tasks in sequence—prioritization, assignment to units of study, and then "unwrapping"—educators will be able to make explicit connections between standards, assessment, curriculum design, and instruction.

Before we begin the actual "unwrapping" process in more detail, let's take a quick look at the standards themselves. Here, reprinted from *Prioritizing the Common Core* (Ainsworth, 2013), is a summary of how the CCSS and CCSSM are organized. This will help explain the distinction between broad, generally worded standards and those we will "unwrap"—the grade-specific Priority Standards.

Organization of the Common Core English Language Arts Standards

The Common Core English language arts standards include 32 College and Career Readiness (CCR) anchor standards divided into four main literacy strands—reading (including literature, informational text, and K–5 foundational skills), writing, speaking and listening, and language. The reading strand has 10 CCR anchor standards, the writing strand has 10, the speaking and listening strand has six, and the language strand six. Each set of anchor standards defines the broad K–12 literacy expectations for college and career readiness (summarized by Maryann D. Wiggs, 2011, p. 27) (Ainsworth, 2013, pp. 4–5). The organization is summarized in Figure 1.1.

Each *broad* anchor standard is accompanied by *grade-specific* standards for every individual grade in kindergarten through grade 8 and for the two high school grade bands, 9–10 and 11–12. These grade-level standards provide the specifics about what

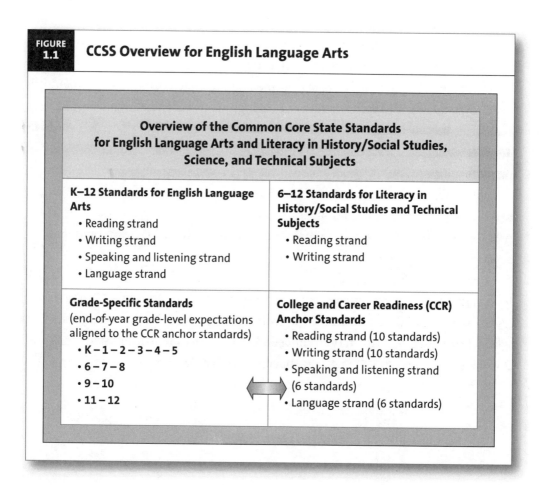

FIGURE 1.1 CCSS Overview for English Language Arts

Overview of the Common Core State Standards for English Language Arts and Literacy in History/Social Studies, Science, and Technical Subjects

K–12 Standards for English Language Arts
- Reading strand
- Writing strand
- Speaking and listening strand
- Language strand

6–12 Standards for Literacy in History/Social Studies and Technical Subjects
- Reading strand
- Writing strand

Grade-Specific Standards
(end-of-year grade-level expectations aligned to the CCR anchor standards)
- K – 1 – 2 – 3 – 4 – 5
- 6 – 7 – 8
- 9 – 10
- 11 – 12

College and Career Readiness (CCR) Anchor Standards
- Reading strand (10 standards)
- Writing strand (10 standards)
- Speaking and listening strand (6 standards)
- Language strand (6 standards)

the corresponding anchor standards mean at each grade level. Together the anchor standards and their related, grade-specific standards explicitly define the knowledge and skills that students must know and be able to demonstrate proficiency in by the end of each grade in order to be prepared for the standards at the next grade level.

Literacy Standards for Science and Technical Subjects, History, and Social Studies

The authors of the Common Core "insist" that literacy be a *shared responsibility* across all content areas. To this end, the K–5 literacy standards for history/social studies, science, and technical subjects are embedded within the K–5 content strands.

However, reading and writing standards for grades 6–12 history/social studies, science, and technical subjects are presented separately (see Figure 1.2). These literacy standards are not intended to replace existing content standards in those content areas, but rather to *supplement* them. Secondary educators in these content areas thus need to determine how they will merge these 10 reading standards and 20 writing standards (19 when excluding the narrative writing standard) with their content-area standards.

FIGURE 1.2	Common Core State Standards—Literacy Standards to Emphasize in History/ Social Studies, Science, Technical Subjects, and Interdisciplinary Writing		
Grade Bands	**History/ Social Studies**	**Science and Technology**	**Interdisciplinary Writing**
Grades 6–8	10	10	20
Grades 9–10	10	10	20
Grades 11–12	10	10	19

Note: These literacy standards are not intended to replace existing content standards in those areas, but rather to *supplement* them.

Organization of the Common Core Math Standards

The K–8 Common Core State Standards for Mathematics (CCSSM) are grouped into three categories: *domains, clusters,* and *standards* (see Figure 1.3). *Domains* are larger groups of related standards (geometry, measurement and data, operations and algebraic thinking, and so on). *Clusters,* within the domains, are groups of related standards. Standards from different domains and clusters may sometimes be closely related. *Standards,* within the clusters, define what students should understand and be able to do at each grade level.

FIGURE 1.3 **Overview of the Common Core State Standards for Mathematics**

Overview of the Structure of the Common Core State Standards for Mathematics	
K–8	**High School**
Grade	Conceptual Category
Domain	Domain
Cluster	Cluster
Standards	Standards

Source: CCSSI, 2010.

Figure 1.4 shows how these three components—domains, clusters, and standards—relate in a grade 3 example from the domain of Number and Operations in Base Ten. The K–5 CCSSM provide students with a solid foundation in whole numbers, addition, subtraction, multiplication, division, fractions, and decimals, with an emphasis on students experiencing "hands-on" learning in number concepts and operations, geometry, and algebra. They are organized into six domains: Counting and Cardinality (kindergarten only), Operations and Algebraic Thinking, Number and Operations in Base Ten (grades K–2 only), Number and Operations in Base Ten and Fractions (grades 3–5 only), Measurement and Data, and Geometry.

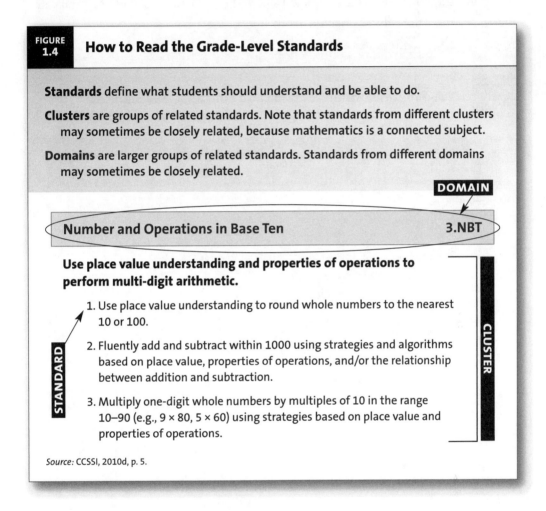

FIGURE 1.4   How to Read the Grade-Level Standards

Standards define what students should understand and be able to do.

Clusters are groups of related standards. Note that standards from different clusters may sometimes be closely related, because mathematics is a connected subject.

Domains are larger groups of related standards. Standards from different domains may sometimes be closely related.

DOMAIN

Number and Operations in Base Ten   **3.NBT**

Use place value understanding and properties of operations to perform multi-digit arithmetic.

STANDARD

1. Use place value understanding to round whole numbers to the nearest 10 or 100.

2. Fluently add and subtract within 1000 using strategies and algorithms based on place value, properties of operations, and/or the relationship between addition and subtraction.

3. Multiply one-digit whole numbers by multiples of 10 in the range 10–90 (e.g., 9 × 80, 5 × 60) using strategies based on place value and properties of operations.

CLUSTER

Source: CCSSI, 2010d, p. 5.

The grades 6–8 CCSSM are organized into six domains: Ratios and Proportional Relationships (grades 6–7 only), Functions (grade 8 only), The Number System, Expressions and Equations, Geometry, and Statistics and Probability.

The high school standards are organized into six conceptual categories—Number and Quantity, Algebra, Functions, Geometry, Statistics and Probability, and Modeling—which will then be assigned to math courses, either traditional or integrated, as proposed in Appendix A of the CCSSM. Modeling is emphasized across *all* conceptual categories.

Whereas nearly all of the *strands* in the English language arts CCSS are consistent in name across all grades, K–12, the *domains* in the math CCSS change names from one grade span to the next (K–5, 6–8) and in the high school *conceptual categories* (grades 9–12). Yet Figure 1.5 shows how these domains and conceptual categories are intentionally connected from one grade span to the next as *learning progressions* across the K–12 grades.

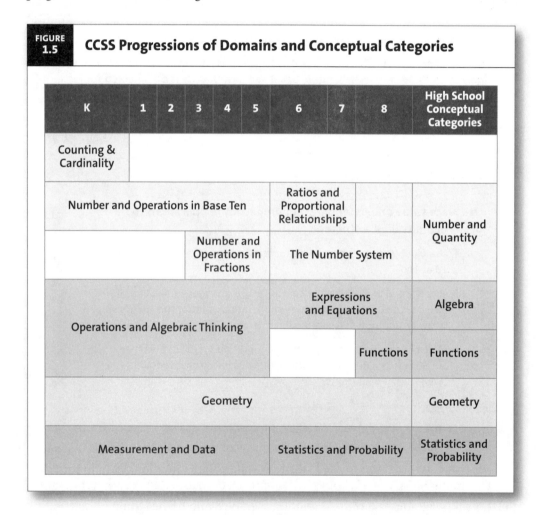

FIGURE 1.5 CCSS Progressions of Domains and Conceptual Categories

K	1	2	3	4	5	6	7	8	High School Conceptual Categories
Counting & Cardinality									
Number and Operations in Base Ten						Ratios and Proportional Relationships			Number and Quantity
			Number and Operations in Fractions			The Number System			
Operations and Algebraic Thinking						Expressions and Equations			Algebra
							Functions		Functions
Geometry									Geometry
Measurement and Data						Statistics and Probability			Statistics and Probability

The Standards for Mathematical Practice

Another major component of the Common Core State Standards in Mathematics is the Standards for Mathematical Practice (SMP). Applicable to every grade level and course, these eight standards describe *how* students are to engage with the mathematical content of each math domain and conceptual category. Applicable to every math domain and conceptual category, they are: (1) Make sense of problems and persevere in solving them; (2) Reason abstractly and quantitatively; (3) Construct viable arguments and critique the reasoning of others; (4) Model with mathematics; (5) Use appropriate tools strategically; (6) Attend to precision; (7) Look for and make use of structure; and (8) Look for and express regularity in repeated reasoning.

It is important to point out that the Standards for Mathematical Practice are neither prioritized nor "unwrapped," but rather are to be emphasized throughout *each and every unit of study* each school year.

"Unwrap" Priority Standards Only

When educators are clear about which standards to "unwrap"—broad or specific—another key question arises: "Do we 'unwrap' *all* of the grade-specific standards?" The answer is no. The reason is twofold: (1) There are too many Common Core standards (particularly in English language arts)—with increased rigor—at each grade level. (2) Not every standard requires the *same* degree of instruction and assessment emphasis. My recommendation, based on years of guiding educators and leaders through the "unwrapping" process and the design of curricular units, learning tasks, and assessments, is to "unwrap" the Priority Standards *only*. Educators who want to also "unwrap" the supporting standards usually find that the result becomes unwieldy with the addition of too many concepts and skills to the graphic organizer. The result is that the sharp focus on the Priority Standards is lost.

So what to do with the supporting standards that are also assigned to the units of study? Rather than "unwrap" these, educators list on the graphic organizer (described in the next chapter) *additional* concepts found in the selected supporting standards and/or they include those concepts in the Unit Vocabulary or "Word Wall" section of the unit planning organizers. In this way, the concepts and skills that support, enhance, and connect to the Priority Standards are intentionally built into the foundation for each unit of study.

In Chapter 2 I will comment upon the three examples of "unwrapped" Common Core State Standards introduced earlier in this chapter, one in English language arts and two in mathematics. These examples will include the "unwrapped" Priority Standards and the related graphic organizers with the concepts, skills, and cognitive skill levels. These same examples will reappear in Chapters 3 and 4 to include the accompanying Big Ideas and Essential Questions, respectively. In this way, you will fully understand each part of the process, see it illustrated along with commentary, and have the opportunity to immediately apply it to your own content area and grade level.

The "Unwrapping" Template

In the *Rigorous Curriculum Design* (Ainsworth, 2010) model for developing new curricula aligned to the Common Core, I constructed a unit planning organizer that design teams could use to create their first-draft units of study. This unit planning organizer is a blank template divided into several sections, each of which is "populated" with the specific information relative to that section. Here are the first parts of that more comprehensive unit template, specific to the "unwrapping" process only, which educators who meet to create curriculum always complete *first*. Please practice with the template in Figure 1.6 as you work through each part of the process.

Your Turn

Because "unwrapping" is very much a hands-on activity, I have included directions following each of the four major parts of the process so that you can experience the method yourself, whether you are a "singleton" or part of a course-alike or grade-level team.

(1) Your first task is to "unwrap" the Priority Standards for a unit of choice. To make this exercise as relevant and meaningful as possible for you, classroom educators should think of an upcoming unit of study that you know you will be teaching in the next month or so.

(2) Working alone or with grade-level or department colleagues, identify the specific Common Core Priority Standards you want to "unwrap." If your school system has not yet determined which Common Core standards are the priorities, and/or has not yet assigned them to curricular units, use your professional judgment to select those high-impact standards you plan to teach during the upcoming unit you select. Find those you would naturally group together for a particular instructional unit focus, not just as they appear together in the Common Core. Often these standards are located in more than one English language arts strand or math domain and will need to be selected and grouped together for more focused instruction.

A word of caution: Be careful not to select too many priorities or the process will become unwieldy as you continue working through the remaining steps. A good rule of thumb is to target no more than four or five Priority Standards for any given unit

FIGURE 1.6 **Rigorous Curriculum Design "Unwrapping" Template**

Subject(s)	
Grade/Course	
Unit of Study	
Pacing	

Priority Common Core State Standards (Bold)
Supporting Standards (Not Bold)

"UNWRAPPED" Priority Standards ONLY

"Unwrapped" Concepts (students need to know)	"Unwrapped" Skills (students need to be able to do)	Taxonomy Levels Bloom's / DOK	

Essential Questions	Corresponding Big Ideas

of study scheduled to last approximately a month. It can be a challenge to limit the number you include, but doing so will keep your focus tighter on those standards you decide are critical for your students to attain. Strive to target and "unwrap" Priority Standards from *more than* one or two English language arts strands or math domains in each unit of study. The ELA strands and math domains are not intended to be taught and assessed in isolation, but rather as an integrated whole that shows the connections *between* strands and *between* domains.

(3) Read through your selected standards, one by one, underlining the key *concepts* (important nouns and noun phrases) and circling the *skills* (the verbs that are usually represented in a phrase or clause). If you are electronically copying and pasting your selected Priority Standards into the related section of the template, it's easier to CAPITALIZE the skills. When working with hard copies of the standards, educators usually circle the verbs. Or they will use two different-colored highlighters or pens, highlighting the concepts in one color and the skills in another. Visually, this can be a useful way to distinguish between concepts and skills.

Remember, the concepts are what the students must know, and the skills are what they must be able to *do with those concepts* (e.g., DETERMINE main idea or CONSTRUCT right angle). If a particular verb appears in its "-ing" form, and it is clearly a skill students need to be able to do, feel free to circle or capitalize it as is. In the next part of the process, you will write it in its root form.

When you are finished, you will be ready for the next dynamic part of the process: creating a graphic organizer that contains all of your "unwrapped" concepts and skills in an easy-to-read visual format.

CHAPTER 2

Create the Graphic Organizer

Now you are ready to create a graphic organizer that represents the "unwrapped" Priority Standards for your selected unit of study. You will be referencing this organizer again and again throughout the unit, using it to create your end-of-unit assessment, pre-assessment, instruction, and related student learning activities. Whether you prefer to create an outline, bulleted list, concept map, or chart, your next task is to organize and arrange the underlined concepts and circled or capitalized skills in the document in a way that makes the most sense to you.

Vary the Format, Not the Concepts and Skills

"Unwrapping" is very much a collaborative process, and teacher teams usually complete the "unwrapping" of each Priority Standard together. However, after educators learn the process, they often want to divide up the "unwrapping" of different standards among themselves to achieve the goal of working smarter, not harder. The only important criterion to remember here is to make sure that the *same* "unwrapped" concepts and skills appear on each educator's graphic organizer, regardless of the particular format used. The educators can then confidently share each other's graphic organizers to plan their own instruction and assessment. In this way, every educator does not have to personally "unwrap" every standard that must be taught but can instead benefit from the collective efforts of colleagues working together with a shared purpose. This respects the professionalism of each educator. However, to promote consistency across the school and district, I recommend deciding upon a *common format* that everyone understands and uses in every grade and content area.

When you have decided on the graphic organizer template you will use, first list all of the underlined concepts together, grouping them under headings where appropriate. Here again are the "unwrapped" English language arts CCSS shown in the previous chapter, now in a chart format (See Figure 2.1) with the key concepts bulleted. Four Priority Standards from three different strands of English language arts and literacy (Reading Informational Text, 6–12 Literacy in History/Social Studies, and Writing) are the focus of this particular unit of study.

- **RI.6.2:** DETERMINE a <u>central idea of a text</u> and <u>how it is conveyed</u> <u>through particular details</u>; PROVIDE a <u>summary</u> of the text <u>distinct</u> <u>from personal opinions or judgments</u>.

- **RI.6.6:** DETERMINE an <u>author's point of view or purpose</u> in a text and EXPLAIN <u>how it is conveyed</u> in the text.

- **RH.6–8.8:** DISTINGUISH among <u>fact, opinion</u>, and <u>reasoned</u> <u>judgment</u> in a text.

- **W.6.2:** WRITE <u>informative/explanatory texts</u> to EXAMINE a <u>topic</u> and CONVEY <u>ideas, concepts, and information</u> through the <u>selection</u>, <u>organization</u>, and <u>analysis</u> of <u>relevant content</u>.

FIGURE 2.1	"Unwrapped" Concepts in Chart Format (ELA Grade 6)

"Unwrapped" Concepts (students need to know)	"Unwrapped" Skills (students need to be able to do)	Taxonomy Levels Bloom's / DOK	

• central idea
  • conveyed through
    • details
    • relevant content
• summary
  • distinct from personal opinions/judgments
  • author's point of view
• author's purpose
  • how conveyed
• fact
• opinion
• reasoned judgment
• informative writing
• explanatory text			

"Unwrapping" the standard and then reorganizing it in this way greatly helps educators understand what the standard means. The specific terms listed on the graphic organizer are the *teachable* concepts that students must learn. Often these same concepts become unit vocabulary terms. It is important to retain the proper Common Core terminology and not use simplified terms instead. Students need to know the "new language" of these standards.

Note that not every underlined concept is included on the graphic organizer. A few underlined nouns (topic, ideas, concepts, information, selection, organization, analysis) may likely be words students are already familiar with or ones the teacher must be sure to incorporate during instruction. Rather than list these underlined terms in the Concepts column, they will instead appear in the Skills column (see next section). The important point to remember is that every concept needs to appear under the Concepts column, the Skills column, or both. It is for the participating educators to analyze the standard completely and make the determinations as to which concepts must be explicitly taught and later assessed.

The Math Graphic Organizer

Here again are the two "unwrapped" Common Core math standard examples from the previous chapter, now shown in chart format with the key concepts bulleted (see Figures 2.2 and 2.3). For ease of illustration, I have focused on only *one* domain in each of the two grade levels: Grade 2 Number & Operations in Base Ten and Grade 8 Statistics & Probability. Whenever it makes sense to do so, however, educators should select Priority Standards from *more than one domain* to match the focus of the particular unit they are planning. This will help students see the mathematical connections between domains.

In these examples, note the grouping of representative concepts under the headings of "Strategies based on" and "Patterns." Whenever appropriate, group like concepts under broader headings. This will help you to identify the Big Ideas later in the process. Again, be sure to retain the proper Common Core standards terminology and not replace what may appear to be more challenging mathematical terms with simplified replacements (e.g., translations, reflections, rotations, *not* "slides, flips, and turns") that might be easier for students to learn but would prevent them from learning the proper mathematical vocabulary.

Grade 2 Number & Operations in Base Ten

- **2.NBT.7**: ADD and SUBTRACT within 1000, US(E)ing concrete models or drawings and strategies based on place value, properties of operations, and/or the relationship between addition and subtraction; RELATE the strategy to a written method. UNDERSTAND that in adding or subtracting three-digit numbers, one adds or subtracts hundreds and hundreds, tens and tens, ones and ones; and sometimes it is necessary to COMPOSE or DECOMPOSE tens or hundreds.

- **2.NBT.9**: EXPLAIN WHY addition and subtraction strategies work, US(E)ing place value and the properties of operations.

FIGURE 2.2	"Unwrapped" Concepts in Chart Format (Math Grade 2)		
"Unwrapped" Concepts (students need to know)	**"Unwrapped" Skills (students need to be able to do)**	**Taxonomy Levels**	
		Bloom's / DOK	

• Numbers within 1000
 	
• Concrete models or drawings and
• Strategies based on
  • Place value
  • Properties of operations
  • Relationship between addition and subtraction
 	
• Strategies to a written method
 	
• Hundreds and hundreds, tens and tens, ones and ones
 	
• Tens or hundreds
 	
• Addition and subtraction strategies
  • Place value
  • Properties of operations			

Grade 8 Statistics & Probability

- **8.SP.1:** CONSTRUCT and INTERPRET <u>scatter plots for bivariate measurement data</u> to INVESTIGATE <u>patterns of association between two quantities</u>. DESCRIBE <u>patterns</u> such as <u>clustering, outliers, positive or negative association, linear association, and nonlinear association</u>.

FIGURE 2.3	"Unwrapped" Concepts in Chart Format (Math Grade 8)		
"Unwrapped" Concepts (students need to know)	**"Unwrapped" Skills (students need to be able to do)**	**Taxonomy Levels**	
		Bloom's / DOK	

• Scatter plots for bivariate measurement data
 	
• Patterns of association between two quantities
 	
• Patterns
  • Clustering
  • Outliers
  • Positive or negative association
  • Linear association
  • Nonlinear association			

It may look as if transferring the underlined concepts from the Priority Standard to the graphic organizer isn't much more than "word shuffling," but the reorganization of the concepts in this way is a big assist to educators wanting to understand a standard's precise meaning. This will become increasingly evident when the skills and taxonomy levels are added in the next part of the process.

Even though the initial task of "unwrapping" is to *separate* concepts from skills, the two remain interrelated. How each skill relates to a particular concept is what determines its corresponding level of cognitive rigor. To decide this, educators reference a thinking skills hierarchy, such as the revised Bloom's Taxonomy (Anderson and Krathwohl, 2001) or Webb's Depth of Knowledge levels (Webb, 1997). Let's look first at the revised Bloom's Taxonomy.

Revised Bloom's Taxonomy: Categories in the Cognitive Process Dimension

Most educators are quite familiar with *The Taxonomy of Educational Objectives* (Bloom, et al., 1956). For decades, understanding the levels of thinking represented in this taxonomy was a cornerstone of required educational methods courses. In recent years, as educators have become increasingly focused on the accurate assessment of student learning, the original taxonomy was revisited and revised by two of Benjamin Bloom's former students, Lorin W. Anderson and David R. Krathwohl.

Unlike the original, the revised framework is two-dimensional. In the newer model, the two dimensions are cognitive process and knowledge. These two components operate like an *X* and *Y* axis: the cognitive level (evident from a verb that represents student learning) would be placed on the horizontal axis, and the type of knowledge (evident from the nouns that represent what the student is to learn) would be placed on the vertical.

The six cognitive processes in the revised taxonomy are *remember, understand, apply, analyze, evaluate,* and *create.* These are just slightly different from the original six levels of Bloom's Taxonomy. The four categories of knowledge in the revised taxonomy are *factual, conceptual, procedural,* and *metacognitive.* This revised taxonomy works well with the "unwrapping" process and later, in designing effective assessment items.

In order to place an objective in the taxonomy, teachers must first "unwrap" a standard to discover what it requires cognitively. It is important for educators working together to collectively agree on the assigned Bloom's level. This consensus will help them decide what must occur instructionally in order for students to achieve the cognitive rigor. Once they have determined the correct placement, they can design appropriate assessment items to match. This predetermination is necessary, because "different types of objectives require different approaches to assessment" (Anderson and Krathwohl, 2001, p. 8).

The following lists contain verbs that *approximate* the particular levels of student learning.

Cognitive Process 1: To *Remember*

"To remember is to retrieve relevant knowledge from long-term memory" (Anderson and Krathwohl, 2001, p. 67).

Verbs associated with this level: choose, define, describe, find, identify, label, list, locate, match, name, recall, recite, recognize, record, relate, retrieve, say, select, show, sort, tell.

Cognitive Process 2: To *Understand*

"To understand is to construct meaning from instructional messages, including oral, written, and graphic communication" (Anderson and Krathwohl, 2001, p. 67).

Verbs associated with this level: categorize, clarify, classify, compare, conclude, construct, contrast, demonstrate, distinguish, explain, illustrate, interpret, match, paraphrase, predict, reorganize, represent, summarize, translate, understand.

Cognitive Process 3: To *Apply*

"To apply is to carry out or use a procedure in a given situation" (Anderson and Krathwohl, 2001, p. 67).

Verbs associated with this level: apply, carry out, construct, develop, display, execute, illustrate, implement, model, solve, use.

Cognitive Process 4: To *Analyze*

"To analyze is to break material into its constituent parts and determine how the parts relate to one another and to an overall structure or purpose" (Anderson and Krathwohl, 2001, p. 68).

Verbs associated with this level: analyze, ascertain, attribute, connect, deconstruct, determine, differentiate, discriminate, dissect, distinguish, divide, examine, experiment, focus, infer, inspect, integrate, investigate, organize, outline, reduce, solve (a problem), test for.

Cognitive Process 5: To *Evaluate*

"To evaluate is to make judgments based on criteria and standards" (Anderson and Krathwohl, 2001, p. 68).

Verbs associated with this level: appraise, assess, award, check, conclude, convince, coordinate, criticize, critique, defend, detect, discriminate, evaluate, judge, justify, monitor, prioritize, rank, recommend, support, test, value.

Cognitive Process 6: To *Create*

"To create is to put elements together to form a coherent or functional whole; reorganize elements into a new pattern or structure; inventing a product" (Anderson and Krathwohl, 2001, p. 68).

Verbs associated with this level: adapt, build, compose, construct, create, design, develop, elaborate, extend, formulate, generate, hypothesize, invent, make, modify, originate, plan, produce, refine, transform.

Add Skills and Revised Bloom's Taxonomy Levels to Graphic Organizer

Now let's refer to these six levels of the revised Bloom's Taxonomy and look again at the first capitalized verb—"DETERMINE"—in the sixth grade English language arts standard, RI.6.2 (see Figure 2.4). It appears in Cognitive Process 4: To Analyze. Write "DETERMINE" in the column opposite "central idea of text" and the numeral "4" in the Bloom's column. To determine the central idea of a text, you have to ANALYZE the text.

FIGURE 2.4	**Determining Skills and Bloom's Levels**	
"Unwrapped" Concepts (students need to know)	**"Unwrapped" Skills (students need to be able to do)**	**Taxonomy Levels** **Bloom's / DOK**

• central idea
   • conveyed through
     • details
     • relevant content
	• **DETERMINE** (central idea *through details*)—ANALYZE*, EVALUATE*, SUPPORT*	4, 5

*Implied by, but not stated in, the standard.

Seems easy enough, right? But this is not just an exercise in finding an isolated verb in one of six alphabetized lists and then writing its corresponding level number on the graphic organizer. There's more to it than that. Notice how "DETERMINE a central idea of a text" is followed by the phrase "how it is conveyed through particular details." This indicates the need to identify a *second* skill level, one that represents the ability to EVALUATE, and SUPPORT ideas. That corresponds to Cognitive Process 5: To Evaluate.

To more accurately represent the thinking skills needed to carry out the given skill, three additional verbs (ANALYZE, EVALUATE, SUPPORT) were added to the graphic organizer. These words are not in the standard; they were added because they more closely identify the *approximate* cognitive level(s) and help explain why there are two cognitive skill numbers (4, 5) listed in the third column. Without those added verbs, another educator might rightly wonder, "The word 'determine' is not in level 5 of the revised Bloom's Taxonomy. Why is level 5 listed here?" Whenever including any such clarifying verbs, always be sure to notate on the graphic organizer with an asterisk that these additions were not part of the original standard.

Figure 2.5 shows the completed graphic organizer for these four Common Core ELA Priority Standards:

- **RI.6.2:** DETERMINE a central idea of a text and how it is conveyed through particular details; PROVIDE a summary of the text distinct from personal opinions or judgments.

- **RI.6.6:** DETERMINE an author's point of view or purpose in a text and EXPLAIN how it is conveyed in the text.

- **RH.6–8.8:** DISTINGUISH among fact, opinion, and reasoned judgment in a text.

- **W.6.2:** WRITE informative/explanatory texts to EXAMINE a topic and CONVEY ideas, concepts, and information through the selection, organization, and analysis of relevant content.

Now the question arises: What do you do if a certain verb you are looking for is not on *any* of the six Bloom's lists? You then have to think about what level of rigor that verb and its matching concept might be. Look again at the last "unwrapped" skill in the middle column of the graphic organizer: "CONVEY ideas, concepts, and information through the selection, organization, and analysis of relevant content." The verb "convey" does not appear on any of the six revised Bloom's Taxonomy lists. So what level of rigor does it indicate? When it is paired with all of the underlined concepts that follow it, the predominant mental skills involved in "conveying" this are *analyze* (level 4) and *evaluate* (level 5).

Two encouraging reminders to keep in mind when striving to assign a cognitive skill level to a verb-concept pairing: (1) Trust your professional judgment, which again underscores the value of educators collaboratively determining these skill levels. (2) Know that you can always revisit and revise your initial decisions later. This often occurs while drafting the assessment items. You zero in on exactly what the "unwrapped" skill and concept are calling for so you can write an assessment question that exactly matches.

FIGURE 2.5	"Unwrapped" Skills in Chart Format (ELA Grade 6)

"Unwrapped" Concepts (students need to know)	"Unwrapped" Skills (students need to be able to do)	Taxonomy Levels Bloom's / DOK	

• central idea
  • conveyed through
    • details
    • relevant content
	• **DETERMINE** (central idea *conveyed through details and relevant content*)—ANALYZE*, EVALUATE*, SUPPORT*	4, 5	

• summary • distinct from personal opinions/judgments	• **PROVIDE** (summary without personal opinions/judgments)	2	
• author's point of view	• **DETERMINE** (author's point of view)—ANALYZE*, INFER*	4	
• author's purpose • how conveyed	• **DETERMINE** (author's purpose) • **EXPLAIN** (how it is conveyed)	2 2	
• fact • opinion • reasoned judgment	• **DISTINGUISH** (fact/opinion/ reasoned judgment)	2	
• informative writing • explanatory text	• **WRITE** (informative/ explanatory texts)	6	
	• **EXAMINE** (topic)—ANALYZE*	4	
	• **CONVEY** (ideas/concepts/ information through selection/ organization/ analysis of relevant content)	4, 5	

*Implied by, but not stated in, the standard.

One other key point worth noting here: When a particular verb appears in more than one of the six revised Bloom's Taxonomy lists, *study each concept it is paired with* to determine the level of cognitive skill rigor. For example, the skill "interpret" requires different cognitive skill levels in the following examples:

INTERPRET (informational text)—Level 2

INTERPRET (*implied* information in text)—Level 4

To interpret informational text requires the learner to *understand* that text, a level two skill. But to interpret *implied* information is more cognitively challenging. It requires the learner to *infer*, a level four skill.

I have often referred to "unwrapping" as a "thinking educator's process." Educators need to keep all of these considerations in mind while determining the cognitive level of each particular skill and related concept listed on the graphic organizer. But doing so will result in their assurance that they clearly understand the standards in focus. This will prove extremely helpful when the time comes to write the assessment questions and plan instruction.

Assigning Revised Bloom's Levels on the Math Graphic Organizer

Figures 2.6 and 2.7 show the Grade 2 and Grade 8 math "unwrapped" Priority Standards and their graphic organizers, now with the skills and revised Bloom's levels added. Unlike the ELA example, note that here only the verbs appear in the center column. The reader must "look left" to match the verb with its related concept(s) in the first column:

- **2.NBT.7**: ADD and SUBTRACT within 1000, US(E)ing concrete models or drawings and strategies based on place value, properties of operations, and/or the relationship between addition and subtraction; RELATE the strategy to a written method. UNDERSTAND that in adding or subtracting three-digit numbers, one adds or subtracts hundreds and hundreds, tens and tens, ones and ones; and sometimes it is necessary to COMPOSE or DECOMPOSE tens or hundreds.

- **2.NBT.9**: EXPLAIN WHY addition and subtraction strategies work, US(E)ing place value and the properties of operations.

FIGURE 2.6	"Unwrapped" Skills in Chart Format (Math Grade 2)

"Unwrapped" Concepts (students need to know)	"Unwrapped" Skills (students need to be able to do)	Taxonomy Levels Bloom's / DOK	
• Numbers within 1000	ADD and SUBTRACT	2	
• Concrete models or drawings, strategies based on: • Place value • Properties of operations • Relationship between addition and subtraction	USE	3	
• Strategy to a written method	RELATE	4	
• Hundreds and hundreds, tens and tens, ones and ones	UNDERSTAND	4	
• Tens or hundreds	COMPOSE and DECOMPOSE	4	
• Addition and subtraction strategies • Place value • Properties of operations	EXPLAIN WHY THEY WORK/USE	4	

• **8.SP.1:** CONSTRUCT and INTERPRET scatter plots for bivariate measurement data to INVESTIGATE patterns of association between two quantities. DESCRIBE patterns such as clustering, outliers, positive or negative association, linear association, and nonlinear association.

The Grade 8 math graphic organizer is much the same as the ones for Grade 2 math and Grade 6 English language arts and literacy, with an important exception. Notice in the Grade 8 chart how the Skills column links two verbs with the preposition "to." The first two skills in the standard, "CONSTRUCT" and "INTERPRET," are linked to "INVESTIGATE." The graphic organizer must therefore represent those

FIGURE 2.7	"Unwrapped" Skills in Chart Format (Math Grade 8)	

"Unwrapped" Concepts (students need to know)	"Unwrapped" Skills (students need to be able to do)	Taxonomy Levels
		Bloom's / DOK
• Scatter plots for bivariate measurement data	CONSTRUCT	4
• Patterns of association between two quantities	to INVESTIGATE	3
• Scatter plots for bivariate measurement data	INTERPRET	
• Patterns of association between two quantities	to INVESTIGATE	5

• Patterns
  • Clustering
  • Outliers
  • Positive or negative association
  • Linear association
  • Nonlinear association
	DESCRIBE	4

connections. If not, the exact meaning of the standard will be lost when the "unwrapped" skills are transferred from the standard to the organizer.

Note too that "CONSTRUCT" and "INTERPRET" are both paired *separately* with "to INVESTIGATE." This is because each verb represents a different skill and corresponding Bloom's level. Without the benefit of the "unwrapping" process, it would be easy to overlook the fact that two *different* skills are both needed in order to achieve the intent of the standard.

This will also generate the need, on occasion, to identify *two* Bloom's levels as shown in the first pair of Grade 8 verbs, "CONSTRUCT to INVESTIGATE." The verb "CONSTRUCT" has been assigned the cognitive level 4 because it is necessary to *analyze* the scatter plots before being able to construct them. The verb "to IN-VESTIGATE" in this context is seen as application, a level 3 skill. The second pair of verbs, "INTERPRET to INVESTIGATE," has been assigned one cognitive level of 5 because interpreting scatter plots involves *evaluating* them. How you *use* the skill is always what determines its level of rigor, not its correspondence to the verbs on the Bloom's lists.

This brings up another important point: not every educator will necessarily agree with the skill levels listed here; some would assign different skill levels to the same verb-noun pair. For example, the last skill in this standard, "DESCRIBE," may at first seem to be a lower-level thinking skill. In this case, it is being used with the related concept "patterns." Close analysis of the different types of patterns named (positive/negative/linear/nonlinear associations, and so on) indicates to me that this kind of "describe" requires a higher level of cognition; thus the assignment of a level 4—analysis.

Keep It Simple

This might be starting to seem too confusing or complex, but it will make more sense as you begin to practice it. The main purpose of identifying the skill level is not to achieve perfection or absolute precision, but to be as thoughtful as possible in identifying the *approximate* skill levels of the "unwrapped" skills and matching concepts. Remember that you can review and revise your initial skill levels whenever you want as you are working through the "unwrapping" process. Often this revision occurs later, when educators are writing assessment questions and taking a closer look at the cognitive skill levels to make sure they are correct. All of this up front work will go a long way toward intentionally aligning both instruction and assessment to the "unwrapped" concepts, skills, and matching cognitive skill levels.

If you create your graphic organizer thoroughly (making sure it includes *every* "unwrapped" concept and skill students need to know and be able to do), you will be able to set aside the standards documents without needing to refer to them again, except as needed for minor clarifications. In my "unwrapping" workshops, I always ask educators after they complete their graphic organizers, "Could you now put away the standards and plan your instruction and assessments entirely by referencing the graphic organizer?" When they can say yes, they feel confident that they have completed the process correctly.

Your Turn, Part 1

(1) Working alone or with grade-level or department colleagues, complete the "Unwrapped" Skills and Bloom's Level columns on your graphic organizer. Write each

circled or capitalized skill adjacent to its matching underlined concept.

(2) Referencing a copy of the revised Bloom's Taxonomy, decide the *approximate* cognitive skill level (1–6) of each verb-concept pair. Remember, you can change your mind and revise your decisions whenever needed. So for now, just make initial decisions.

(3) When you are finished, make sure that you have carefully represented each and every "unwrapped" concept and skill on the graphic organizer with its approximate cognitive skill level.

(4) Put aside the graphic organizer for now. You will revisit it to add Depth of Knowledge (DOK) levels, described in the next section.

Webb's Depth of Knowledge and the Common Core

The other taxonomy of cognitive skills that has seen a marked increase in use since the widespread adoption of the Common Core beginning in 2010 is Webb's Depth of Knowledge (1997). Much of the attention on DOK has come from the high-profile reference to this taxonomy by the Smarter Balanced Assessment Consortium (SBAC) and the Partnership for Assessment of Readiness for College and Careers (PARCC) in their design of the new national assessments aligned to the Common Core. Both consortia reference the DOK scale to closely align their constructed-response assessment questions (short-response, extended-response, and performance tasks) to the standards and their inherent levels of rigor.

Educators and professional developers share differences of opinion as to how and when the DOK scale should be used—during the assignment of skill levels while "unwrapping" or later in the creation of assessments. My position is that the standards and identified levels of rigor must be determined *first* so that the subsequent design of assessment questions directly aligns with the predetermined levels of rigor.

The DOK framework is frequently used to correctly identify the levels of rigor of assessment *tasks* created by external sources (such as SBAC and PARCC). However, keep in mind that *educators* are the ones who will be *creating their own* formative and summative assessments matched to the "unwrapped" concepts, skills, and levels of rigor. To do this, they must first know whether they are setting out to write a level 1, 2, 3, or 4 assessment question or task. The assignment of DOK (and Bloom's) levels is a fluid process; it can and should be reviewed and revised as needed during the development of assessments. Determining the DOK levels *first* respects both approaches. The assessment question must match the level of rigor in the standard, and the level of rigor must equal the demand of the assessment question. One approach becomes the check for the other.

Another key point: In the examples throughout the remainder of this book, typically only one DOK level is identified for each skill-concept pair. This one-to-one correspondence is not meant to oversimplify the process and ignore the fact that occasionally *several* skills and concepts must be considered together when assigning a DOK level. And when that combination of skills occurs, the DOK level of the assessment question or task will need to reflect that combination.

Again, my purpose here is to provide educators with a doable, practical way of ensuring that they match assessment, curriculum, and instruction to the *standards-based* levels of rigor first. As you work through the process of assigning DOK levels to your own "unwrapped" concepts and skills, this should all become clear and make good sense. The information in the next section from Dr. Karin Hess regarding the application of the DOK process will assist you in your understanding.

Selection of DOK Guiding Documents for "Unwrapping"

Many state departments of education and professional development organizations have prepared helpful materials explaining the Depth of Knowledge scale of cognitive demand originated by Dr. Norman Webb in 1997 and its role in assessing and evaluating curriculum, developing assessments (formative and summative), and determining students' knowledge and attainment of the Common Core standards. I have selected for use with the "unwrapping" process the work of Dr. Karin Hess, who has done much to raise the awareness and use of DOK levels through her published papers and, more recently, her updated publication for the Common Core Institute, *A Guide for Using Webb's Depth of Knowledge with Common Core State Standards* (2013). You can view this entire document online at http://cliu21cng. wikispaces.com/file/view/WebsDepthofKnowledgeFlipChart.pdf/457670878/ WebsDepthofKnowledgeFlipChart.pdf. Several excerpts from this publication and others by Dr. Hess (*Linking Research with Practice, 2013*) follow:

> Norman Webb's Depth-of-Knowledge (DOK) schema has become one of the key tools educators can employ to analyze the cognitive demand (complexity) intended by the standards, curricular activities, and assessment tasks. Webb (1997) developed a process and criteria for systematically analyzing the alignment between standards and test items in standardized assessments. Since then the process and criteria have demonstrated application to reviewing curricular align-

ment as well. The model categorizes assessment tasks by different levels of cognitive expectation, or depth of knowledge, required to successfully complete the task. Hess (2004–2012) further articulated the model with content-specific descriptions for use by classroom teachers and organizations conducting alignment studies. The table below outlines the DOK levels followed by a description of each level:

DOK LEVEL	DESCRIPTION OF LEVEL
1	Recall & Reproduction
2	Skills & Concepts
3	Strategic Thinking & Reasoning
4	Extended Thinking

Level 1: Recall & Reproduction

Curricular elements that fall into this category involve basic tasks that require students to recall or reproduce knowledge and/or skills. The subject matter content at this level usually involves working with facts, terms, details, calculations, principles, and/or properties. It may also involve use of simple procedures or formulas. There is little or no transformation of the target knowledge or skill required by the tasks that fall into this category. A student answering a Level I item either knows the answer or does not; that is, the answer does not need to be figured out" or "solved."

Level 2: Skills & Concepts

Level 2 includes the engagement of mental processing beyond recalling, reproducing, or locating an answer. This level generally requires students to compare or differentiate among people, places, events, objects, text types, etc.; apply multiple concepts when responding; classify or sort items into meaningful categories; describe or explain relationships, such as cause and effect, character relationships; and provide and explain examples and non-examples.

A Level 2 "describe or explain" task requires students to go beyond a basic description or definition to predict a possible result or explain "why" something might happen. The learner makes use of information provided in context to determine intended word meanings, which tools or approach is appropriate to find a solution (e.g., in a math word problem), or what characteristics to pay attention to when making observations.

At this level, students are asked to transform/process target knowledge before responding. Example mental processes that often denote this particular level include: summarize, estimate, organize, classify, extend, and make basic inferences.

Level 3: Strategic Thinking & Reasoning

Tasks and classroom discourse falling into this category demand the use of planning, reasoning, and higher-order thinking processes, such as analysis and evaluation, to solve real-world problems or explore questions with multiple possible outcomes. Stating one's reasoning and providing relevant supporting evidence are key markers of DOK 3 tasks.... Tasks at this level require an in-depth integration of conceptual knowledge and multiple skills to reach a solution or produce a final product. DOK 3 tasks and classroom discourse focus on in-depth understanding of one text, one data set, one investigation, or one key source, whereas DOK 4 tasks expand the breadth of the task using multiple texts or sources, or multiple concepts/disciplines to reach a solution or create a final product.

Level 4: Extended Thinking

Curricular elements assigned to this level demand extended and integrated use of higher-order thinking processes such as critical and creative-productive thinking, reflection, and adjustment of plans over time. Students are engaged in conducting multifaceted investigations to solve real-world problems with unpredictable solutions. Employing and sustaining strategic thinking processes over a longer period of time to solve the problem or produce an authentic product is a key feature of curricular objectives assigned to DOK 4. Key aspects that denote this particular level typically include authentic problems and audiences, and collaboration within a project-based setting.

Helpful Guidelines for Determining DOK Levels

Accompanying each DOK level, Hess (2013) has included representative verbs, teacher roles, student roles, possible products, potential activities, and potential questions to help educators design curricula, instruction, and assessments aligned to the cognitive demand of the respective levels. She has also included the following bulleted list of general guidelines for understanding the purpose and function of each level. These guidelines (italicized emphasis added) are helpful to educators when they prepare to complete the DOK column on the graphic organizer of the "unwrapped" standards.

- The DOK level assigned should reflect the level of work students are most commonly required to perform in order for the response to be deemed proficient, such as in rubric descriptions describing proficient performance.

- The DOK level should reflect the *complexity* of cognitive processes demanded by the learning or assessment objective and task, rather than its *difficulty*. Ultimately, the DOK level describes the depth of understanding required by a task, not whether or not the task is considered "difficult."

- If there is a question regarding which of two levels a standard addresses,…
  it is appropriate to *assign the highest level* as the "DOK ceiling" for the task,
  but also provide opportunities at the lower DOK levels as an instructional progression (e.g., summarizing a text/DOK 2 before analyzing a text/DOK 3; making observations/DOK 2 before conducting investigation/DOK 3) (Hess,
  2004–2006).

- The DOK level should be assigned based upon the *cognitive demand* (mental
  processing) required by the central performance described in the objective or
  task.

- The task or objective's central verb(s) alone is/are not sufficient to assign a DOK
  level. *Developers must consider "what comes after [the] verb"—the complexity
  of the task and content/concepts—*in addition to the mental processing required by the requirements set forth in the objective [Webb, 1997].

Revised Bloom's Taxonomy and DOK Charts

Dr. Hess developed three user-friendly matrices to show the relationship between the
six levels of the revised Bloom's Taxonomy and the four levels of Webb's Depth of
Knowledge. One chart is specific to close reading in English language arts and
history/social studies, the second to math and science, and the third to written and
oral communications across content areas. When educators are assigning Bloom's and
DOK levels to their "unwrapped" skills and matching concepts on the graphic organizer, they use the chart specific to their content-area focus. Reproduced in Figure 2.8,
courtesy of Dr. Hess, is the English language arts and history/social studies matrix.

Notice the list of alphabetized verbs beneath each of the six revised Bloom's Taxonomy levels in the first column. These verbs differ from the lists presented earlier
in this chapter. Even though the six Bloom's levels remain constant, there are many
versions of the actual lists of verbs. This can cause inconsistencies and disagreement
between educators when they are using different lists. I recommend using the earlier revised Bloom's Taxonomy document when first assigning the Bloom's levels.
You can then cross-reference your choices with Dr. Hess' Bloom's levels and revise
your selections as needed.

An ongoing challenge to educators engaged in the "unwrapping" process using
only the revised Bloom's scale has been the varying interpretations of what a particular verb in isolation means. Without the accompanying concept for each verb, there
can be confusion (and disagreement) among educators: "But is this a Level 2 or Level
4? All we have to go on is the verb itself."

| FIGURE 2.8 | **Karin Hess's Cognitive Rigor Matrix for ELA (Close Reading) and History/Social Studies** |

Hess Cognitive Rigor Matrix (Reading): Applying Webb's Depth-of-Knowledge Levels to Bloom's Cognitive Process Dimensions				
Revised Bloom's Taxonomy	**Webb's DOK Level 1** Recall & Reproduction	**Webb's DOK Level 2** Skills & Concepts	**Webb's DOK Level 3** Strategic Thinking/ Reasoning	**Webb's DOK Level 4** Extended Thinking
Remember Retrieve knowledge from long-term memory, recognize, recall, locate, identify	• Recall, recognize, or locate basic facts, terms, details, events, or ideas explicit in texts • Read words orally in connected text with fluency & accuracy	Use these Hess CRM curricular examples with most close reading or listening assignments or assessments in any content area.		
Understand Construct meaning, clarify, paraphrase, represent, translate, illustrate, give examples, classify, categorize, summarize, generalize, infer a logical conclusion, predict, compare/contrast, match like ideas, explain, construct models	• Identify or describe literary elements (characters, setting, sequence, etc.) • Select appropriate words when intended meaning/definition is clearly evident • Describe/explain who, what, where, when, or how • Define/describe facts, details, terms, principles • Write simple sentences	• Specify, explain, show relationships; explain why (e.g., cause-effect) • Give non-examples/examples • Summarize results, concepts, ideas • Make basic inferences or logical predictions from data or texts • Identify main ideas or accurate generalizations of texts • Locate information to support explicit-implicit central ideas	• Explain, generalize, or connect ideas using supporting evidence (quote, example, text reference) • Identify/ make inferences about explicit or implicit themes • Describe how word choice, point of view, or bias may affect the readers' interpretation of a text • Write multi-paragraph composition for specific purpose, focus, voice, tone, & audience	• Explain how concepts or ideas specifically relate to other content domains (e.g., social, political, historical) or concepts • Develop generalizations of the results obtained or strategies used and apply them to new problem-based situations
Apply Carry out or use a procedure in a given situation; carry out (apply to a familiar task), or use (apply) to an unfamiliar task	• Use language structure (prefix/suffix) or word relationships (synonym/antonym) to determine meaning of words • Apply rules or resources to edit spelling, grammar, punctuation, conventions, word use • Apply basic formats for documenting sources	• Use context to identify the meaning of words/phrases • Obtain and interpret information using text features • Develop a text that may be limited to one paragraph • Apply simple organizational structures (paragraph, sentence types) in writing	• Apply a concept in a new context • Revise final draft for meaning or progression of ideas • Apply internal consistency of text organization and structure to composing a full composition • Apply word choice, point of view, style to impact readers'/viewers' interpretation of a text	• Illustrate how multiple themes (historical, geographic, social, artistic, literary) may be interrelated • Select or devise an approach among many alternatives to research a novel problem

Source: © Karin K. Hess (2009, updated 2013). Hess Cognitive Rigor Matrix (CRM) in Local Assessment Toolkit. Permission to use only with full citation. khess@nciea.org or kar_hes@msn.com.

FIGURE 2.8

Karin Hess's Cognitive Rigor Matrix for ELA (Close Reading) and History/Social Studies (continued)

	Hess Cognitive Rigor Matrix (Reading): Applying Webb's Depth-of-Knowledge Levels to Bloom's Cognitive Process Dimensions			
Revised Bloom's Taxonomy	**Webb's DOK Level 1** Recall & Reproduction	**Webb's DOK Level 2** Skills & Concepts	**Webb's DOK Level 3** Strategic Thinking/ Reasoning	**Webb's DOK Level 4** Extended Thinking
Analyze Break into constituent parts, determine how parts relate, differentiate between relevant-irrelevant, distinguish, focus, select, organize, outline, find coherence, deconstruct (e.g., for bias or point of view)	• Identify whether specific information is contained in graphic representations (e.g., map, chart, table, graph, T-chart, diagram) or text features (e.g., headings, subheadings, captions) • Decide which text structure is appropriate to audience and purpose	• Categorize/compare literary elements, terms, facts/details, events • Identify use of literary devices • Analyze format, organization, & internal text structure (signal words, transitions, semantic cues) of different texts • Distinguish: relevant-irrelevant information; fact/opinion • Identify characteristic text features; distinguish between texts, genres	• Analyze information within data sets or texts • Analyze interrelationships among concepts, issues, problems • Analyze or interpret author's craft (literary devices, viewpoint, or potential bias) to create or critique a text • Use reasoning, planning, and evidence to support inferences	• Analyze multiple sources of evidence, or multiple works by the same author, or across genres, time periods, themes • Analyze complex/abstract themes, perspectives, concepts • Gather, analyze, and organize multiple information sources • Analyze discourse styles
Evaluate Make judgments based on criteria, check, detect inconsistencies or fallacies, judge, critique	"UG"— unsubstantiated generalizations = stating an opinion without providing any support for it!		• Cite evidence and develop a logical argument for conjectures • Describe, compare, and contrast solution methods • Verify reasonableness of results • Justify or critique conclusions drawn	• Evaluate relevancy, accuracy, and completeness of information from multiple sources • Apply understanding in a novel way, provide argument or justification for the application
Create Reorganize elements into new patterns/ structures, generate, hypothesize, design, plan, produce	• Brainstorm ideas, concepts, problems, or perspectives related to a topic, principle, or concept	• Generate conjectures or hypotheses based on observations or prior knowledge and experience	• Synthesize information within one source or text • Develop a complex model for a given situation • Develop an alternative solution	• Synthesize information across multiple sources or texts • Articulate a new voice, alternate theme, new knowledge or perspective

Source: © Karin K. Hess (2009, updated 2013). Hess Cognitive Rigor Matrix (CRM) in Local Assessment Toolkit. Permission to use only with full citation. khess@nciea.org or kar_hes@msn.com.

It is critical to *approximate as closely as possible* the level of each skill-concept pair, because you must soon design assessment questions to match that same level of rigor. If you assign a level that is too low, the matching assessment question will likely not be an accurate measure of students' attainment of that skill, and the related classroom instruction will not be at the matching level of rigor. Whenever this uncertainty of which level to select occurred in my workshops, I always advised going with the higher of the two levels in question. My rationale was this: it's better to aim too high than too low, especially with regard to the design of your assessment questions, which need to be appropriately matched to the level of rigor.

The DOK descriptors—written as *phrases* in each of the four columns—provide more helpful guidance for accurately determining the approximate skill level than do the lists of isolated verbs in the revised Bloom's Taxonomy. When preparing to assign a particular DOK level to an "unwrapped" verb-concept, read down the *entire column* to locate the phrase that most closely approximates the intent of the verb-concept pair you are focused on, irrespective of the section in which that description appears. When you locate the phrase that most closely matches, the number of that column is the number you write on your graphic organizer.

Assigning DOK Levels to the English Language Arts Graphic Organizer

Let's revisit the ELA graphic organizer from earlier in the chapter to see how this works (see Figure 2.9). Looking at just the first entry of "unwrapped" concepts and related skills on the graphic organizer, what is the DOK level?

FIGURE 2.9   **Determining DOK Levels (ELA)**

"Unwrapped" Concepts (students need to know)	"Unwrapped" Skills (students need to be able to do)	Taxonomy Levels Bloom's / DOK	
• central idea • conveyed through • details • relevant content	• **DETERMINE** (central idea *conveyed through details and relevant content*)—ANALYZE*, EVALUATE*, SUPPORT*	4, 5	?

*Implied by, but not stated in, the standard.

The answer is 2. Why? Reading down the Level 1 column of Figure 2.8, there are no descriptive phrases that match the skill-concept pair in focus. Moving over to the Level 2 column, in the first section of phrases (second block), the fifth bullet states, "Identify main ideas or accurate generalizations of texts." This is a close match to the "unwrapped" concept and skill "DETERMINE (central idea)." Yet the remaining

FIGURE 2.10	**Completed "Unwrapping" Chart (ELA Grade 6)**		
"Unwrapped" Concepts (students need to know)	**"Unwrapped" Skills** (students need to be able to do)	**Taxonomy Levels**	
		Bloom's	**DOK**

• central idea
  • conveyed through
    • details
    • relevant content
	• **DETERMINE** (central idea *conveyed through details and relevant content*)—ANALYZE*, EVALUATE*, SUPPORT*	4, 5	2

• summary • distinct from personal opinions/judgments	• **PROVIDE** (summary without personal opinions/judgments)	2	2
• author's point of view	• **DETERMINE** (author's point of view)—ANALYZE*, INFER*	4	3
• author's purpose • how conveyed	• **DETERMINE** (author's purpose) • **EXPLAIN** (how it is conveyed)	2 2	3 3
• fact • opinion • reasoned judgment	• **DISTINGUISH** (fact/opinion/ reasoned judgment)	2	2
• informative writing • explanatory text	• **WRITE** (informative/explanatory texts)	6	3, 4
	• **EXAMINE** (topic)—ANALYZE*	4	2
	• **CONVEY** (ideas/concepts/ information through selection/ organization/ analysis of relevant content)	4, 5	3

*Implied by, but not stated in, the standard.

concept, "conveyed through details and relevant content" must also be assigned a DOK level. The very next bullet in the same section, "Locate information to support explicit/implicit central ideas," communicates the same intent as "conveyed through details and relevant content." Therefore, DOK Level 2 is the level assigned to the complete concept-skill pair.

Continuing this same process with the remaining "unwrapped" skills and related concepts, Figure 2.10 shows all of the assigned DOK levels. Note the addition of capitalized verbs after "DETERMINE (author's point of view)" and "EXAMINE (topic)." They communicate the intended meaning of the skill-concept to make the assignment of the Bloom's *and* DOK levels easier to determine. The last entry, "CONVEY (ideas/concepts/ information through selection/organization/analysis of relevant content)" although not a perfect match, aligns closest with Level 3: Strategic Thinking and Reasoning (the last bullet in the third section of descriptors), "Use reasoning, planning, and evidence to support inferences."

Keep in mind there will often be discussion and occasional disagreement when colleagues collaborate to assign the revised Bloom's Taxonomy and Webb's DOK levels. That's OK! The conversations around these cognitive level assignments are of great value because educators who "agree to disagree" will support their positions and ultimately arrive at a shared conclusion. In the process, they will have gained clarity and understanding about the degree of rigor and cognitive challenge inherent in each of the "unwrapped" skills and concepts. This will enable them to better design aligned assessment questions, determine appropriate curriculum, and plan related instruction.

Adding DOK Levels to the Math Graphic Organizer

The same process used to determine and assign DOK levels to the "unwrapped" Common Core English language arts and literacy standards represented on the graphic organizer applies also to mathematics. Reproduced in Figure 2.11 is the *math and science* cognitive skills matrix, again through the courtesy of Dr. Karin Hess.

FIGURE 2.11	Karin Hess's Cognitive Rigor Matrix for Math and Science

Hess Cognitive Rigor Matrix (Math/Science): Applying Webb's Depth-of-Knowledge Levels to Bloom's Cognitive Process Dimensions				
Revised Bloom's Taxonomy	**Webb's DOK Level 1** Recall & Reproduction	**Webb's DOK Level 2** Skills & Concepts	**Webb's DOK Level 3** Strategic Thinking/ Reasoning	**Webb's DOK Level 4** Extended Thinking
Remember Retrieve knowledge from long-term memory, recognize, recall, locate, identify	• Recall, observe, & recognize facts, principles, properties • Recall/identify conversions among representations or numbers (e.g., customary and metric measures)	Use these Hess CRM curricular examples with most mathematics or science assignments or assessments		
Understand Construct meaning, clarify, paraphrase, represent, translate, illustrate, give examples, classify, categorize, summarize, generalize, infer a logical conclusion, predict, compare/contrast, match like ideas, explain, construct models	• Evaluate an expression • Locate points on a grid or numbers on a number line • Solve a one-step problem • Represent math relationships in words, pictures, or symbols • Read, write, compare decimals in scientific notation	• Specify and explain relationships (e.g., non-examples/ examples; cause-effect) • Make and record observations • Explain steps followed • Summarize results or concepts • Make basic inferences or logical predictions from data/observations • Use models/diagrams to represent or explain mathematical concepts • Make and explain estimates	• Use concepts to solve non-routine problems • Explain, generalize, or connect ideas using supporting evidence • Make and justify conjectures • Explain thinking/reasoning when more than one solution or approach is possible • Explain phenomena in terms of concepts	• Relate mathematical or scientific concepts to other content areas, other domains, or other concepts • Develop generalizations of the results obtained and the strategies used (from investigation or readings) and apply them to new problem situation
Apply Carry out or use a procedure in a given situation; carry out (apply to a familiar task), or use (apply) to an unfamiliar task	• Follow simple procedures (recipe-type directions) • Calculate, measure, apply a rule (e.g., rounding) • Apply algorithm or formula (e.g., area, perimeter) • Solve linear equations • Make conversions among representations or numbers, or within and between customary and metric measures	• Select a procedure according to criteria and perform it • Solve routine problem applying multiple concepts or decision points • Retrieve information from a table, graph, or figure and use it to solve a problem requiring multiple steps • Translate between tables, graphs, words, and symbolic notations (e.g., graph data from a table) • Construct models given criteria	• Design investigation for a specific purpose or research question • Conduct a designed investigation • Use concepts to solve non-routine problems • Use & show reasoning, planning, and evidence • Translate between problem & symbolic notation when not a direct translation	• Select or devise approach among many alternatives to solve a problem • Conduct a project that specifies a problem, identifies solution paths, solves the problem, and reports results

Source: © Karin K. Hess (2009, updated 2013). Hess Cognitive Rigor Matrix (CRM) in Local Assessment Toolkit. Permission to use only with full citation. khess@nciea.org or kar_hes@msn.com.

FIGURE 2.11	Karin Hess's Cognitive Rigor Matrix for Math and Science *(continued)*

Hess Cognitive Rigor Matrix (Math/Science): Applying Webb's Depth-of-Knowledge Levels to Bloom's Cognitive Process Dimensions				
Revised Bloom's Taxonomy	**Webb's DOK Level 1** Recall & Reproduction	**Webb's DOK Level 2** Skills & Concepts	**Webb's DOK Level 3** Strategic Thinking/ Reasoning	**Webb's DOK Level 4** Extended Thinking
Analyze Break into constituent parts, determine how parts relate, differentiate between relevant-irrelevant, distinguish, focus, select, organize, outline, find coherence, deconstruct	• Retrieve information from a table or graph to answer a question • Identify whether specific information is contained in graphic representations (e.g., table, graph, T-chart, diagram) • Identify a pattern/trend	• Categorize, classify materials, data, figures based on characteristics • Organize or order data • Compare/contrast figures or data • Select appropriate graph and organize & display data • Interpret data from a simple graph • Extend a pattern	• Compare information within or across data sets or texts • Analyze and draw conclusions from data, citing evidence • Generalize a pattern • Interpret data from complex graph • Analyze similarities/differences between procedures or solutions	• Analyze multiple sources of evidence • Analyze complex/abstract themes • Gather, analyze, and evaluate information
Evaluate Make judgments based on criteria, check, detect inconsistencies or fallacies, judge, critique	"UG"— unsubstantiated generalizations = stating an opinion without providing any support for it!		• Cite evidence and develop a logical argument for concepts or solutions • Describe, compare, and contrast solution methods • Verify reasonableness of results	• Gather, analyze, & evaluate information to draw conclusions • Apply understanding in a novel way, provide argument or justification for the application
Create Reorganize elements into new patterns/structures, generate, hypothesize, design, plan, produce	• Brainstorm ideas, concepts, or perspectives related to a topic	• Generate conjectures or hypotheses based on observations or prior knowledge and experience	• Synthesize information within one data set, source, or text • Formulate an original problem given a situation • Develop a scientific/mathematical model for a complex situation	• Synthesize information across multiple sources or texts • Design a mathematical model to inform and solve a practical or abstract situation

Source: © Karin K. Hess (2009, updated 2013). Hess Cognitive Rigor Matrix (CRM) in Local Assessment Toolkit. Permission to use only with full citation. khess@nciea.org or kar_hes@msn.com.

FIGURE 2.12	**Determining DOK Levels (Math, Part 1)**

"Unwrapped" Concepts (students need to know)	"Unwrapped" Skills (students need to be able to do)	Taxonomy Levels	
		Bloom's / DOK	
• Numbers within 1000	**ADD** and **SUBTRACT**	2	2

Figure 2.12 shows the first entry in the graphic organizer of "unwrapped" concepts and skills for grade 2 math. Reading down the Level 2 column of the math DOK matrix (Figure 2.11), the first two descriptors in the second box—"Select a procedure according to criteria and perform it" and "Solve routine problem applying multiple concepts or decision points"—are a pretty close match to the skill-concept pair "Add and subtract numbers within 1000."

FIGURE 2.13	**Determining DOK Levels (Math, Part 2)**

"Unwrapped" Concepts (students need to know)	"Unwrapped" Skills (students need to be able to do)	Taxonomy Levels	
		Bloom's / DOK	

• Concrete models or drawings and strategies based on
  • Place value
  • Properties of operations
  • Relationship between addition and subtraction
	USE	3	2

The third descriptor in the same box of the Level 2 column in Figure 2.11—"Retrieve information from a table, graph, or figure and use it to solve a problem requiring multiple steps"—matches fairly closely the second pairing of skill and concepts listed on the graphic organizer, "Use concrete models or drawings based on . . . ," as shown in Figure 2.13.

Continuing the same process using the DOK math and science thinking skills matrix, all of the DOK levels have now been added to our Grade 2 math graphic organizer in Figure 2.14.

FIGURE 2.14 **Completed "Unwrapping" Chart (Math Grade 2)**

"Unwrapped" Concepts (students need to know)	"Unwrapped" Skills (students need to be able to do)	Taxonomy Levels Bloom's / DOK	
• Numbers within 1000	ADD and SUBTRACT	2	2
• Concrete models or drawings and strategies based on • Place value • Properties of operations • Relationship between addition and subtraction	USE	3	2
• Strategies to a written method	RELATE	4	3
• Hundreds and hundreds, tens and tens, ones and ones	UNDERSTAND	4	2
• Tens or hundreds	COMPOSE and DECOMPOSE	4	3
• Addition and subtraction strategies • Place value • Properties of operations	EXPLAIN WHY THEY WORK/USE	4	3

It can seem a bit more challenging when there are *two* math skills linked by the preposition "to" that must both be considered when determining the DOK level (see Figure 2.15). In the case of the revised Bloom's Taxonomy levels, this necessitated assigning two levels, 4 and 3. Using the DOK scale, it only requires one: Level 3.

Reading down the Level 2 column of the math and science matrix (Figure 2.11), the descriptors do not seem to indicate the rigor needed to carry out this part of the "unwrapped" standard. The complete skill ("construct to investigate") applied to

FIGURE 2.15	Determining DOK Levels (Math, Part 3)			

"Unwrapped" Concepts (students need to know)	"Unwrapped" Skills (students need to be able to do)	Taxonomy Levels	
		Bloom's / DOK	
• Scatter plots for bivariate measurement data • Patterns of association between two quantities	CONSTRUCT to INVESTIGATE	4 3	3

both mathematical concepts ("scatter plots for bivariate measurement data" and "patterns of association between two quantities") requires strategic thinking and reasoning. In the Level 3 column, however, four phrases listed in the second section—"Design investigation for a specific purpose or research question," "Conduct a designed investigation," "Use concepts to solve non-routine problems," and "Use & show reasoning, planning, and evidence"—are more representative of what the "unwrapped" standard is requiring students to know and be able to do. Therefore, DOK Level 3 can be assigned to this complete concept-skill pair.

The next "unwrapped" skill on the graphic organizer ("*interpret* to investigate," Figure 2.16), when applied to the same two mathematical concepts ("scatter plots for bivariate measurement data" and "patterns of association between two quantities"), also requires strategic thinking and reasoning. Reading down the Level 3 column of Figure 2.11, three phrases listed in the third section—"Compare information within or across data sets or texts," "Analyze and draw conclusions from data, citing evi-

FIGURE 2.16	Determining DOK Levels (Math, Part 4)			

"Unwrapped" Concepts (students need to know)	"Unwrapped" Skills (students need to be able to do)	Taxonomy Levels	
		Bloom's / DOK	
• Scatter plots for bivariate measurement data • Patterns of association between two quantities	INTERPRET to INVESTIGATE	5	3

dence," and "Interpret data from complex graph"—certainly represent a close approximation to what this "unwrapped" standard requires.

However, the point could also be made that engaging in this skill, "interpret to investigate," requires *extended thinking.* Reading down the Level 4 column (see Figure 2.11), this is represented in the phrase, "Gather, analyze, and evaluate information to draw conclusions." Therefore, either DOK Level 3 or 4 could be assigned to this entire concept-skill pair. Again, when you are uncertain about which of two levels is the correct one, go with the higher level. This will require educators to "teach up," but students who understand and can demonstrate a Level 4 skill would most likely be capable of also demonstrating a Level 3 skill.

The final "unwrapped" concept-skill pair, "DESCRIBE patterns," seems to be best reflected in the DOK Level 3 column descriptor, "Generalize a pattern" (see Figure 2.11).

The completed math graphic organizer for this "unwrapped" Priority Common Core math standard with the inclusion of DOK levels is shown in Figure 2.17.

FIGURE 2.17	Completed "Unwrapping" Chart (Math Grade 8)			

"Unwrapped" Concepts (students need to know)	"Unwrapped" Skills (students need to be able to do)	Taxonomy Levels	
		Bloom's / DOK	
• Scatter plots for bivariate measurement data • Patterns of association between two quantities	**CONSTRUCT** to **INVESTIGATE**	4 3	3
• Scatter plots for bivariate measurement data • Patterns of association between two quantities	**INTERPRET** to **INVESTIGATE**	5	3 or 4

• Patterns
  • Clustering
  • Outliers
  • Positive or negative association
  • Linear association
  • Nonlinear association
	DESCRIBE	4	3

Remember the Purpose

Again, keep in mind that the purpose in providing these examples is to demonstrate the process of assigning *closely approximated* revised Bloom's Taxonomy and DOK levels. It is not to provide the uncontested "right" answers. As stated earlier, "healthy debate" when colleagues collaborate to assign the Bloom's and DOK levels is a necessary and valuable part of the entire process to help educators gain greater understanding of the rigor and cognitive challenge inherent in each of the "unwrapped" skills and concepts. This will enable them to better design aligned assessment questions, determine appropriate curricula, and plan related instruction.

For further information regarding the useful application of Webb's Depth of Knowledge, visit www.karin-hess.com, or visit the Center for Assessment's Web site at www.nciea.org, click on "publications" in the navigation bar, search for "Karin Hess," and read her published papers on the use of DOK in ELA and math.

Another Consideration When Assigning DOK Levels to Common Core Math Standards

Lori Cook, a Professional Development Associate at The Leadership and Learning Center, shared with me cautionary information from a WestEd report for educators to consider when they are assigning DOK levels to their "unwrapped" Common Core math standards and designing related assessment questions. The message reinforces the idea of "teaching up" and "assessing up" when assigning DOK levels and creating *classroom* assessment questions.

> "*It should be noted that while the majority of the mathematics content knowledge as described by the Standards for Mathematical Content was rated at DOK levels 1 and 2, it is not necessarily the case that assessment items would be developed at the same DOK levels. Developers of the summative assessment items/tasks may decide to require students to apply the Standards for Mathematical Practice in varied and complex ways, resulting in assessment items/tasks at DOK levels 3 or 4.*"
>
> **—Edynn Sato, Rachel Lagunoff, and Peter Worth, 2011**

Other Perspectives about Assigning DOK Levels

As emphasized throughout this chapter, it is important to "unwrap" standards and ensure that each standard is assigned a level based on the taxonomy tables *before* educators design aligned assessment items. Writing the assessment questions directly matched to the "unwrapped" concepts, skills, and cognitive levels (both the revised Bloom's Taxonomy and Webb's Depth of Knowledge) is a critical requirement. Creation of the related assessment is the very next step that follows the "unwrapping" process. Indicating the DOK level next to each assessment question as well as on the "unwrapping" graphic organizer makes this connection explicit and directs assessment design.

Lisa Cebelak, who is also a Professional Development Associate at The Leadership and Learning Center, shared with me her advice to educators when she is leading them through the "unwrapping" process:

> "During the 'unwrapping' process, there should not be a choice of either using the revised Bloom's Taxonomy *or* DOK. When educators 'skip' Bloom's and instead use only DOK, the powerful conversations around *how* to teach the standard disappear. As a facilitator of this process, I feel that Bloom's underscores the importance of collaboration and discussion around teaching that is much needed. So many educators still teach in isolation. These conversations are very important to help them grow in their understanding of this powerful process."

Going on, Lisa offers another option for educators to consider with regard to the *timing* of when this task takes place:

> "With regard to the Common Core English language arts and literacy standards, I advocate postponing the assigning of a DOK level *until* the educators are ready to write the assessment questions. For example, in ELA/literacy, as soon as you create a constructed-response question, it could increase the initial assignment of DOK level simply due to the fact that students are being asked to write."

Lisa's comment illustrates the "back and forth," or circular process, that takes place between assigning the level of thinking to the "unwrapped" skill and designing the matching assessment questions.

Lisa continues:

> "When scaffolding a Priority Standard so that it is taught
> throughout the year in different units of study, that Priority
> Standard can take on different contexts depending on the part of
> the standard you are addressing in each particular unit. While that
> 'unwrapped' standard might be a DOK Level 1 or 2 in the first
> unit of study, it could quickly become a DOK Level 3 or 4 by the
> third or fourth unit of study, if the targeted part of that standard
> indicates a step up in rigor."

These additional considerations explain why I often refer to "unwrapping" as a thinking educator's process: the professional discussion this practice elicits is invaluable. Yet the intent of including these other perspectives here is not to confuse your understanding of how to complete the graphic organizer part of the "unwrapping" process, but rather to underscore its foundational connection to the design of assessment questions. In my years of experience guiding educators through this process, I have always asked them to complete the assignment of Bloom's and DOK levels *during* the graphic organizer step, informing them that the very next task is to create common formative assessment questions and authentic performance tasks for the unit of study. Repeatedly I emphasize the importance of writing those questions and tasks so that they are directly aligned to the levels of rigor they have already determined, and encourage them to make any and all revisions necessary to keep that alignment deliberate. Sometimes this means changing the DOK levels to match the assessment questions and tasks, but more often it spotlights the need to increase the level of rigor in the *questions.*

Again, Remember the Purpose

Assigning Bloom's and DOK cognitive levels to "unwrapped" skills can at first seem somewhat daunting. Don't let yourself feel overwhelmed by the task. Bloom's Taxonomy and Webb's DOK are simply *tools* that can be used to inform and improve instruction. As with any set of tools, practice makes using them easier. The most important benefit is the *collaborative process* of thinking about cognitive levels of rigor with your colleagues in advance of any assessment design and instructional planning.

Your Turn, Part 2: Add the Depth of Knowledge Levels

(1) Now you are ready to complete your graphic organizer by adding the Depth of Knowledge (DOK) levels next to the revised Bloom's Taxonomy levels assigned to the "unwrapped" concepts and skills.

(2) Reference Karin Hess' cognitive rigor matrix chart specific to either English language arts (Figure 2.8) or math (Figure 2.11). Decide the *approximate* thinking skill level (1–4) of each verb-concept pair. Remember, you can change your mind and revise your decisions whenever needed.

(3) When you are finished, ensure that you have carefully represented each and every "unwrapped" concept and skill on the graphic organizer with its approximate level of rigor for both Bloom's *and* DOK. Ask yourself if you could, in confidence, put the standards away and plan all instruction and assessment by referencing the organizer only. Review your work and double check each entry on the graphic organizer to make sure. Then place your "unwrapped" version of the standards next to the original standards themselves. Notice how much more user-friendly your graphic organizer is than the compacted sentences in the standards. Think how much easier this will make your unit planning!

Note: The completed graphic organizer will be much longer than the original "wrapped" Common Core standards. It may seem that the process of "unwrapping" has therefore complicated rather than simplified the standards. Because the concepts and skills flow so logically in sentence format, an educator does not always realize how much substance these standards contain until they "unwrap" and represent them all on the graphic organizer. But look at how many specific (and rigorous) concepts and skills those individual Priority Standards include—concepts and skills that you may have unintentionally overlooked had you not "unwrapped" them first.

What's Next?

Now that the graphic organizer is finished, you are ready to determine the Big Ideas. The purpose of the Big Ideas is to help students discover *why* these concepts and skills are important for them to learn. In the next chapter, you will see how to derive Big Ideas from the "unwrapped" Priority Standards and why doing so is one of the most powerful instructional strategies educators can use to help students retain what they have been taught long after instruction ends.

Critiquing Your Graphic Organizer

The following excerpt from the Rigorous Curriculum Design Unit Development Guide (created for educators to evaluate the quality of the units they designed) will assist you in evaluating the quality of the "unwrapping" and graphic organizer steps you have just completed. It functions like a rubric or scoring guide. Check the first column of each criterion you believe you have completed correctly. Highlight any criteria that you have yet to complete or want to revise.

"Unwrapped" Priority Standards ONLY		
	Essential Element	**Comment(s)/Feedback**
	Underlines Teachable Concepts (Nouns, Noun Phrases) and CAPITALIZES Skills (Verbs) Students Are to Know/Do	
	Connects Skills to Concepts on Graphic Organizer with Parenthetical Side-By-Side Notation, e.g., • DETERMINE (main idea) • CONVERT (fraction to decimal)	
	Identifies Approximate Levels of Bloom's (1–6) and Depth of Knowledge (1–4) for Each Skill-Concept Pair	
	Graphic Organizer Represents *All* "Unwrapped" Concepts and Skills from Priority Standards ONLY	

CHAPTER 3

Decide the Big Ideas

What exactly are Big Ideas anyway? I like to think of them as "light bulb moments," those sudden flashes of illumination when a student says, "Oh, I get it!" and goes on to articulate the meaning he or she has suddenly come to understand.

Big Ideas originate with the educator who thinks deeply, in advance of any instructional planning, about what the end learning goals for students should be for a particular unit of study. The educator then guides students *during* the unit to discover these Big Ideas for themselves by the *end* of the unit. This backwards-planning approach to standards-based unit design is an intentional way of aligning standards, assessment, curriculum, and instruction.

Although extremely beneficial to educators, ultimately the Big Ideas provide the greatest benefit to *students* because:

- Big Ideas represent those "aha!" realizations, discoveries, or conclusions students reach *on their own* either during or after instruction.

- Big Ideas are key generalizations students are able to articulate in their own words after their "I get it" moment.

- Big Ideas bring relevancy to students by answering their unspoken mental question: "Why do I have to learn this anyway?" or "When will I ever use this in real life?"

- Big Ideas *endure* in students' minds and help them apply those insights to future learning. That is why they are often referred to as "enduring understandings" (Wiggins and McTighe, 2005).

Here are a few stand-alone examples of Big Ideas derived from Common Core English language arts and math standards in different grade levels:

- Retelling the story helps me comprehend what I read.

- Knowing the author's message helps me understand what I read.

- Symbolism is used in literature to represent something more than its literal meaning.

- Knowing the parts of speech will make us better writers.

- The place-value system is based on groups of ten.

- Quantities can be represented in different ways and are still the same quantity.

- Diagrams, models, and equations help you visualize and solve word problems.

- The area of a polygon can be determined by composing rectangles or decomposing into triangles.

Big Ideas are not limited to English language arts and literacy and mathematics, even though the focus of this book is on how to apply the "unwrapping" process to the Common Core State Standards. Here are a few Big Idea examples from other content areas and grade levels:

- Geographic, political, cultural, and religious structures work together to ensure the survival and advancement of all civilizations.

- Energy can change forms, but never disappears.

- Teamwork promotes cooperation and positive interaction among individuals.

- What you eat and do can affect your health now and in the future.

- Music performance incorporates a variety of literature from various genres, styles, and cultures.

- Knowing another language can help you communicate in other cultures.

- Tires and wheels need to be compatible and uniform for proper function.

Your graphic organizer of "unwrapped" concepts, skills, and levels of cognitive rigor (identified from the revised Bloom's and Webb's DOK taxonomies) represents the "what" and the "how" of the particular standards in focus. The concepts are the "what" that students need to know; the skills and cognition levels are "how" they need to demonstrate them. Now let's consider the "why"—the *reasons* these concepts and skills are important for students to understand and be able to do. I call these reasons the Big Ideas and define them as follows:

> **Big Ideas** are the three or four foundational understandings—
> main ideas, conclusions, or generalizations derived from the unit's
> "unwrapped" concepts—that educators want their students to
> discover and state in their own words by the end of the unit of study.
> Written as *complete sentences*, not phrases, Big Ideas convey to
> *students* the benefit or value of learning the standards in focus that
> they are to remember long after instruction ends.

Deciding the Big Ideas works best when it is done collaboratively. Grade-level or course-alike educators bounce ideas off one another until they hit upon the wording of their Big Ideas. To encourage educators to brainstorm and not get bogged down in the precise wording of a Big Idea statement, I always say to them, "Don't get it right; get it written. You can always wordsmith it later."

Why Big Ideas?

Sadly, much of what I learned in high school and college I simply memorized for a specific test. Once the test was over, so was much of my retention of that particular information. I didn't understand why that was so at the time. Only when I became an educator years later did I come to understand that I had had no larger framework or structure in which to place the voluminous number of facts I was striving to remember, nor did I see much relevancy of the information to the whole of my life. And because I never again needed most of that information, it remained "out of sight, out of mind."

In *"Unwrapping" the Standards* (2003), I excerpted a persuasive article in support of Big Ideas titled "The Standards Juggernaut." In it, educational consultant Marion Brady (2000) states: "Give adults the exams they took a few years earlier in high school or college, and their poor performance will prove that facts that are not made part of an often-used, larger scheme of meaning are soon forgotten" (p. 650).

Brady goes on to say what many educators are realizing even more today: Students need "large-scale mental organizers" or "Big Ideas" to help them organize and make sense of the myriad facts they are expected to learn. The lessons from brain research have underscored the fact that the human brain organizes information according to patterns. Unless educators deliberately help their students connect the concepts and skills being taught to *prior learning* through some type of organizational structure, Brady (2000) concludes that "facts will continue to come first" with little chance that "some master pattern will eventually emerge to bind (the facts) together in a way that makes useful sense" (p. 650).

Educators need to help students connect the dots of understanding. In order for students to discover these larger concepts *on their own*, they need learning opportunities that allow them to "wrestle with" ideas and understand them at a deep level. "Key principles and generalizations [are] . . . the 'big ideas' that transfer through time and across cultures" (Erickson, 2000, p. 83). Big Ideas are "the important understandings that we want students to 'get inside of' and retain after they've forgotten many of the details" (Wiggins and McTighe, 1998, p. 10).

In his extensive meta-analyses of educational research presented in *Visible Learning* (2009), John Hattie writes: "Teachers are successful to the degree that they can move students from single to multiple ideas, and then relate and extend these ideas (so that) learners construct and reconstruct knowledge and ideas. It is not the knowledge or ideas, but rather the learner's construction of the knowledge and ideas that is critical" (p. 37).

The Deep End of the Pool

The term "Big Idea" often seems a bit abstract. In fact, for years educators have said to me whenever they got to this part of the process, "I was humming right along, underlining concepts and capitalizing skills, and now I'm struggling to come up with the Big Ideas. It's like I've been thrown into the deep end of the pool."

For the majority of educators I have worked with, identifying Big Ideas does not come easily. Why? Because most teachers will confide that they, like me, were not taught to think about making insightful connections during their own educational experience. Yet their recognition of the importance of doing this, coupled with a corresponding willingness to find out how, is rooted in a strong desire to help students become able to grasp Big Ideas on their own.

It is not enough simply to say to students, "Here's the Big Idea you need to know," and then proceed to tell them what that Big Idea is. If it were this easy, we could simply tell students how everything relates to everything else and be done. We would no longer see students engaged in the struggle to make their own connections between present and past learning—*the critical factor in the learning process.*

As the saying goes, "If teaching were merely 'telling,' we would all be so smart we wouldn't know what to do with ourselves!" We know that what lasts is what we realize and conclude on our own. When students independently discover the Big Ideas for themselves (a discovery guided by their teacher), they are far more likely to retain those understandings.

How the Graphic Organizer Helps Identify Big Ideas

Big Ideas come from the "unwrapped" *concepts*, not the "unwrapped" skills, because the concepts represent the essential understandings we want the students to derive from a standards-based unit. When educators start thinking about what the Big Ideas are for their unit of study, they look at the "Unwrapped" Concepts column of their graphic organizer and start brainstorming what the three or four important "takeaways" from the study of those concepts might be. This is not to minimize the importance of the skills, however. It is in the *exercise of those related skills* during instruction and related activities that students arrive at the "aha" understandings about the concepts. Thus, concepts and skills *together* lead to students' realization of the Big Ideas.

Educators have repeatedly said to me that they like using the graphic organizer to identify their Big Ideas because it gives them a practical way of moving from the "concrete" (the underlined concepts that students need to learn) to the "abstract" (the key understandings or generalizations they want students to draw from the particular standard).

Often it is easier, and more manageable, to look at each of the bulleted headings in the Concepts column and think about what the corresponding Big Idea might be *for that heading* and its related sub-points. Because the Big Ideas are not usually self-evident, grouping the concepts under headings and then looking at one section at a time is an easy way to start. This is not to say there must always be a one-to-one correspondence of Big Ideas with major headings; often two Big Ideas can be derived from one section.

English Language Arts and Literacy Big Ideas

To make this abstract concept more concrete, let's see how Big Ideas can be determined from the "unwrapped" Common Core State Standards in English language arts and literacy. Revisiting the English language arts example from the previous two chapters, the first heading "central idea" is followed by its indented sub-points (see Figure 3.1).

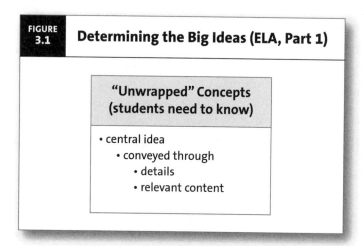

FIGURE 3.1　Determining the Big Ideas (ELA, Part 1)

**"Unwrapped" Concepts
(students need to know)**

- central idea
  - conveyed through
    - details
    - relevant content

Big Ideas are not definitions to be memorized. Educators would certainly want students to know what a central idea *is*, such as "The main or central idea is a sentence or generalization that tells mostly what the text is about." But beyond just the definition, they would want students to understand its application, *how the central idea can be communicated.* So the Big Idea in this instance could be worded something like this:

You can convey or explain a central idea by supporting it with details and relevant content.

This statement of understanding goes beyond a simple definition of "central idea" to evoke deeper thought on the part of the student.

Let's look at the rest of the graphic organizer (Figure 3.2) to decide how the Big Ideas could be derived from the other "unwrapped" concepts.

With a little combining of the bulleted concepts, three major concepts emerge: (1) summary; (2) author's point of view and purpose; and (3) fact, opinion, and reasoned judgment. The remaining two, "informative writing and explanatory text," could be folded in with one or more of those major concepts. The following two Big Ideas address *all* of these concepts in a connected way:

An effective summary of informational text is free of personal opinions and judgments.

An author of informational text tries to convey a particular point of view through relevant facts and without bias.

Together, these three Big Ideas represent the key understandings educators would want their students to take away from the unit of study focused on these particular

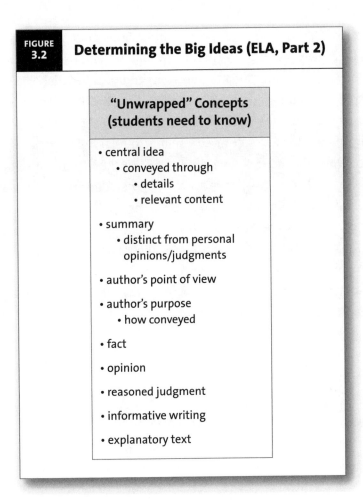

FIGURE 3.2 Determining the Big Ideas (ELA, Part 2)

"Unwrapped" Concepts
(students need to know)

- central idea
  - conveyed through
    - details
    - relevant content
- summary
  - distinct from personal opinions/judgments
- author's point of view
- author's purpose
  - how conveyed
- fact
- opinion
- reasoned judgment
- informative writing
- explanatory text

Priority Standards. Certainly they would expect students to be able to elaborate or provide examples in support of each Big Idea statement, but the *essence* of what students needed to understand, retain, and apply to future learning would be captured in these Big Ideas.

Math Big Ideas

I have observed during my years leading educators through the "unwrapping" of individual state standards that the Big Ideas in mathematics often look more like *foundational understandings* ("The position of a digit determines its number") rather than perceptive insights ("Math formulas are actually just shortcuts that help me solve problems more quickly"). This is still proving to be true when determining

Big Ideas for the "unwrapped" Common Core math standards, although I am not recommending that math Big Ideas remain only on that level. Certainly educators want to help students make larger connections and thus broaden their mathematical understandings, but foundational understandings are often a necessary first step.

As a former math teacher, whenever I used to think about what the Big Ideas for a math unit should be, the resulting statements were usually expressed more as important *foundational understandings* because I knew these represented key ideas that students absolutely had to grasp in order to be prepared for math concepts and skills yet to come that year or in succeeding grade levels.

To see how to determine math Big Ideas from "unwrapped" Common Core concepts, let's look again at the first column of the Grade 2 math graphic organizer shown in the previous chapter (see Figure 3.3).

Even though there are several "unwrapped" concepts listed on this graphic organizer, what students really need to grasp for themselves are two Big Ideas that collectively represent *all* of these "unwrapped" concepts:

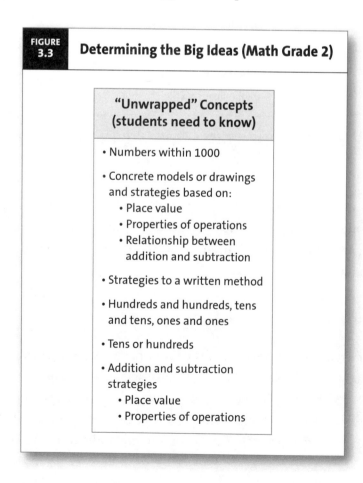

FIGURE 3.3 **Determining the Big Ideas (Math Grade 2)**

"Unwrapped" Concepts (students need to know)

- Numbers within 1000

- Concrete models or drawings and strategies based on:
  - Place value
  - Properties of operations
  - Relationship between addition and subtraction

- Strategies to a written method

- Hundreds and hundreds, tens and tens, ones and ones

- Tens or hundreds

- Addition and subtraction strategies
  - Place value
  - Properties of operations

Some strategies are faster or more efficient for adding and subtracting big numbers.

Addition and subtraction are inverse operations.

The intent is not to limit student understanding to only these two Big Ideas. Certainly students would need to understand the purpose and value of those "unwrapped" concepts not specifically named in the Big Ideas for this unit of study (e.g., numbers within 1000, place value) Additional examples of Big Ideas for this same "unwrapped" Priority Standard appear in the Topical Big Ideas section later in this chapter.

To see how to derive a math Big Idea from the Grade 8 "unwrapped" Common Core concepts, let's revisit the first column of the eighth grade math graphic organizer shown in the previous chapter (see Figure 3.4). The major headings are about scatter plots and the different kinds of patterns of association.

Here is one possible Big Idea that could address the combination of all these related concepts:

Lines of best fit help you visualize the patterns in data.

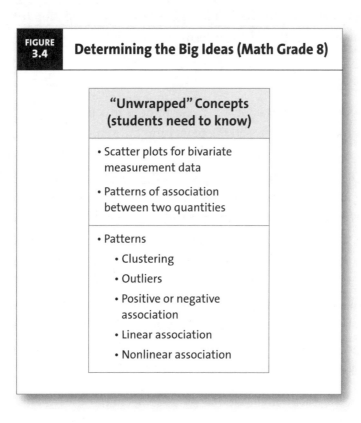

FIGURE 3.4 **Determining the Big Ideas (Math Grade 8)**

"Unwrapped" Concepts (students need to know)

- Scatter plots for bivariate measurement data
- Patterns of association between two quantities

- Patterns
  - Clustering
  - Outliers
  - Positive or negative association
  - Linear association
  - Nonlinear association

Math educators might decide they want *two* Big Ideas for this particular set of "unwrapped" concepts, the one for scatter plots and patterns of association, and the other for the various types of patterns (represented in the sub-points), such as this:

> *Mathematical patterns can be determined or identified in multiple ways and used for different problem-solving situations.*

Educators make the decision about how many Big Ideas are needed for a unit of study. Sometimes there is a need for three or four Big Ideas and other times only one or two. The bottom line is that the Big Ideas for any unit should collectively represent *all* of the "unwrapped" Priority Standards concepts for that unit.

Why "Unwrap" Only to "Re-Wrap"?

One of the issues that may arise when math educators are collaborating to determine the Big Ideas is that the process can begin to *seem* redundant or even unnecessary, especially when nearly the entire standard has been underlined, as shown again in this Grade 8 Common Core Statistics and Probability standard.

> **8.SP.1:** CONSTRUCT and INTERPRET scatter plots for bivariate measurement data to INVESTIGATE patterns of association between two quantities. DESCRIBE patterns such as clustering, outliers, positive or negative association, linear association, and nonlinear association.

It may look as if all any educator needs to do is to separate the standard into its concepts and skills, reposition all the parts onto the graphic organizer, and then reassemble it as a Big Idea. Math educators may rightly ask: "Why not just leave the standard in its original form and pull out the Big Idea directly from it?" It is because the act of analyzing and breaking apart the standard ("unwrapping") provides absolute *clarity* about the specific concepts and skills that the educator must teach and the students must learn. But then the separate elements have to be put back together again ("re-wrapped") as Big Ideas to represent the end learning goals: the "takeaways" that students need to discover and remember on their own by the conclusion of the unit of study. And it requires a paraphrase or synthesis of the standard, not just a recitation of it in its original form. This entire deconstruction-reconstruction process results in educators feeling they know the standard "inside and out" *before* they ever begin assessment design and instructional planning.

Student-Worded Big Ideas

Adults often exchange intellectual ideas using language that is beyond the understanding of most students. Because educators are typically master communicators, they know inherently how to communicate complex ideas in an understandable way to their students, whatever age their students may be. That is why, after articulating the Big Ideas in language they themselves might use, a powerful next step in the Big Idea identification process is for educators to think how to write those Big Ideas in student-friendly wording, to consider how *students* might say them in simpler language.

Because of my 24 years of teaching experience in the classroom, I am used to thinking from the perspective of "what's in it for the students?" Whenever I am trying to determine the Big Ideas, I look at the "Unwrapped" Concepts column of the graphic organizer and ask myself: "Okay, so what? If I were to teach my students these concepts and skills, what would *I* want them to realize at a deeper level of understanding than mere recall of information?" This leads me to identify what I hope *students* will deeply understand about the concepts and skills related to the "unwrapped" standard. How will they express these Big Ideas in their own words?

I always remember the quiet wisdom of Jane Cimolino, my mentor teacher with 35 years of classroom experience who first introduced me to the concept of Big Ideas in the mid-1990s. As we planned an integrated history/social science and language arts unit for a combination class of fifth and sixth grade students, Jane said to me, "The study of history should never be reduced to memorizing a mountain of facts that students will rarely ever remember. So I always try to think of the three or four Big Ideas I want the students to be able to explain to me in their own words after instruction ends. I then strive to help them connect these Big Ideas to their own lives. If I don't, history has no real relevancy and meaning for them."

Putting Jane's wisdom into practice at the time, I wrote these four Big Ideas for my Ancient Egypt and Mesopotamia unit:

1. Civilizations require geographic, political, economic, religious, and social structures in order to survive and thrive.

2. Each structure plays a unique and interconnected role with other structures for the survival of the civilization.

3. The effects of human actions combined with environmental factors determine whether a civilization ceases to exist or continues to survive.

4. Contemporary civilizations parallel those of the past.

At the conclusion of our unit, I asked my students: "So what do you think were the most important things you learned during this particular unit of study?"

One student exclaimed, "I didn't know that every civilization on earth back then had the same basic ways of organizing their society."

Another added, "Or that those ways all worked together to keep their civilizations going."

And this last one proved Jane's assertion that students must be able to see the connections between what we teach them in the classroom and their own lives in the real world: "Our society today is a lot like those that aren't around any longer."

The students had indeed expressed my original Big Ideas in their own words, and as I listened to their responses, I thought their versions expressed more succinctly and accurately the essential understandings I wanted them to have than did mine. What teacher of this content area wouldn't be thrilled to hear his or her students be able to articulate these insights in this way?

Educators have often said to me, "I usually think in terms of how students say things anyway, so I just naturally write my Big Ideas in words my students would most likely use."

After you and your colleagues have drafted your Big Ideas, ask yourselves, "How would the students say these?" It may help to think of how to make the Big Ideas *conversational.* The easiest way to do this is to look at an adult-worded Big Idea, take the essence of that statement, and then substitute simpler language.

Examples of Student-Worded Big Ideas

Here are a few English language arts Big Idea examples that illustrate this "translation" from adult-worded to student-friendly statements:

1. Narratives need a specific setting and supporting details to advance plot.
   Stories need a place to happen with details that keep readers interested.

2. Informational writing develops a central idea and provides details to support it.
   Informational writing always has a main idea that the writer backs up with supporting details.

3. Different kinds of writing communicate information for a variety of

purposes and audiences.
Writers need to know how to say what they mean in different ways for different people.

4. Knowing the differences between facts, opinions, and inferences helps you make your own decisions about what you read.
Don't believe everything you read.

5. Effective writers need to revise their work as many times as needed in order to improve it.
The first time you write something is not the last!

These math examples also illustrate the transition from adult-worded to student-friendly Big Ideas:

1. The position of a digit in a number determines its value.
Where a digit is in a number tells me what it's worth.

2. Multiplication and division are inverse operations.
Multiplication and division are opposites, the way subtraction is the opposite of addition.

3. Mathematical formulas and estimates both provide shortcuts for determining needed mathematical information.
Math formulas are shortcuts I can use to help me solve problems faster.

4. Selecting and using interchangeable measurement units helps to make sense of quantities in the real world.
The measurement unit that's best to use depends on what you are measuring.

Educators often ask me if their Big Ideas are "okay." Before I show them the specific criteria that reflect well-written Big Ideas (included in the "Your Turn" and "Critiquing Your Big Ideas" sections at the end of this chapter), I respond to their question by asking them this: "Would you be happy if your students could say these Big Ideas *by themselves in their own words* by the conclusion of the unit?" They usually reply with exultations such as, "I'd be thrilled" or "I'd be turning cartwheels." That is the best measure that the Big Ideas are indeed "okay."

Topical Big Ideas—A Pathway to Broad Big Ideas

Big Ideas can be *topical* ("Fractions represent quantities less than, equal to, or greater than one whole," applicable to math only), *broad* ("People can justify their conclusions with data," applicable to several content areas), or *both* ("Objects can be compared and classified by their different attributes," applicable to math and science).

Topical Big Ideas relate primarily to a particular unit of study or section of the standards. The following topical Big Idea in reading is specific to standards that emphasize story elements and how they are arranged: "All events in a story—present, past, and future—play a strategic part in its conclusion."

Broad Big Ideas are the generalizations derived from one area of study that connect to many standards and even several subject matter areas, such as "Research brings together divergent viewpoints."

Big ideas—whether topical, broad, or both—help students scaffold their understanding so they can eventually make further generalizations and connections to other units of study within a discipline and to other disciplines as well.

Examples of Topical Big Ideas

Again, topical Big Ideas relate specifically to the "unwrapped" Priority Standards concepts for a particular unit of study. Figure 3.5 shows again the Grade 2 Common Core math graphic organizer representing the Number and Operations in Base Ten domain that appeared earlier in the chapter. Here are the three related Big Ideas. After reading them, think how second graders might say them in their own words.

1. The place-value system is based on groups of ten.

2. To compare numbers you must use place value.

3. A quantity can be rearranged in different ways and it is still the same quantity.

Each one of these baseline Big Ideas is critical to building students' number sense in mathematics. Often topical Big Ideas represent the "building blocks" we want to be sure students achieve relative to a particular unit of study—foundational math understandings they will need to build upon in future learning.

Topical Big Ideas about the Writing Process

The widely used, sequential steps of the writing process (prewriting, drafting, revising, editing, and publishing) can also help to illustrate the idea of *topical* Big Ideas in English language arts.

The first step of the writing process is to brainstorm ideas. The topical Big Idea

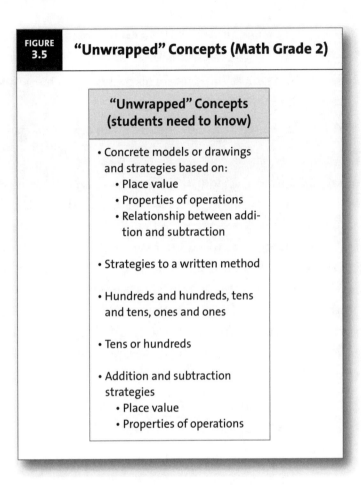

FIGURE 3.5 — "Unwrapped" Concepts (Math Grade 2)

> **"Unwrapped" Concepts (students need to know)**
>
> • Concrete models or drawings and strategies based on:
>   • Place value
>   • Properties of operations
>   • Relationship between addition and subtraction
>
> • Strategies to a written method
>
> • Hundreds and hundreds, tens and tens, ones and ones
>
> • Tens or hundreds
>
> • Addition and subtraction strategies
>   • Place value
>   • Properties of operations

might be, "Prewriting helps you plan what you are going to write about." The second step is to write the first draft. The topical Big Idea might be, "Writing a first draft helps you get your ideas written in an organized way." Continuing on in the same manner, the benefit of each of the remaining steps of the writing process could also be expressed with a topical Big Idea.

Broad Big Ideas in English Language Arts

But there are also *broad* Big Ideas, the larger generalizations often derived from several topical ideas. For example, the five *topical* ideas of the writing process above could be represented in this one *broad* Big Idea: "Writing is a process that involves many steps."

Consider these broad Big Ideas that represent multiple ELA standards that span several grade levels:

1. Fiction and nonfiction forms of writing each have their own unique formats, vocabulary, language, and style.

2. Proficient writers choose different forms of writing to meet their specific purpose for particular audiences.

3. Effective writing supports its major points with relevant facts and details.

Once educators become accustomed to identifying *topical* Big Ideas, they can consider how to move from *topical* Big Ideas to *broader* Big Ideas. A helpful question to begin this would be: "What connections can I make between these unit-based Big Ideas to those that extend beyond one unit of study?" By expanding your own understanding in this way, you will be better able to teach your students how to eventually make such broader generalizations by themselves.

To help students learn how to generalize their thinking to broader Big Ideas, topical Big Ideas are a necessary starting point. They are the "cognitive springboards" to help students learn how to think bigger and make larger connections. For these reasons, the majority of Big Ideas presented in this book are *topical* Big Ideas.

More Than Just One Sentence

The Big Idea statement represents the kernel of understanding we want students to comprehend independently and remember indefinitely. It is usually represented by a single statement. However, students certainly should be expected to expound on that single statement if asked to do so, just as they are taught to write a topic sentence and then elaborate upon that main idea with supporting detail sentences. Otherwise, the Big Idea may be reduced to a factual statement response that does not reveal whether the student has grasped its larger importance.

For example: "Estimation comes close to an actual number" is a necessary starting point for a student, but it is really only a definition. The true *Big Idea* that the student would hopefully be able to state as an elaboration to that definition would be, "Whether you need to estimate or find the actual answer depends on the situation." That statement clearly shows that the student understands the value or benefit of knowing when estimation is and isn't needed.

Not a "Cookie Cutter" Process

Writing Big Ideas can be challenging, tricky, and even frustrating at first. There is no "cookie cutter" approach to doing so. I've always encouraged educators to first brainstorm their Big Ideas and then go back and revise them until they are happy with the results, just as they encourage students to revise their first drafts of an important piece of writing. Repeated here is the encouragement stated earlier in the chapter: "Don't get it right; get it written and then wordsmith it later." As with almost every challenging new task, the more one does it, the easier it gets. The mind starts to think in terms of Big Ideas and becomes increasingly articulate in identifying them.

Workshop participants have always said at the end of the day that it was very helpful to look at first-draft Big Ideas created and shared by other workshop participants and then immediately review their own first drafts. This helped them revise any Big Ideas that may have been too broad or too narrow and to recognize the ones that are "just right." It has helped them identify the Big Ideas that are topical and the ones that are broader in nature, and rework those that need just a bit more "tweaking." This collaborative learning process results in a quality enhancement of everyone's Big Ideas. It's always fun to see which Big Ideas shared by workshop participants get the "ooh" or "ahh" response or head nods from the audience—that intuitive recognition that the Big Idea being shared has expressed an essential truth or captured the essence of an important realization relevant to the standards in focus.

How Many Big Ideas?

Jane Cimolino used to caution me about having too many Big Ideas. She would say, "If we want to help the students really understand ancient civilizations, we need to focus on only *three or four* Big Ideas for a particular unit. Otherwise we are not going to achieve the depth we need to reach for students to remember the information that is most important."

There is no set rule as to how many Big Ideas an educator should identify for a unit of study. This is a matter of professional choice. It depends on the number and complexity of the standards assigned to the unit. In several grade levels, for example, one Common Core math standard is literally the length of a paragraph, and it is packed with concepts and skills that students must know and be able to do. That one standard may require two or three Big Ideas to capture its breadth and depth, whereas the concepts in two or three single-sentence standards can be represented with one Big Idea.

The number of Big Ideas also depends on the grade level (usually there are fewer in lower grades and *perhaps* there are more in higher grades) and on the planned length of the unit. I recommend identifying only as many Big Ideas as needed to collectively represent the "unwrapped" concepts and skills students need to learn in that unit. But as a general rule of thumb, this number should not exceed four, if at all possible. More than four Big Ideas for one unit of study can prove difficult for students to grasp on a deep level.

Helping students arrive at the Big Ideas calls to mind a nugget of Far Eastern wisdom about teaching that I read more than a quarter of a century ago: True education is not a "pumping in" of information, but a "drawing out" from the learner the knowledge already present within. The educator who helps students "draw from their own understanding within" gives students the gift of learning how to think for themselves.

Big Ideas Contain a Benefit

A Big Idea statement often contains within it a *benefit* for learning. This example of a high school English Big Idea provides a good illustration: "Literary devices enhance and deepen fiction's impact upon the reader." Instead of an educator trying to "tell" students why literary devices are important, wouldn't it be exciting if students, upon completion of a novel that was rich in literary devices, could announce to the teacher, "Now I understand why you made us learn metaphors, allusion, satire, and irony! That novel we just read was so much more interesting because you taught us those literary devices, then asked us to identify them in the novel, and tell why they were important to the story. The literary devices really got me into the imaginary world of the author. Now I understand *why* this is a great book!"

Because the students, on their own, have identified the Big Idea, stated it in their own words, and discovered the benefit for learning it, the likelihood is high that they will retain this understanding long after the unit is over. Identifying such a benefit of Big Ideas is especially valuable considering the number of times educators must listen to students moan, "Why do we have to learn this?"

The benefit of learning is often expressed by the inclusion in the Big Idea of the word "help." The student understands that if he or she learns this or that, it will *help* him or her in some way. In one of the "unwrapped" Grade 4 Common Core math standards within the Measurement and Data domain, the Big Idea is, "Diagrams, models, and equations *help* visualize and solve word problems." Another Big Idea from a Grade 5 math standard in the Number and Operations-Fractions domain is,

"Benchmark fractions and estimates *help* to verify the reasonableness of an answer." The *help* is received by the student to "visualize and solve word problems" or to "verify the reasonableness of an answer."

Should We Post the Big Ideas in the Classroom?

Educators occasionally ask, "If the Big Ideas are so important, why not post them on the classroom wall beside the standards we are learning? Then we can simply announce to students, 'This is what you will be learning during this unit.'"

Even though it is a powerful practice for an educator to think about and identify the Big Ideas for a particular unit of study prior to instruction, simply announcing the Big Ideas to students at the inception of a unit eliminates their motivation to discover those desired end results of learning for themselves. From the students' point of view, this may sound as if the teacher is saying, "I have already realized these Big Ideas, and now you get to have that same experience. Lucky you!" Remember that the power of Big Ideas lies in the expectation that students will *discover them on their own*.

To promote student interest and engagement, consider posting instead open-ended *Essential Questions* on the classroom walls at the beginning of an instructional unit. Then announce to students that they will be exploring these questions in depth during the unit and that by the time the unit is over, they will be able to answer or respond to these questions with "Big Ideas" stated in their own words.

Along with the Essential Questions, many educators also post on large chart paper for the duration of the unit a student-friendly version of the graphic organizer of "unwrapped" concepts and skills and point out to students the specific concepts and skills they are learning each day. This is more effective than simply posting the standards on the wall and announcing to students, "Today we will be learning Common Core Standard 4!" It helps the students see the direct connections between what they are learning that day and the bigger picture of the entire unit.

Guidelines to Determine Big Ideas

Here are a few questions to ask yourself when determining your own Big Ideas from the Priority Standards you "unwrap":

- Will this Big Idea help students understand the benefit of learning the Priority Standards in this unit?

- Will this Big Idea help students make connections to prior learning?

- Will this Big Idea help students prepare for more abstract ideas or generalizations in subsequent units and grade levels?

- Will this Big Idea endure?

- Will students remember this Big Idea long after instruction ends?

Your Turn

(1) Refer again to the "Unwrapped" Concepts column on your graphic organizer. Think and discuss with colleagues these two questions:

- "What are the main or essential understandings we want the students to discover on their own after learning these 'unwrapped' concepts and skills?"

- "What do *we* think is important for our students to understand as a result of studying this particular combination of concepts and skills?"

(2) *Practice* writing your first-draft Big Ideas. Keep this simple. Brainstorm two, three, or four Big Ideas without worrying about the exact wording. Remember, you can always go back and revise or wordsmith them later.

(3) If you are having difficulty or are not sure exactly what to write, break the process down by focusing on just *one* bulleted heading on the graphic organizer at a time. Ask this question, specific to your particular concepts:

- "What is the Big Idea about *structural elements of literature*?"

- "What is the Big Idea about *literary devices*?"

OR

- "What is the Big Idea about *mathematical patterns*?"

- "What is the Big Idea about *two- and three-dimensional shapes*?"

The answers you come up with are likely to be the topical Big Ideas you are looking for.

(4) Educators always appreciate seeing examples of Big Ideas either before or after they draft their own. If it would be helpful to you, refer again to the various examples in this chapter and also to the particular chapter of English language arts and math examples for the grade that is closest to your own (see grade-span exam-

ple Chapters 5 through 8). Then make any changes to your own Big Ideas based on the ideas you get from the examples.

(5) Ask yourself and/or your colleagues these two guiding questions: "Would I/we be happy if my/our students could state these Big ideas in their own words?" and "Do my/our Big Ideas represent foundational understandings and/or convey the benefit for learning these particular standards?"

(6) Once you have your Big Ideas in reasonably good shape, see if you can "translate" them into student-friendly language. Think how the students might express them.

Along with your graphic organizer of "unwrapped" concepts, skills, and levels of rigor (from the revised Bloom's and Webb's DOK), your Big Ideas will be your road map and your guide as you design your end-of-unit assessment and plan and deliver instruction. At the conclusion of the next chapter, you will write Essential Questions, review and refine your Big Ideas, and see if those Big Ideas indeed are the desired responses to your Essential Questions.

Critiquing Your Big Ideas

Here is the related excerpt from the Rigorous Curriculum Design Unit Development Guide that is specific to evaluating the quality of your Big Ideas. Again, check the first column of each criterion you believe you have completed correctly. Highlight any criteria that you have to complete or want to revise.

Big Ideas	
Essential Element	**Comment(s)/Feedback**
Represent Desired Student Responses to Teacher's Essential Questions	
Written Succinctly in Complete Statements (3 to 4 Maximum)	
Reflect Explicit and/or Inferential Connections Students Are to Make and Retain After Instruction Concludes	
Convey Value or Long-Term Benefit of Learning to Students	
Topical Statements (Specific to Priority Standards in Focus) that Could Lead to Broader Generalizations	
Link Directly to "Unwrapped" Priority Standards, Not to Curriculum Materials	
Represent *All* "Unwrapped" Priority Standards Collectively	

CHAPTER 4

Write the Essential Questions

Thoughtfully worded questions posed to students by the teacher, with the expectation that students will think and respond, encourage active listening versus passive inattention. It is much easier to "tune out" the voice of a teacher lecturing than it is to "tune in" to an instructional and thought-provoking *dialogue* that requires active participation by the learner.

At some point in my long and fulfilling career as a classroom educator, I began "telling" less and "asking" more. It probably had something to do with the fact that I realized I was working harder than many of my students, doing too much of their thinking for them. Trying to motivate reluctant learners was exhausting and frustrating when, despite my best efforts, they just were not responding. When I began transferring more of the responsibility for their learning to *them*—by posing worthwhile questions and waiting for them to think and reply—they began to get more involved. In time, many students who had been quiet and unresponsive to classroom instruction and related activities became more engrossed and engaged. They began asking *their own* questions about whatever we were learning instead of just answering mine. Not surprisingly, they began saying, "School isn't boring anymore."

Big Ideas: The Responses to the Essential Questions

Questions stimulate thought and generate answers. At the beginning of a unit of study educators post—in a prominent location in the classroom or instructional space—two to four questions written in bold, colorful lettering. They explain to their students that these questions are a special type of question known as "Essential Questions," and that by the end of the unit of study, they want all students to be able to respond to each of these Essential Questions with a corresponding "Big Idea" expressed in their own words. This is reflected in the following definition:

Essential Questions are engaging, open-ended questions that educators use to spark student interest in learning the content of the unit about to commence. Even though plainly worded, they carry with them an underlying rigor. Responding to them in a way that demonstrates genuine understanding requires more than superficial thought. Along with the "unwrapped" concepts and skills from the Priority Standards, educators use the Essential Questions *throughout the unit* to sharply focus curriculum, instruction, and assessment.

To illustrate the close question-answer relationship between the Essential Questions and the Big Ideas for a unit of study, Figure 4.1 shows the Big Ideas and Essential Questions for the three examples of "unwrapped" Common Core standards in English language arts and literacy and in mathematics shown in the previous chapters. Note the intentional side-by-side placement to demonstrate how the Big Ideas are the intended student responses to the teacher's Essential Questions.

Sixty grade-specific examples are included in Chapters 5–8 that show the close connections between the Essential Questions and the corresponding Big Ideas. Here are a few other introductory examples selected from various grades to represent "unwrapped" Common Core standards in English language arts and math.

Examples of ELA Essential Questions and Corresponding Big Ideas

How do you know if the main idea is really the main idea?
(Main ideas must be supported by key details.)

What are conclusions and generalizations? How do we determine them?
(We draw conclusions and make generalizations from what we read and from our own experiences.)

Why is it important to use standard English conventions in our writing?
(We want others to read our writing the way we meant it to be read.)

FIGURE 4.1	Essential Questions and Corresponding Big Ideas

English Language Arts Grade 6	
Essential Questions	**Corresponding Big Ideas**
How can you convey a central idea when writing informative or explanatory texts?	You can convey or explain a central idea by supporting it with details and relevant content.
What makes a summary of informational text effective?	An effective summary of informational text is free of personal opinions and judgments.
How does an author of informational text convey a personal point of view?	An author of informational text tries to convey a particular point of view through relevant facts and without bias.

Math Grade 2	
Essential Questions	**Corresponding Big Ideas**
Which strategy works best to add and subtract big numbers? Why?	Some strategies are faster or more efficient for adding and subtracting big numbers.
How are addition and subtraction related?	Addition and subtraction are inverse operations.

Math Grade 8	
Essential Questions	**Corresponding Big Ideas**
Why are lines of best fit helpful?	Lines of best fit help visualize the patterns in data.
How are mathematical patterns used?	Mathematical patterns can be determined or identified in multiple ways and used for different problem-solving situations.

Why read more than one text on the same topic?
(By reading multiple texts about a topic, you can consider different points of view.)

How does an author's personal experience influence the stories he or she tells?
(Authors draw on their personal experiences to reflect the larger cultural issues they want readers to reflect on, and to bring about social change.)

How are we influenced by what others write?
(Personal opinions gain strength when supported by facts and reasons.)

How do authors create interesting literary characters?
(Authors use specific details and examples in literature to describe how characters live, think, feel, and act.)

Examples of Math Essential Questions and Corresponding Big Ideas

Are there different ways to add and subtract numbers?
(A variety of strategies help you add and subtract numbers.)

How can I model and solve word problems using mathematical representations?
(Equations and/or numerical patterning show me how to model and solve word problems.)

How do I determine if my answer is reasonable?
(Mental math and estimation strategies help me determine the reasonableness of an answer.)

What kinds of strategies can you use when solving word problems? Why are they useful?
(Diagrams, models, and equations help visualize and solve word problems.)

Why do I graph ordered pairs and how do I use them?
(Graphing ordered pairs helps me predict and compare data.)

Why learn math formulas and algorithms? How can they help us in real life?
(The different math formulas, algorithms, strategies, and skills are all tools to simplify the problem-solving process.)

What are the different sets of real numbers? How do you determine which set each number belongs to?
(Every number has a decimal expansion and can be categorized as rational or irrational.)

Standards-Based Essential Questions

Questions to inform instruction and assessment for a particular unit of study are referred to by many names, including Guiding Questions, Focus Questions, Enduring Questions, Essential Questions, and others. I prefer the term "Essential Questions" because I see the role of these questions as *essential* to advancing student understanding of the standards in focus.

Essential Questions are not ordinary questions. Because they are derived from the "unwrapped" Priority Standards, they are, in truth, *standards-based questions*. This is an important distinction to make since the Common Core standards are the critical focus upon which the vast majority of United States K–12 education is now based and because the national assessments developed by the Smarter Balanced Assessment Consortium (SBAC) and the Partnership for Assessment of Readiness for College and Careers (PARCC) are directly aligned to the Common Core standards. It is therefore *essential* that students become able to respond correctly and effectively to these thoughtfully designed questions.

When educators pose the Essential Questions to students at the beginning of an instructional unit, they are advertising up front the learning goals they expect students to meet. This practice of making learning intentions explicit to students in advance of instruction (Hattie, 2009 and 2012) is associated with greater than average student learning gains.

Educators use the Essential Questions and "unwrapped" concepts, skills, and levels of cognitive rigor as reference points for the unit assessments they create, making sure that their assessment questions directly align with these elements. After the end-of-unit assessment is designed, they use the Essential Questions and "unwrapped" concepts, skills, and levels of cognitive rigor as *instructional filters* for planning lessons and learning activities that will advance student understanding toward those end learning goals.

As students move through the lessons and activities, they are developing their understanding of the "unwrapped" concepts and skills and formulating their realization of the Big Ideas. The oral and written responses students give through formal and informal assessments aligned to the Essential Questions provide the evidence as to whether or not the students have met the particular Priority Standards upon which they are based. The *degree* to which students demonstrate proficiency on the unit assessments determines the degree to which they have learned the "unwrapped" concepts and skills of the Priority Standards for that unit.

The Power of Questioning Techniques

Educators have long known the power of using questioning techniques to engage students and evoke insightful responses from them. The research strongly supports using questioning, but the questions need to represent a blend of surface knowledge and deep understanding.

It is the "why" and "how" questions educators ask that will always move student thinking to a higher level, because the "why" and "how" questions require the learner to *process* the information in any number of ways. This is not to undermine the value of students acquiring a knowledge base through the judicious use of "who, what, where, and when" questions posed by the teacher. The problem is that too often learning can stop with lower-level recall if educators do not deliberately ask higher-level questions. When this is the case, students accumulate a body of facts but are not shown how to extend their knowledge into the interpretative, synthesis, evaluative, and creative levels. It is in these higher levels that students integrate the new information they are studying with their own prior knowledge, make connections to other areas of study, and learn how to reason, infer, and draw insightful conclusions.

In *Visible Learning for Teachers* (2012), John Hattie states that expert teachers create classroom climates "in which error is welcomed, in which student questioning is high, in which engagement is the norm" (p. 26). He cites a study by Brualdi (1998) who counted between 200 and 300 questions asked by each teacher per day, but the majority of those were low-level cognitive questions: 60 percent recall of facts, 20 percent procedural. Hattie concludes: "More effort needs to be given to framing questions that are worth asking—ones that open the dialogue in the classroom so that teachers can 'hear' students' suggested strategies" (p. 75).

Hattie also cites the research of Rich Mayer and his colleagues (Mayer, 2004 and 2009; Mayer, et al., 2009). They are studying educators "using questioning in classes to promote active learning [so] that students attend to relevant material, mentally organize the selected material, and integrate the material with prior knowledge so that they advance in their knowing and understanding" (Hattie, 2012, p. 75).

Attributes of Effective Questions

Here are a few attributes or characteristics of effective questions to keep in mind when you and your colleagues are drafting and refining your own Essential Questions:

- Cannot be answered with a "yes" or "no"
- Have no single obvious right answer
- Cannot be answered from rote memory (simple recall of facts)
- Match the rigor of the "unwrapped" Priority Standard
- Go beyond who, what, when, and where to how and why

In his instructive article, "What Is a Good Guiding Question?" (1998), Rob Traver of the Massachusetts Department of Education offers these characteristics of guiding (essential) questions:

- Open-ended, yet focus inquiry into a specific topic
- Non-judgmental, but answering them requires high-level cognitive work
- Contain "emotive force" and "intellectual bite," such as "Whose America is it?" and "When are laws fair?"
- Succinct—"a handful of words that demand a lot."

Questions that cannot be answered with a simple "yes" or "no" or with the mere recall of facts indeed demand more of students. These questions can set the purpose for learning that requires students to think, make connections, draw conclusions, and justify their responses with supporting details. Effective questioning techniques lie at the heart of a thinking curriculum.

"One-Two Punch" Essential Questions

Reflecting on my own teaching experience, I believe that the very best questions expect students to effectively respond to *both* lower- and higher-level types of questioning. I call these types of combination inquiries "one-two punch" questions.

The "one-two punch" is a two-part question. The first part asks students to demonstrate their *recall* of information. It validates the need to acquire a knowledge base about the question at hand. But the second part asks students to *apply* that information. It communicates the message that facts alone are not enough; they must be utilized if they are to be of real value.

Here are a few examples of "one-two punch" Essential Questions. Note how they ask students for specific knowledge and then challenge them to go beyond mere recall.

- *What is the writing process? Why do accomplished writers use it?*
- *What is point of view? How does it affect the story?*
- *What are the differences between fact and opinion? When is it appropriate to use fact or opinion?*
- *How do people use data? Why are certain representations of data more useful than others?*
- *Which strategy works best for me to add and subtract big numbers? Why?*
- *What are linear equations? How can we use them in real life?*

I always like to share with educators an example from one of my own first attempts at writing a "one-two punch" question. Here is my first-draft pairing of an Essential Question about literary devices with its corresponding Big Idea in parentheses:

How do literary devices enhance and deepen fiction's impact upon the reader?
(Literary devices enhance and deepen fiction's impact upon the reader.)

Notice anything amiss? The question is a nearly verbatim rephrasing of the Big Idea, giving the answer the *students* are expected to provide. No further learning is needed. It's understandable how this can happen, because the Big Ideas are determined *before* writing the Essential Questions. Too much "Big Idea wording" may unintentionally creep into the questions if you're not careful.

A way of making sure that you do not "give away" the Big Idea in the Essential Question is to look at the Big Idea and think, "If that's the answer, then what is the question?" The goal is to write a more succinct, open-ended question (whether a single question or a two-part question) that allows *students* to supply the important content contained in the Big Idea.

With this guideline in mind, look how much more "mileage" an educator would get in terms of student understanding if the flawed Essential Question about literary devices were revised as a "one-two punch" question:

What are literary devices? Why do authors use them?
(Literary devices enhance and deepen fiction's impact upon the reader.)

In responding to the first part of the Essential Question, students would need to demonstrate recall of knowledge (definitions of specific literary devices). But the second part of the question requires more of students; they must determine the author's purpose for using those devices (to enhance and deepen fiction's impact on the reader).

"One-Two Punch" Questions in Math

"One-two punch" Essential Questions work equally well in math. But again, be careful that you don't give away the Big Idea in the Essential Question, as is the case in the following first-draft question with the corresponding Big Idea in parentheses beneath it:

How can a fraction, decimal, and percentage represent the same numerical amount differently?
(A fraction, decimal, and percentage can represent the same numerical amount differently.)

To revise this math Essential Question, I turned it into a "one-two punch" as follows:

What is equivalency? How can equivalency be expressed?
(A fraction, decimal, and percentage can represent the same numerical amount differently.)

Another characteristic example of a "one-two punch" math Essential Questions is this:

What is estimation? When and how do we use it?

Let's revisit the example of a Big Idea presented in the previous chapter: "Estimation comes close to an actual number." This Big Idea answers the first Essential Question, but it only provides a *definition* of estimation. This still has merit because it represents a foundational understanding that students need to acquire. A second Big Idea, "Whether you need to estimate or find the actual answer depends on the situation," would match the second question. It clearly would show that the student understands the value or benefit of knowing when estimation is and isn't needed.

Occasionally workshop participants will comment, "It was much easier for me to write the Essential Questions than it was to come up with the Big Ideas." Writing an open-ended question to elicit the already identified answer may simply be easier to do because the deepest thinking has already taken place in the determination of the Big Idea. Others say they are just better able to "see the question first." The truth is it's not a hard and fast rule which you determine first (although doing the heavy lifting of determining the Big Idea first is my recommendation). Honor your own process. What *is* important is to maintain the question-answer relationship between your Big Ideas and your Essential Questions.

Write Engaging Essential Questions

You may have written your Essential Questions correctly, but what if they are static and do not achieve their primary purpose: to motivate students to want to explore them and discover the Big Idea answers? Here is where you can be creative!

Imagine how the following Essential Questions derived from several different content areas could stimulate student interest:

- *How can journalists who write opinion pieces or editorials get readers to agree or disagree with them?*
- *How are area and perimeter relevant to home improvement?*
- *Why are there little lines on my ruler?*
- *How can an author "capture" an audience?*
- *Why is social media so important to people today?*
- *Are resources renewable?*
- *Why do people create art?*
- *Are rights equal for everyone? What makes you think so?*
- *Are all of the pioneers really gone?*
- *What makes something alive? Are there any nonliving things that have life characteristics?*
- *Is there a solution to every mathematical problem? How do you know?*
- *Why should you be physically active?*

- *As a speaker, why do you need to know your audience?*

- *Why write your own music?*

- *Why is teamwork a necessary life skill?*

- *Why is the wheel assembly important to a moving vehicle?*

Strive to make your Essential Questions *relevant* to students. Design them so they help students understand their connections to real life. Think how the particular Big Idea would apply in the world. Often students complain that school has no connection to their day-to-day lives. Show them through creative wording of your Essential Questions that it does.

I remember the following *engaging* Essential Question created by Gary Colburn and his table colleagues at Harrison School, Stockton Unified School District, in Stockton, California: *"Why can't I write something only once?"*

By use of this question Gary led his students to their discovery of the Big Idea about the value of the writing process, stated in their own words: *"Writing takes a lot of rewriting. The first time you write is not the last!"* Imagine the gratitude of every educator in later grades who no longer had to persuade and cajole students to work through the steps of the writing process because those students had already realized the reason for doing so in a prior grade!

I had the privilege and good fortune to know and work with Pre-K through high school educators in West Haven, Connecticut, over a period of several years. They gave real impetus to my ongoing advocacy for educators to create *engaging* Essential Questions.

A second-grade team of West Haven educators had "unwrapped" Connecticut science standards and determined their initial Big Ideas as follows:

1. Like poles repel and unlike poles attract.

2. Some materials absorb more liquid than other materials.

3. Change of temperature can affect the state of matter.

4. Plants need sunlight, water, and nutrients.

When they wrote their first-draft Essential Questions, the educators were lukewarm in their enthusiasm about them. I encouraged them to "get creative" and think about more motivational and relevant questions to engage their students. Here is what they came up with:

1. Why does the magnet stick to the refrigerator?

2. *After a swim, would you rather dry yourself off with a napkin or a bath towel?*

3. *Why should you eat a popsicle quickly on a hot day?*

4. *What would happen if I kept my plants in the closet over summer vacation?*

Showing how the Big Ideas represent the desired student responses to the Essential Questions, here they are together. The creativity should come from the Essential Questions, *not* the Big Ideas that represent solid insights students need to acquire:

1. *Why does the magnet stick to the refrigerator?*
(Like poles repel and unlike poles attract.)

2. *After a swim, would you rather dry yourself off with a napkin or a bath towel?*
(Some materials absorb more liquid than other materials.)

3. *Why should you eat a popsicle quickly on a hot day?*
(Change of temperature can affect the state of matter.)

4. *What would happen if I kept my plants in the closet over summer vacation?*
(Plants need sunlight, water, and nutrients.)

A few months later I was conducting an "unwrapping" session in Hartford, Connecticut, and shared these West Haven science examples. Ben McLane, a sixth-grade science educator at Wish School, put his own creative spin onto his first-draft Essential Question to correspond with his Big Idea: "Heat changes particle movement."

• *(First draft) How does heat affect the motion of particles?*

• *(Revised) Why is Play-Doh® harder to play with after it's been in the refrigerator?*

Since that time, I have continued to show these same examples to audiences all over the country. Educators catch on immediately to the possibilities and are eager to apply the idea to their own Essential Questions. One excellent example for an "unwrapped" Common Core math standard from a team of eighth-grade math educators in Woodridge, Illinois, is this pair of Essential Questions to match the Big Idea: "Using coordinates of a two-dimensional object helps to understand and apply transformations."

- *(First draft) What must math problem solvers do to accurately determine the effect of transformation of a two-dimensional figure on a coordinate plane?*
- *(Revised) Why do the words on my T-shirt read backwards in the mirror?*

Compare the difference between the examples in both pairs; it's clear which of the two Essential Questions would be more engaging to students.

Into the Classroom—A Powerful Use of Essential Questions

After educators have written and rewritten their Essential Questions to make them creative, engaging, and matched to their Big Ideas for the unit of study, how can they most effectively use these questions in their classrooms to motivate their students and focus instruction? At the end of each and every lesson, spend a few minutes asking students to reflect and make immediate connections between the posted Essential Questions and what they just learned.

My all-time favorite story to illustrate this powerful way of regularly using Essential Questions in the classroom is still, after more than 10 years, one from high school math educator Sue Sims in Vista Unified School District, Vista, California. First published in *"Unwrapping" the Standards* (Ainsworth, 2003), its timelessness bears retelling here because it reveals a powerful educational practice that continues to resonate with educators in all grades and content areas. Teachers who have heard this story have later told me they applied it in their own classrooms with the same wonderful results. I include it here in hopes that you will consider using your own Essential Questions in the same way.

Mrs. Sims had invited me to visit her geometry class to show me how she was implementing these ideas in her instructional program. Her schedule was tight, especially because each instructional period at her high school was only 42 minutes in duration. On the morning of my visit, there were only a few minutes of class time remaining, so I sat down at the back of the classroom to wait to meet with her. Looking around, I noticed she had written her Essential Questions for the current unit of study in colorful, large letters on narrow butcher paper and posted them around the perimeter of the classroom near the ceiling. These questions asked:

- *What is the Pythagorean theorem? When and how is it used?*

- *What is the perimeter of a geometric shape, and how is it found? What is the area of a geometric shape?*

- *How do you calculate the area of triangles, rectangles, parallelograms, and trapezoids?*

- *What is a linear equation? What are two methods that can be used to graph a linear equation?*

My attention was brought back to Mrs. Sims asking the students to put away their books and materials and to give her their undivided attention. She then announced, "Now I want all of you to look up at our Essential Questions for this geometry unit posted around the room. Think about what we just finished doing in class this morning. Which question did we work on today?"

Instead of the silence I expected from students who were well aware that the passing bell was about to ring, several raised their hands. One answered, "The graphing calculator activity we did matches that Essential Question there," and pointed to one of the four questions on the chart paper. Another student chimed in, "Yes but it also connects to that question there," pointing to one of the other questions. A few other students voiced similar connections.

This continued for about four minutes until the passing bell rang, and Mrs. Sims dismissed the class. Walking back to where I was seated, I expressed my surprise and enthusiasm for the self-reflection opportunity she had provided her students—an idea that had never occurred to me to use with my own students even though I had taught *her* the value of posting the questions on the walls. During that brief exchange between Mrs. Sims and her students, I understood why my own classroom's posted questions had become little more than "wallpaper" after the first week.

She replied, "I have to really discipline myself on such a tight bell schedule to conclude the lesson and assign homework early enough to allow me these last four minutes for students to reflect upon their learning and bring closure to the lesson. This is proving to be the most important part of each of my lessons."

Mrs. Sims had recognized the importance of helping her students identify and connect the new information and skills they had gained in that particular lesson with her ultimate learning goals for the unit. Her Essential Questions were clearly guiding her instruction, and she was reminding her geometry students daily that these questions represented what she expected them to know by the conclusion of the unit.

She then walked me over to one of her cabinets to show me her students' test results from the previous unit of study. I was seeing several A's, B's, and only a few C's—and this was not an honors class but a regular tenth-grade math class representing the full range of student learning needs. Mrs. Sims commented, "In eighteen years as a high school math teacher, I have never had results like this. I'm certain that it's because the Essential Questions keep me focused on what my students need to understand and be able to do. This guides my instructional planning, the choice of curriculum materials and textbook assignments I select, and the design of my end-of-unit test."

And what was, for me, the "icing on the cake" was her requirement that the students, before turning in their completed unit tests to her, turn their exams over and write their Big Idea responses to the Essential Questions. In this way, she had a multiple-format assessment that included computation problems, constructed-response problems, and the evidence of the degree to which the students had attained the Big Ideas. The students' work provided highly persuasive evidence supporting her powerful practice of daily helping students make the connections between the Essential Questions, "unwrapped" concepts and skills, daily lessons, and end-of-unit assessment.

As she walked me to her classroom door, Mrs. Sims thanked me for introducing the "unwrapping" process to her and concluded: "When this unit is over, I will put up the Essential Questions for the next unit and repeat the same process. This has done so much to improve my teaching and the performance of my students!"

Taking This Practice One Step Further

Educators regularly administer ongoing, short formative assessments to gauge student understanding during a unit of study. They then use those formative assessment results to differentiate their instruction to specifically meet individual student learning needs. One way to incorporate the practice of providing students with quick, end-of-lesson reflection opportunities is to ask them to write one or two sentences in a journal about what they just learned that class period relative to the Essential Questions. This will provide them, and the teacher who can quickly read through these student journals two or three times a week, with a written record of their understanding of the Big Ideas as it develops throughout the unit.

In *Rigorous Curriculum Design* (Ainsworth, 2010), I included the following narrative from an educator in West Haven, Connecticut, who had heard me tell the story of my experience visiting Mrs. Sims' classroom. I have shared it again here to show

another way educators can gather ongoing evidence of student understanding during the unit of study.

"Near the end of the class period, [she] distributed colored Post-It® note squares
to each student. She asked the students to write what they thought the Big Idea was
for each of the unit's Essential Questions. Then she asked the students to share their
individual responses with the other students in their cooperative groups, encouraging them to add any additional information they heard from their group members
to their own individual Post-It notes. When finished, the students signed their names
on their notes and posted them on the appropriate chart papers displaying the Essential Questions as they exited the class.

"The educator said that by the time two or three classes had posted their responses, the hundreds of colorful squares created quite a visual display. Yet the power
in the practice became evident when she saw the visible evidence of her students'
learning, [formative assessment] evidence that she was able to use in the days that
followed to further clarify and deepen her students' understanding of the unit's Big
Ideas" (Ainsworth, 2010, p. 156).

Whether we ask students to process their own learning verbally or in writing, the
regular, consistent practice of asking them to connect each day's lesson to the Essential Questions is what will keep students moving successfully along the highway to
the end destination of the Big Ideas.

Including the Essential Questions
on the End-of-Unit Assessment

Because students know at the beginning of an instructional unit that they will be
expected to answer the Essential Questions at the conclusion of a unit, educators
often utilize the Essential Questions as a part of their end-of-unit assessment. They
simply add a final section to the assessment that lists the three or four Essential Questions with space after each one for students to write their Big Idea responses. Younger
students, second language learners, or special needs students who are not yet writing independently and/or fluently can respond orally—individually, in small groups,
or as part of a whole-class discussion.

This is a wonderful way to differentiate assessment because it allows students to
demonstrate as much as they have individually learned relative to the Essential Questions. Also, since the Big Ideas have been derived from the "unwrapped" Priority
Standards, student responses will almost certainly include the understanding and

application of the specific "unwrapped" concepts and skills that students have learned during daily instruction and related activities.

When students are assessed in this way, they are often amazed to realize how much they have learned as they write responses that reflect "all they know" about each Essential Question. The important point is to make sure that educators, beginning as early as kindergarten, set up the conditions for students to respond orally or in writing with their own Big Ideas. This holds students accountable for explaining what they learned during the unit and for developing their own conceptual understanding of the standards in focus.

Spiraling the Essential Questions across the Four Grade Spans

Debbie Higdon, Program Manager of English Language Arts for the San Diego Unified School District in San Diego, California, wanted to be sure that the Essential Questions representative of the "unwrapped" Common Core State Standards were showing the necessary progression of rigor as they developed across the K–12 spectrum. Working with her colleagues, she created the following charts as a way to confirm these progressions from one year to the next (Grade 12 is yet to be completed).

As stated before, the Common Core ELA standards are intentionally "spiraled," or progressed, from one grade to the next to ensure that students acquire the needed prerequisite concepts and skills in one grade in order to be educationally prepared for the standards at the next grade. Figure 4.2 shows a work-in-progress chart of the Essential Questions in the Reading strands of Literature and Informational Text from primary to secondary grades. This is an excellent way for educators and leaders to gain a "big picture" perspective of whether or not the needed *learning progressions* from one grade to the next are indeed reflected in the Essential Questions that are derived from the "unwrapped" Priority Standards at each of those grade levels.

FIGURE 4.2	Essential Questions Learning Progressions Chart

Kindergarten	1st Grade	2nd Grade	3rd Grade	4th Grade	5th Grade
How do we learn about our world? What is this really about? How are these texts the same? Different? Who would you recommend this to? Why?	What is the main topic? What are the key details? Why is it important to read a variety of texts? What makes an informational writing piece effective?	Why did the author write the article? What does the author want us to know? What is the main idea of a text? What does the author want us to know?	What is the central message, lesson, or moral? How do you know? What is your opinion? How does/do the text(s) support your opinion? What are the common themes, setting, plots, or characters of the texts?	What is a theme? Why is it important to understand theme? How can the theme of a text be determined? What is point of view? How does point of view affect the story? Why is it important to speak and write correctly?	Why do readers and writers need to read a variety of sources on a particular topic? What is the difference between a topic, central idea, and details?

6th Grade	7th Grade	8th Grade
How does an author structure the text to determine the central idea? What does an effective summary include? How does knowing the genre affect the way you read a text? How does the author choose what information to include, exclude, and illustrate to support the central idea? How does textual information allow the reader to determine the central idea?	How can I develop an informed understanding of a topic or event? How does reading, viewing, and analyzing multiple sources build depth of knowledge of a topic? How can I communicate an informed point of view on a given topic or event?	How do authors support the central idea(s)? How do you know a central idea is a central idea? Why do readers examine multiple points of view? How do we determine the reliability of a point of view? How do we connect individuals, ideas, and events? Why do we use multiple resources to conduct research? What are the differences between fact and opinion? When is it appropriate to use fact or opinion? What makes research meaningful? What does it mean to be a critical reader? Who do we believe and why?

FIGURE 4.2	Essential Questions Learning Progressions Chart *(continued)*	

9th Grade	10th Grade	11th Grade
Why would you read and write a summary?	How do you identify the central idea?	Why do authors use literary devices?
How do you find the main idea?	What are the different types of textual evidence?	
What is the purpose of informational/explanatory text?	How do you determine relevant evidence to support a central idea?	
How do we decide the value of an argument?	Why does an author use an explanatory text?	
Why is listening important in a discussion?	What are different purposes for writing?	
How do authors make us believe their ideas?	How do you structure an informational/explanatory text to convey your idea?	
	How does an author unfold information to express ideas in an informative/explanatory text?	
	What is academic language and why do authors use this type of language?	
	How does academic language influence your understanding of the text and impact your writing?	
	What is a credible source?	
	What criteria do you use to find a credible source?	

Your Turn

Now it's your turn to write your first-draft Essential Questions to correspond with the Big Ideas you drafted during the previous step of the process. Here are the directions for doing so:

(1) Look again at each of your Big Ideas and focus on the first one. Ask yourself and/or the colleagues you are collaborating with, "If that Big Idea statement is the desired student answer or response, what could the Essential Question be?"

(2) Following this same procedure, practice writing a first-draft Essential Question for each of your Big Ideas. Decide whether any of your questions would be more effective if written as "one-two punch" questions.

(3) Check each question to be sure that it asks for the desired student answer or response. Make sure that you have not unintentionally "given away" the Big Idea by restating it in the question.

(4) If your first-draft questions seem fairly routine or ordinary, see if you can make them more engaging, relevant, and motivational for students by writing them *creatively*, as illustrated by the engaging Essential Questions presented earlier in this chapter.

(5) Remember that you can revise your Essential Questions (and Big Ideas) until you are satisfied with the results. Often educators will "tweak" their Big Ideas after they write their Essential Questions so that they are more clearly reflective of what the end learning goals for students should be. The process of writing and revising Essential Questions and Big Ideas is very fluid. One informs the other.

Critiquing Your Essential Questions

Here is the related excerpt from the Rigorous Curriculum Design Unit Development Guide to evaluate the quality of your Essential Questions. Again, check the first column of each criterion you believe you have completed correctly. Highlight any criteria that you have to complete or want to revise. Use these criteria as guides to confirm that you have produced well-written Essential Questions.

Essential Questions		
	Essential Element	**Comment(s)/Feedback**
	Represent Learning Goals for Unit of Study	
	Reflect *Content* and *Rigor* of "Unwrapped" Priority Standards	
	Include Higher-Level Questions, e.g., • Why do authors use literary devices? • When and how do we use estimation in daily life?	
	Are Written in Student-Friendly Language	
	Are Written in Engaging, Creative Wording	
	Require Thought, Discussion, Investigation to Answer	
	Lead Students to Their Own Discovery of Big Ideas	

PART TWO:

The Examples

In the next four chapters, you will see 60 examples of "unwrapped" Common Core State Standards in English language arts and literacy and in mathematics that are specific to nearly every grade level, K–12. These examples are part of the Rigorous Curriculum Design units of study that educators created while participating in multiple workshop sessions that I conducted in their school districts. Keep in mind these examples are "works in progress," first- and second-draft products that their contributing educators have most likely continued to revise and improve as they developed the related units of study.

The wording of the introduction to each of these four chapters is essentially the same. Because readers are likely to be most interested in seeing grade-specific examples in the grade span that most closely corresponds to the one they teach—and will likely turn to that chapter first—the introductory information at the beginning of these four chapters is repeated so as to be comprehensive for all grade levels.

I would encourage those in the elementary grades to review the examples in both the primary and upper elementary grade chapters to see how the "unwrapped" standards, graphic organizers, Big Ideas, and Essential Questions progress across the K–5 grades. Upper elementary teachers will likely benefit from reviewing some of the middle school examples also.

The same recommendation holds true for those in secondary grades. Middle school and high school math and English language arts and literacy educators will benefit from looking at examples across the 6–12 range of grade levels.

Making Connections:
How "Unwrapping" Fits Into the Big Picture

After you have completed your review of one or more of the grade-span example chapters, please look ahead to Chapter 9: *Connecting "Unwrapping" the Standards to the Big Picture*. There you will see how the entire "unwrapping" process fits within the larger scope of curricular unit design, a framework that includes the creation of the end-of-unit assessment, the pre-assessment, authentic learning tasks, resources and materials, and instructional strategies to meet the diverse learning needs of all students.

CHAPTER 5

Primary Grade Examples

One of the most beneficial features of the original *"Unwrapping" the Standards* (2003) book was its inclusion of more than 85 examples of "unwrapped" standards, Big Ideas, and Essential Questions specific to each grade span, K–2, 3–5, 6–8, and 9–12, from numerous content areas. Educators always appreciate seeing examples: especially Big Ideas and Essential Questions. These concrete samples greatly help to convey what the explanatory content describes. For these reasons, I knew it was important to include in this volume similar examples of "unwrapped" Common Core State Standards in English language arts and literacy and in mathematics.

Four school systems that I have worked closely with, two in the eastern United States and two in the West, graciously responded to my request for "unwrapped" Common Core examples created by their educators. The two east coast districts are West Hartford and Bloomfield, both in Connecticut. The two west coast districts are San Diego Unified School District in California and McMinnville School District in Oregon. It was my great privilege over a period of many months to lead their educators and leaders through the Rigorous Curriculum Design framework I created to help educators write new curricula for the Common Core. The four parts of the "unwrapping" process were the first steps they followed in developing their curricular units of study in English language arts and literacy and in math that later included unit-specific formative and summative assessments, authentic performance tasks, instructional resources, and differentiated instructional strategies.

I always encourage educators and curriculum writers to follow the framework of "unwrapping" and curriculum design as prescribed, but then to "make the process their own" by customizing the format for their units of study. Reprinted here are the first sections of the Rigorous Curriculum Design Unit Planning Organizer you have seen throughout the previous explanatory chapters. Many grade-level or course-level design teams in the four districts used this template as is; others chose to modify it somewhat. To respect their particular district formatting, I have included the graphic organizers as they were submitted to me. Because you now understand the complete "unwrapping" process, you will be able to understand the content represented in these district examples even when it varies from the original format. Also, note that not every district included both Bloom's *and* DOK cognitive levels on their initial graphic organizers.

I have organized these grade-span examples by district and by content area, rather than interspersing all the examples for each grade level. This will make each district's examples "self-contained" and hopefully easier for you to read and understand.

Rigorous Curriculum Design Unit Planning Organizer

Subject(s)	
Grade/Course	
Unit of Study	
Pacing	

Priority Common Core State Standards (Bolded) Supporting Standards

"UNWRAPPED" Priority Standards

"Unwrapped" Concepts (students need to know)	"Unwrapped" Skills (students need to be able to do)	Taxonomy Levels	
		Bloom's / DOK	

Essential Questions	Corresponding Big Ideas

ELA EXAMPLES

Rigorous Curriculum Design ELA Unit Planning Organizer
Kindergarten: San Diego Unified School District

Subject(s)	English Language Arts—Reading Literature
Grade/Course	Kindergarten
Unit of Study	Unit 5: Characters Are Amazing
Pacing	

Priority Common Core State Standards

READING LITERATURE:

RL.K.9: With prompting and support, compare and contrast the adventures and experiences of characters in familiar stories.

RL.K.7: With prompting and support, describe the relationship between illustrations and the story in which they appear.

WRITING:

W.K.1: Use a combination of drawing, dictating, and writing to compose opinion pieces in which they tell a reader the topic or the name of the book they are writing about and state an opinion or preference about the topic or book.

W.K.3: Use a combination of drawing, dictating, and writing to narrate a single event or several loosely linked events, tell about the events in the order in which they occurred, and provide a reaction to what happened.

LANGUAGE:
L.K.1b: Use frequently occurring nouns and verbs.
L.K.1c: Form regular plural nouns orally by adding /s/ or /es/.
L.K.1d: Understand and use question words.
L.K.1f: Produce and expand complete sentences in shared language activities.
L.K.5d: Distinguish shades of meaning among verbs describing the same general action (e.g., walk, march, strut, prance) by acting out the meanings.

"UNWRAPPED" Priority Standards
(Note: Priority *Language* Standards listed above were not "unwrapped" for inclusion here.)

RL.K.9: With prompting and support, COMPARE AND CONTRAST the adventures and experiences of characters in familiar stories.

RL.K.7: With prompting and support, DESCRIBE the relationship between the illustrations and the story in which they appear.

W.K.1: Use a combination of drawing, dictating, and writing to COMPOSE opinion pieces in which they TELL a reader the topic or the name of the book they are writing about and STATE an opinion or preference about the topic or book.

W.K.3: Use a combination of drawing, dictating, and writing to NARRATE a single event or several loosely linked events, TELL about the events in the order in which they occurred, and PROVIDE a reaction to what happened.

"Unwrapped" Concepts (students need to know)	"Unwrapped" Skills (students need to be able to do)	Taxonomy Levels	
		Bloom's / DOK	
• Adventures/experiences of characters • In familiar stories	• **COMPARE/CONTRAST** (adventures/ experiences of characters)	2	2
• Relationships between • Illustrations/Story	• **DESCRIBE** (relationships btw illustrations/story) *ANALYZE*	4	3
• Opinion Pieces	• **COMPOSE** (opinion pieces) *EVALUATE*	5	3
• Topic or name of book	• **TELL** (topic or name of book) *IDENTIFY*	1	1
• Opinion or preference about topic or book	• **STATE** (opinion or preference) *UNDERSTAND*	2	2
• Single Event or Loosely Linked Events	• **NARRATE** (single event or loosely linked events)	1	1
• Events in order as occurred	• **TELL** (events in order as occurred) *SEQUENCE; UNDERSTAND*	2	1
• Reactions	• **PROVIDE** (reactions)	3	2

Essential Questions	Corresponding Big Ideas
Why is it important to know about the characters in a story? How does thinking and talking about characters help you to understand a story? How does comparing and contrasting characters help you as a reader?	1. Characters act and feel in different ways and that tells the reader who they are as a "person." The interactions between characters are what the story is about. (Student version) We know who a character is by how they look, think, and feel. The things characters do is what the story is about. Knowing how the characters are alike and different helps me understand what the story is all about.
Why are there pictures in a story?	2. Pictures help to tell the story.
Why should you share your opinions about topics/ideas with others in writing?	3. Writing my opinions shows others I understand the story and what I like or don't like about it.
Why does the order of the story matter? Can I start my story at the end? How come?	4. I write stories in the order they happen so people can understand them.

Source: Kindergarten RCD Curriculum Design Team, San Diego Unified School District, San Diego, CA

Rigorous Curriculum Design ELA Unit Planning Organizer
Grade 1: San Diego Unified School District

Subject(s)	English Language Arts—Reading Literature
Grade/Course	Grade 1
Unit of Study	How Stories and Poems Work
Pacing	26 days

"Unwrapped" Common Core Priority Standards

READING LITERATURE:

RL.1.2: RETELL stories, including key details, and DEMONSTRATE understanding of their central message or lesson. READ poetry and DETERMINE central message as well.

RL.1.3: DESCRIBE characters, settings, and major events in a story, USING key details.

WRITING:

W.1.3: WRITE narratives in which they RECOUNT two or more appropriately sequenced events, INCLUDE some details regarding what happened, USE temporal words to signal event order, and PROVIDE some sense of closure.

"Unwrapped" Concepts (students need to know)	"Unwrapped" Skills (students need to be able to do)	Taxonomy Levels Bloom's / DOK	
• Key Details • Stories	RETELL (stories through details)	1	1
• Central Message • Stories • Poetry	DETERMINE (central message in stories and poems) *INFER, ANALYZE*	4, 5	3
• Characters, settings, & major events	DESCRIBE (story elements using key details)	↓	↓
• Narrative writing • Sequenced events with details	WRITE (narrative—two+ sequenced events with details)	2	1
• Temporal words	USE (temporal words to signal order)	3, 6	2
• Sense of closure	PROVIDE (closure)	↓	↓

Essential Questions	Corresponding Big Ideas
What are story elements? Why are they needed? How do they help the reader?	Understanding how stories work (characters, setting, plot, problem, solution) helps readers make sense of the story and determine the central message.
What is a central message? How do readers find it in a story?	A central message is the lesson about life that a reader can learn from a story.
How do authors create a personal story?	Narrative writing includes details and has a clear beginning, middle, and end.

Source: 1st Grade RCD Curriculum Design Team, San Diego Unified School District, San Diego, CA

Rigorous Curriculum Design ELA Unit Planning Organizer
Grade 2: San Diego Unified School District

Subject(s)	Fiction—Comparing Literary Elements across Text (fairytales, fables, folktales across cultures) Writing—Personal Narrative; Opinion
Grade/Course	Grade 2
Unit of Study	Comparing Literary Elements across Text
Pacing	26 days

"Unwrapped" Common Core Priority Standards

READING LITERATURE:

RL.2.2: RECOUNT stories, including fables and folktales from diverse cultures, and DETERMINE their central message, lesson, or moral.

RL.2.3: DESCRIBE how characters in a story respond to major events and challenges.

RL.2.9: COMPARE and CONTRAST two or more versions of the same story (e.g., Cinderella stories) by different authors or from different cultures.

WRITING:

W.2.1: WRITE opinion pieces in which they INTRODUCE the topic or book they are writing about, STATE an opinion, SUPPLY reasons that support the opinion, USE linking words (e.g., because, and, also) to connect opinion and reasons, and PROVIDE a concluding statement or section.

W.2.3: WRITE narratives in which they RECOUNT a well-elaborated event or short sequence of events, including details to DESCRIBE actions, thoughts and feelings, USE temporal words to signal event order, and PROVIDE a sense of closure.

"Unwrapped" Concepts (students need to know)	"Unwrapped" Skills (students need to be able to do)	Taxonomy Levels Bloom's / DOK	
• Stories (fables, folktales, cultures)	• RECOUNT (fables and folktales from diverse cultures)	1	1
• Central message, lesson or moral	• DETERMINE (central message, lesson or moral)	4	3
• Characters	• DESCRIBE (how characters respond to events and challenges)	3	3
• Similarities and differences	• COMPARE/CONTRAST (two or more versions same story, different author and different cultures)	4	3

• Opinion Piece
  • Topic
  • Opinion
  • Reasons
  • Linking words
  • Concluding statement
	• WRITE (opinion piece)
	  • Introduce (topic)
	  • State (opinion)
	  • Supply (reasons)
	  • Use (linking words)
	  • Provide (concluding statement)
		6	4

• Narrative
  • Well-elaborated event
  • Sequence of events
  • Details
  • Temporal words
  • Closure
	• WRITE (narrative)
	  • Recount (well-elaborated event or sequence of events)
	  • Describe (details)
	  • Use (temporal words)
	  • Provide (closure)
		3	3

Essential Questions	Corresponding Big Ideas
How does a character's behaviors/actions affect what happens in stories?	A character's behaviors/actions affect the outcome of a story.
Why is it important to understand characters in a story?	Understanding the character helps me to determine the central lesson, message, or moral.
Why do you think some stories have been told all over the world by different authors?	Exploring literature from different cultures teaches us about how people around the world are the same and different and what they value.
How do writers convey their opinions effectively?	Writers need to support their ideas and opinions with evidence from the text.

Source: 2nd Grade RCD Curriculum Design Team, San Diego Unified School District, San Diego, CA

McMinnville School District—Kindergarten

UNIT NUMBER THREE	Opinion 1
Unit Length	**December 2, 2013–January 24, 2014** 26-day unit with 3-day buffer

"Unwrapped" PRIORITY Standards	**W.K.1:** USE a combination of drawing, dictating, and writing to COMPOSE opinion pieces in which they TELL a reader the topic or the name of the book they are writing about and STATE an opinion or preference about the topic or book (e.g., My favorite book is…).
	
	SL.K.1: PARTICIPATE in collaborative conversations with diverse partners about kindergarten topics and texts with peers and adults in small and larger groups.
	   A. FOLLOW agreed-upon rules for discussions (e.g., listening to others and taking turns speaking about the topics and texts under discussion).
	   B. CONTINUE a conversation through multiple exchanges.
	
	RI.K.8: With prompting and support, IDENTIFY the reasons an author gives to support points in a text.

"Unwrapped" PRIORITY Standards Graphic Organizer	Concepts	Skills	Bloom's
	Opinion Piece	COMPOSE	3
	Combination of drawing, dictation, and writing	USE	6
	Topic or name of book	TELL	1
	Opinion or preference about topic or book	STATE	1, 6*
	Collaborative conversations; kindergarten topics and texts; peers and adults; small and larger groups	PARTICIPATE	3
	Agreed-upon rules for discussions	FOLLOW	3
	Conversation through multiple exchanges	CONTINUE	3
	Reasons author gives to support points	IDENTIFY	1, 4*
	*The literal level of the verbs (STATE and IDENTIFY) is level 1; but what the task requires students to do requires a higher level of cognitive thinking.		

Supporting Standards	**RL.K.1:** With prompting and support, ask and answer questions about key details in a text. **RL.K.3:** With prompting and support, identify characters, settings, and major events in a story. **SL.K.6:** Speak audibly and express thoughts, feelings, and ideas clearly. **SL.K.2:** Confirm understanding of a text read aloud or information presented orally or through other media by asking and answering questions about key details and requesting clarification if something is not understood.
Essential Questions	• Why do you have that opinion? • How do we share our opinions?
Big Ideas	• Conversations are important to express our opinions. • We support opinions with reasons.

Source: Kindergarten RCD Team, McMinnville School District, McMinnville, Oregon

McMinnville School District—Grade 1

UNIT NUMBER TWO	Explanatory One		
Unit Length	**October 17–November 27, 2013** 23 days with a 3-day buffer		
"Unwrapped" PRIORITY Standards	**W.1.2:** WRITE informative/explanatory texts in which they NAME a topic, SUPPLY some facts about the topic, and PROVIDE some sense of closure. **RI.1.4:** ASK and ANSWER questions to help DETERMINE or CLARIFY the meaning of words and phrases in a text. **RL.1.5:** EXPLAIN major differences between books that tell stories and books that give information, DRAWING on a wide reading of a range of text types.		

	Concepts	Skills	Bloom's
"Unwrapped" PRIORITY Standards Graphic Organizer	Informative/explanatory texts	WRITE	6
	A topic	NAME	1
	Facts about the topic	SUPPLY	3
	Sense of closure	PROVIDE	3
	Questions	ASK	4
	Questions	ANSWER	3
	Meaning of words and phrases in a text	CLARIFY	4
	Differences between books that tell stories and books that give information	EXPLAIN	4
	Wide range of text types	DRAW ON	1

Supporting Standards	**W.1.7:** Participate in shared research and writing projects (e.g., explore a number of "how-to" books on a given topic and use them to write a sequence of instructions). **RI.1.1:** Ask and answer questions about key details in a text. **RI.1.6:** Distinguish between information provided by pictures or other illustrations and information provided by the words in a text. **RI.1.7:** Use the illustrations and details in a text to describe its key ideas. **RI.1.9:** Identify basic similarities in and differences between two texts on the same topic (e.g., in illustrations, descriptions, or procedures). **SL.1.6:** Produce complete sentences when appropriate to task and situation.
Essential Questions	• How does a writer make their writing easy for others to understand? • What do you do when you don't know what a word means? • How are books written differently?
Big Ideas	• Writers can organize writing by including a topic sentence, facts about the topic, and a closing sentence that finishes off the writing. • You ask and answer questions to help understand the meaning of the word. • Some books tell stories, some books give information.

Source: Grade 1 RCD Team, McMinnville School District, McMinnville, Oregon

McMinnville School District—Grade 2

UNIT NUMBER FOUR	Narrative Two
Unit Length	**January 27–March 7, 2014** 25-day unit with 3-day buffer

"Unwrapped" PRIORITY Standards	**W.2.3: WRITE** narratives in which they **RECOUNT** a well-elaborated event or short sequence of events, include details to **DESCRIBE** actions, thoughts, and feelings, **USE** temporal words to signal event order, and **PROVIDE** a sense of closure.
	
	RL.2.6: ACKNOWLEDGE differences in the points of view of characters, including by **SPEAKING** in a different voice for each character when **READING** dialogue aloud.
	
	L.2.1: DEMONSTRATE command of the conventions of standard English grammar and usage when writing or speaking.
	
	    F. **PRODUCE, EXPAND, AND REARRANGE** complete simple and compound sentences (e.g., The boy watched the movie; The little boy watched the movie; The action movie was watched by the little boy).
	
	L.2.2: DEMONSTRATE command of the conventions of standard English capitalization, punctuation, and spelling when writing.
	
	    C. **USE** an apostrophe to **FORM** contractions and frequently occurring possessives.

	Concepts	Skills	Bloom's
"Unwrapped" PRIORITY Standards Graphic Organizer	Narratives	WRITE	3
	Well-elaborated events or short sequence of events	RECOUNT	1 (2, 3)*
	Actions, thoughts, feelings	DESCRIBE	2
	Temporal words	USE	3
	Sense of closure	PROVIDE	3
	Differences in points of view	ACKNOWLEDGE	4
	Conventions of standard English grammar	DEMONSTRATE	3
	Simple and compound sentences	PRODUCE, EXPAND, and REARRANGE	3
	Conventions of standard English capitalization, punctuation, and spelling	DEMONSTRATE	3
	Contractions and possessives	USE	3

*The literal level of the verb RECOUNT is level 1; but what the task requires students to do requires a higher level of cognitive thinking.

McMinnville School District—Grade 2 *(continued)*

Supporting Standards	RL.2.4: Describe how words and phrases (e.g., regular beats, alliteration, rhymes, repeated lines) supply rhythm and meaning in a story, poem, or song.
	
	RL.2.10: By the end of the year, read and comprehend literature, including stories and poetry, in the grades 2–3 text complexity band proficiently, with scaffolding as needed at the high end of the range.
	
	SL.2.5: Create audio recordings of stories or poems; add drawings or other visual displays to stories or recounts of experiences when appropriate to clarify ideas, thoughts, and feelings.
	
	L.2.1: Demonstrate command of the conventions of standard English grammar and usage when writing or speaking.
	    a. Use collective nouns (e.g., group).
	    b. Form and use frequently occurring irregular plural nouns (e.g., feet, children).
	    c. Use reflexive pronouns (e.g., myself, ourselves).
	    d. Form and use the past tense of frequently occurring irregular verbs.
	    e. Use adjectives and adverbs, and choose between them depending on what is to be modified.

Essential Questions	• How do details and organization help the reader? • Why is it important to use standard English conventions in our writing?
Big Ideas	• A reader uses details such as descriptive words, well-elaborated ideas, and points of view. They also use organizational structures such as temporal words, simple and compound sentences, and conclusions. • We want others to read our writing the way we meant it to be read.

Source: Grade 2 RCD Team, McMinnville School District, McMinnville, Oregon

West Hartford Public Schools English/Language Arts: Grade K

Unit 7: Show and Tell

Pacing Guide: This unit is designed to be implemented over the course of 25 days with 3 buffer days.

UNIT OVERVIEW

In this unit, Show and Tell, students will integrate their informational text reading strategies in order to participate in independent research. Students will learn how to look to multiple sources to answer a question. Students will ask a research question, choose sources and then find the answer to their research question. A final presentation to peers will require the student to speak clearly and share some sort of visual. During presentations, students will be expected to listen attentively and ask questions. Teachers will have the freedom to integrate nonfiction topics of their choice and integrate science and social studies topics. A series of assured learning experiences are included that will scaffold the research project and ask students to apply and practice their new skills in both small-group and whole-group formats. Additionally, StoryTown will be utilized as the core resource as referenced in the learning plan for phonological awareness activities and phonics skills application. Library books, Scholastic Ready-To-Go library books, and Scholastic Content Area Guided Reading materials will be used to teach the Priority Standards and comprehension skills in addition to a variety of informational texts from the school library.

STANDARDS

RI.K.9: With prompting and support, identify basic similarities in and differences between two texts on the same topic (e.g., in illustrations, descriptions, or procedures).

RI.K.3: With prompting and support, describe the connection between two individuals, events, ideas, or pieces of information in a text.

RI.K.8: With prompting and support, identify the reasons an author gives to support points in a text.

W.K.8: With guidance and support from adults, recall information from experiences or gather information from provided sources to answer a question.

W.K.6: With guidance and support from adults, explore a variety of digital tools to produce and publish writing, including in collaboration with peers.

W.K.7: Participate in shared research and writing projects (e.g., explore a number of books by a favorite author and express opinions about them).

SL.K.6: Speak audibly and express thoughts, feelings, and ideas clearly.

SL.K.2: Confirm understanding of a text read aloud or information presented orally or through other media by asking and answering questions about key details and requesting clarification if something is not understood.

SL.K.5: Add drawings or other visual displays to descriptions as desired to provide additional detail.

RF.K.1: Demonstrate understanding of the organization and basic features of print.
  d. Recognize and name all upper- and lower-case letters of the alphabet.
RF.K.2: Demonstrate understanding of spoken words, syllables, and sounds (phonemes).
  b. Count, pronounce, blend, and segment syllables in spoken words.
  c. Blend and segment onsets and rimes of single-syllable spoken words.
  d. Isolate and pronounce the initial, medial vowel, and final sounds (phonemes) in three-phoneme (consonant-vowel-consonant, or CVC) words. (This does not include CVCs ending with /l/, /r/, or /x/.)
  e. Add or substitute individual sounds (phonemes) in simple, one-syllable words to make new words.

STANDARDS *(continued)*

R.F.K.3: Know and apply grade-level phonics and word analysis skills in decoding words.
 a. Demonstrate basic knowledge of one-to-one letter-sound correspondences by producing the primary sound or many of the most frequent sounds for each consonant.
 b. Associate the long and short sounds with common spellings (graphemes) for the five major vowels.
 c. Read common high-frequency words by sight (e.g., the, of, to, you, she, my, is, are, do, does).
 d. Distinguish between similarly spelled words by identifying the sounds of the letters that differ.

L.K.1: Demonstrate command of the conventions of standard English grammar and usage when writing or speaking.
 a. Print many upper- and lower-case letters.
 b. Use frequently occurring nouns and verbs.
 f. Produce and expand complete sentences in shared language activities.

L.K.2: Demonstrate command of the conventions of standard English capitalization, punctuation, and spelling when writing.
 d. Spell simple words phonetically, drawing on knowledge of sound-letter relationships.

L.K.5: With guidance and support from adults, explore word relationships and nuances in word meaning.
 a. Sort common objects into categories (e.g., shapes, foods) to gain a sense of the concepts the categories represent.
 c. Identify real-world connections between words and their use (e.g., note places at school that are colorful).

L.K.6: Use words and phrases acquired through conversations, reading and being read to, and responding to texts.

Priority
Supporting
Skills

"UNWRAPPED" STANDARDS			
Standard	**"Unwrapped" Concepts (students need to know)**	**"Unwrapped" Skills (students need to be able to do)**	**Bloom's/ Webb's DOK**
RI.K.9	**Similarities and differences between two texts on the same topic**	**IDENTIFY (similarities and differences between two texts on the same topic)**	**4/4 Analyze/ Extended Thinking**
RI.K.3	Connection between two individuals, events, ideas, or pieces of information in a text	DESCRIBE (connection between two individuals, events, ideas, or pieces of information in a text)	4/3 Analyze/ Strategic Thinking
RI.K.8	Reasons an author gives to support points in a text	IDENTIFY (reasons an author gives to support points in a text)	2/3 Understand/ Strategic Thinking
W.K.8	**Information from provided sources to answer a question**	**RECALL (information from provided sources to answer a question)**	**3/2 Apply/Skills & Concepts**
W.K.6	Variety of digital tools to produce and publish writing	EXPLORE (variety of digital tools to produce and publish writing) • INCLUDING (collaboration with peers)	2/2 Understand/ Skills & Concepts
W.K.7	Shared research & writing projects	PARTICIPATE (shared research & writing projects)	4/2 Analyze/ Strategic Thinking
SL.K.6	**Thoughts, feelings, and ideas**	**SPEAK AUDIBLY & EXPRESS (thoughts, feelings, and ideas clearly)**	**1/1 Remember/ Recall**
SL.K.2	Understanding of a text read aloud or information presented orally or through other media	CONFIRM (understanding of a text read aloud or information presented orally or through other media) • ASKING & ANSWERING (questions about key details) • REQUESTING (clarification if something is not understood)	2/2 Understand/ Concepts & Skills
SL.K.5	Drawings or other visual displays	ADD (drawings or other visual displays to description) to PROVIDE (additional detail)	2/1 Understand/ Recall

FOUNDATIONAL SKILLS				
StoryTown Lessons	Phonemic Awareness	Phonics RF.K.1d/L.K.1a	High Frequency Words RF.K.3c Bold = Bedrock	Language L.K.5c/L.K.6(Robust) L.K.2c(Writing)
27 Theme 9	phoneme substitution RF.K.2e	consonant Q RF.K.1d/RF.K.3a L.K.1a—print upper- and lowercase letters	that, have	L.K.1f—complete sentences T192, T208 L.K.5a— identify/classify T184
28 Theme 10	Review RF.K.2b syllable blending syllable segmentation syllable deletion RF.K.2c onset-rime blending	phonograms: -ug & -up RF.K.3, T274 L.K.2d—spell simple words, T262–263, T274–275, T304–305, T314–315	Review: that, have	
29 Theme 10	Review: RF.K.2d phoneme isolation: initial, middle, final phoneme identity: initial, final phoneme identity: medial phoneme categorization: initial, final phoneme categorization, medial	RF.K.3b—review short vowels L.K.2d—spell simple words T352–353, T366–367, T382–383, T293–393	Review: **you, look,** for, **the,** there, **are,** little, give, me, **like, and, come,** here	L.K.1b—action verbs, T364 L.K.1f—complete sentences, T338, T363
magic –e long vowels	Extending the Common Core State Standards Teacher Support Book T12—long a; T18—long I; T25—long o; T34—long e; T42—long u	Extending the Common Core State Standards Teacher Support Book fast track T53 review long vowels, T53–T74	**Note:** *The West Hartford Kindergarten RCD Curriculum Team uses Harcourt's StoryTown program to help educators plan out the teaching of letters, skills, and sight words. This table shows how the team matched the CCSS foundational skills to specific StoryTown lessons planned for this unit of study.*	

ESSENTIAL QUESTIONS	BIG IDEAS
How do I compare what I have learned about a topic from two different resources?	I can compare what I have learned about a topic from two different resources by looking for similarities and differences in the information gathered.
How do I share what I have learned during my research?	I can share the research questions I asked and the information/details gathered to answer the questions through dictating, drawing, and writing.
How do I present information so that others can understand?	I speak loudly and clearly when I share my thoughts, feelings, and ideas so that others can understand me.

Source: Kindergarten RCD Curriculum Design Team, West Hartford Public Schools, West Hartford, CT

West Hartford Public Schools English/Language Arts: Grade 1

Unit 1: Oh, The Places You'll Go!

Pacing Guide: This unit is designed to be implemented over the course of 22 days with 3 buffer days.

UNIT OVERVIEW

In this introductory unit, Oh, The Places You'll Go!, first graders will explore the differences between literature and informational text, practice asking and answering questions about key details within texts, and learn how to share their opinions in writing. StoryTown texts (big books, main and paired selections, etc.) will be used to teach the Priority Standards and comprehension skills. Students will also learn the rules for collaborative conversations and practice speaking and listening in both the whole group and small groups. Additionally, StoryTown will be utilized as the core resource as referenced in the skills section for reading foundational skills and language standards. A series of assured learning experiences are included that ask students to apply and practice their new skills in a structured format.

This unit planner should inform the majority of your direct instruction and influence small-group activities; however, it is not intended to cover the entire scope of daily literacy in your classroom. Small-group reading instruction including guided reading should continue to occur regularly as in past years. StoryTown leveled readers should be used in order (since they match phonics skills) along with additional leveled texts you may have. Additionally, students should read and write independently on a regular basis.

STANDARDS

RL.1.5: Explain major differences between books that tell stories and books that give information, drawing on a wide reading of a range of text types.

RL.1.1: Ask and answer questions about key details in a text.

RI.1.1 Ask and answer questions about key details in a text.

RF.1.1: Demonstrate understanding of the organization and basic features of print.

a. Recognize the distinguishing features of a sentence (e.g., first word, capitalization, ending punctuation).

RF.1.2: Demonstrate understanding of spoken words, syllables, and sounds (phonemes).

a. Distinguish long from short vowel sounds in spoken single-syllable words.

c. Isolate and pronounce initial, medial vowel, and final sounds (phonemes) in spoken single-syllable words.

RF.1.3: Know and apply grade-level phonics and word analysis skills in decoding words.

a. Know the spelling-sound correspondences for common consonant digraphs.

b. Decode regularly spelled one-syllable words.

f. Read words with inflectional endings.

L.1.1: Demonstrate command of the conventions of standard English grammar and usage when writing or speaking.

a. Print all upper- and lower-case letters.

b. Use common, proper, and possessive nouns.

i. Use frequently-occurring prepositions (e.g., during, beyond, toward).

L.1.2: Demonstrate command of the conventions of standard English capitalization, punctuation, and spelling when writing.

d. Use conventional spelling for words with common spelling patterns and for frequently occurring irregular words.

e. Spell untaught words phonetically, drawing on phonemic awareness and spelling conventions.

L.1.4: Determine or clarify the meaning of unknown and multiple-meaning words and phrases based on grade 1 reading and content, choosing flexibly from an array of strategies.

c. Identify frequently occurring root words (e.g., look) and their inflectional forms (e.g., looks, looked, looking).

L.1.5. With guidance and support from adults, demonstrate understanding of word relationships and nuances in word meanings.

a. Sort words into categories (e.g., colors, clothing) to gain a sense of the concepts the categories represent.

c. Identify real-life connections between words and their use (e.g., note places at home that are cozy).

W.1.1: Write opinion pieces in which they introduce the topic or name the book they are writing about, state an opinion, supply a reason for the opinion, and provide some sense of closure.

W.1.8: With guidance and support from adults, recall information from experiences or gather information from provided sources to answer a question.

SL.1.1: Participate in collaborative conversations with diverse partners about grade 1 topics and texts with peers and adults in small and larger groups.

a. Follow agreed-upon rules for discussions (e.g., listening to others with care, speaking one at a time about the topics and texts under discussion).

SL.1.2: Ask and answer questions about key details in a text read aloud or information presented orally or through other media.

SL.1.6: Produce complete sentences when appropriate to task and situation.

Priority
Supporting
Skills

"UNWRAPPED" STANDARDS			
Standard	"Unwrapped" Concepts (students need to know)	"Unwrapped" Skills (students need to be able to do)	Bloom's/ Webb's DOK
RL.1.5	Major differences between books that tell stories and books that give information	EXPLAIN (major differences between books that tell stories and books that give information)	4/2 Analyze/Skills & Concepts
RL.1.1/ RI.1.1	Questions about key details in a text	ASK & ANSWER (questions about key details in a text)	2/1 Understand/ Recall
W.1.1	Opinion pieces	WRITE (opinion pieces) • INTRODUCE (topic or name the book) • STATE (opinion) • SUPPLY (reason for the opinion) • PROVIDE (sense of closure)	3/2 Apply/Skills & Concepts
W.1.8	Information from experiences or provided sources	RECALL (information from experiences or provided sources) to ANSWER (question)	3/2 Apply/Skills & Concepts
SL.1.1	Collaborative conversations with diverse partners about grade 1 topics and texts	PARTICIPATE (collaborative conversations with diverse partners about grade 1 topics and texts) • FOLLOW (agreed-upon rules for discussions)	3/1 Apply/ Recall
SL.1.2	Questions about key details in a text read aloud or information presented orally or through other media	ASK & ANSWER (questions about key details in a text read aloud or information presented orally or through other media)	2/1 Understand/ Recall
SL.1.6	Complete sentences	PRODUCE (complete sentences when appropriate to task and situation)	2/1 Understand/ Recall

ESSENTIAL QUESTIONS	BIG IDEAS
How do I actively participate in collaborative conversations?	I actively participate in collaborative conversations by following agreed-upon rules.
How do I determine whether a text is literature or informational text?	I look to see if the text is telling me a story or giving me information when determining if it is literature or informational text.
How do I share my opinion with others in writing?	I share my information in writing by introducing the topic or book title, stating my opinion, supplying a reason to support this opinion, and providing a sense of closure.

Source: Grade 1 RCD Curriculum Design Team, West Hartford Public Schools, West Hartford, CT

West Hartford Public Schools English/Language Arts: Grade 2

Unit 3: Open Books/Open Minds

Pacing Guide: This unit is designed to be implemented over the course of 20 days with 3 buffer days.

UNIT OVERVIEW

There are three Priority Standards in this unit, two for reading for literature and one for writing of narrative text. The focus in reading for literature is on recounting stories and how the events in the story help determine the central message, lesson, or moral. The second reading for literature standard focuses on describing how the characters in a story respond to major events and challenges in a story. This unit will include fables, folktales, and narrative stories that include a strong lesson or central message.

The following definitions can be used to define the key terms in this unit.

Recount: to tell about the story elements and most important details in a concise but detailed way; an intermediate step between retelling and summarizing; the message/lesson/moral should be included when applicable

Lesson: a principle an author intends to teach a reader

Message: the point, moral, or meaning of a story

Moral: a lesson learned from a story or event (commonly associated with a fable)

Fable: a story that commonly uses animals as characters that is meant to teach a useful lesson

Folktale: a story passed down orally from one generation to another by the people of a country or region

Narrative: a story or description of events that may or may not be true

The students will be asked to create a short fable or narrative with a strong message or lesson. The focus in writing is on moving students through the entire writing process including planning, drafting, editing, revising, and publishing using a digital tool. Students will be given the opportunity to practice their speaking and listening skills through the creation of an audio recording and drawings or other visual displays, and incorporating them into their digital presentation of their writing. Students will create at least one narrative writing piece, but may be given the opportunity to create more than one piece as time allows.

STANDARDS

RL.2.2: Recount stories, including fables and folktales from diverse cultures, and determine their central message, lesson, or moral.

RL.2.3: Describe how characters in a story respond to major events and challenges.

RL.2.1: Ask and answer such questions as who, what, where, when, why, and how to demonstrate understanding of key details in a text.

RL.2.7: Use information gained from the illustrations and words in a print or digital text to demonstrate understanding of its characters, setting, or plot.

RF.2.3: Know and apply grade-level phonics and word analysis skills in decoding words.

   a. Distinguish long and short vowels when reading regularly spelled one-syllable words.

   c. Decode regularly spelled two-syllable words with long vowels.

   d. Decode words with common prefixes and suffixes.

   f. Recognize and read grade-appropriate irregularly spelled words.

W.2.3: Write narratives in which they recount a well-elaborated event or short sequence of events, include details to describe actions, thoughts, and feelings, use temporal words to signal event order, and provide a sense of closure.

W.2.5: With guidance and support from adults and peers, focus on a topic and strengthen writing as needed by revising and editing.

W.2.6: With guidance and support from adults, use a variety of digital tools to produce and publish writing, including in collaboration with peers.

W.2.8: Recall information from experiences or gather information from provided sources to answer a question.

L.2.2: Demonstrate command of the conventions of standard English capitalization, punctuation, and spelling when writing.

   c. Use an apostrophe to form contractions and frequently occurring possessives.

   d. Generalize learned spelling patterns when writing words.

L.2.6: Use words and phrases acquired through conversations, reading and being read to, and responding to texts, including using adjectives and adverbs to describe (e.g., When other kids are happy that makes me happy).

SL.2.5: Create audio recordings of stories or poems; add drawings or other visual displays to stories or recounts of experiences when appropriate to clarify ideas, thoughts, and feelings.

SL.2.6: Produce complete sentences when appropriate to task and situation in order to provide requested detail or clarification.

Priority
Supporting
Skills

"UNWRAPPED" STANDARDS			
Standard	"Unwrapped" Concepts (students need to know)	"Unwrapped" Skills (students need to be able to do)	Bloom's/ Webb's DOK
RL.2.2	Stories	RECOUNT (stories including fables and folktales from diverse cultures)	2/1 Understand/ Recall
	Central message, lesson, or moral	DETERMINE (central message, lesson, or moral)	4/2 Analyze/Skills & Concepts
RL.2.3	Character's response to major events and challenges	DESCRIBE (character's response to major events and challenges)	2/2 Understand/ Skills & Concepts
RL.2.1	Questions	ASK and ANSWER (who, what, when, where, why, and how questions) to DEMONSTRATE (understanding of key details in literary and informational texts)	2/1 Understand/ Recall
RL.2.7	Information gained from the illustrations and words in a print or digital text	USE (information gained from the illustrations and words in a print or digital text) to DEMONSTRATE (understanding of its characters, setting, or plot)	3/2 Apply/Skills & Concepts
W.2.3	Narratives	WRITE (narratives) to RECOUNT (well elaborated event or short sequence of events) • INCLUDE (details to describe actions, thoughts, and feelings) • USE (temporal words to signal event order) • PROVIDE (sense of closure)	2/3 Understand/ Strategic Reasoning
W.2.5	Topic	FOCUS ON (topic) and STRENGTHEN (writing) by REVISING and EDITING (with guidance and support from adults and peers)	3/3 Apply/ Strategic Thinking
W.2.6	Digital Tools	USE (variety of digital tools) to PRODUCE and PUBLISH (writing in collaboration with peers with guidance and support from adults)	2/2 Apply/Skills & Concepts
W.2.8	Information from experiences	RECALL (information from experiences) to ANSWER (questions) in writing	2/1 Understand/ Recall

"UNWRAPPED" STANDARDS *(continued)*			
Standard	"Unwrapped" Concepts (students need to know)	"Unwrapped" Skills (students need to be able to do)	Bloom's/ Webb's DOK
SL.2.5	Audio recordings of stories or poems	CREATE (audio recordings of stories/poems)	2/1 Understand/ Recall
	Drawings or other visual displays	ADD (drawings or other visual displays to stories or recounts of experiences) to CLARIFY (ideas, thoughts, and feelings)	2/1 Understand/ Recall
SL.2.6	Complete sentences	PRODUCE (complete sentences when appropriate to task and situation) to PROVIDE (requested detail or clarification)	3/1 Apply/Recall & Reproduction

ESSENTIAL QUESTIONS	BIG IDEAS
When recounting a story what do I include?	I recount a story by including the key details from the beginning, middle, and end, and the story's central message, lesson, or moral.
What affects the way a character acts in a story?	A character acts in response to major events and challenges in a story.
What does a writer do to prepare a story for publication?	A writer revises and edits with peers and adults to create a published narrative that includes a beginning, middle, and end with elaborated events told in order.

Source: Grade 2 RCD Curriculum Design Team, West Hartford Public Schools, West Hartford, CT

MATH EXAMPLES

Rigorous Curriculum Design Math Unit Planning Organizer
Kindergarten: San Diego Unified School District

Subject(s)	Math
Grade/Course	Kindergarten
Unit of Study	Fingers and Toes (Counting from 1–20)
Pacing	
Overview of Unit	In this unit students will use concrete models, drawings, and strategies based on place value to add and subtract numbers within 1000. They will come to understand the Big Ideas that some strategies are more effective when adding and subtracting larger numbers, and that addition and subtraction are inverse operations.

Priority Common Core State Standards
Supporting Standards

K.CC.3: WRITE numbers from 0 to 20. REPRESENT a number of objects with a written numeral 0–20 (with 0 representing a count of no objects).

K.CC.4: UNDERSTAND the relationship between numbers and quantities; CONNECT counting to cardinality.

K.CC.5: Count to answer "how many?" questions about as many as 20 things arranged in a line, a rectangular array, or a circle, or as many as 10 things in a scattered configuration; given a number from 1–20, count out that many objects.

K.CC.4.a: When counting objects, SAY the number names in the standard order, PAIRING each object with one and only one number name and each number name with one and only one object.

K.CC.4.b: UNDERSTAND that the last number name said tells the number of objects counted. The number of objects is the same regardless of their arrangement or the order in which they were counted.

K.CC.6: IDENTIFY whether the number of objects in one group is greater than, less than, or equal to the number of objects in another group, e.g., by USING matching and counting strategies.

K.CC.7: Compare two numbers between 1 and 10 presented as written numerals.

"Unwrapped" Concepts (students need to know)	"Unwrapped" Skills (students need to be able to do)	Taxonomy Levels	
		Bloom's / DOK	
K.CC.3: Numbers from 0–20	WRITE	1	1
K.CC.3: Number of objects with written numeral 0–20	REPRESENT	1	1
K.CC.4a: each object with one and only one number name	PAIR	3	2
K.CC.4a: each number name with one and only one object	PAIR	3	2
K.CC.4b: Last number name said tells number of objects counted (regardless of their arrangement or order)	UNDERSTAND	3	2
K.CC.6: Whether the number of objects in one group is greater than, less than, or equal to the number of objects in another group	UNDERSTAND IDENTIFY	3 4	2 3

Essential Questions	Corresponding Big Ideas
How do I know how many I have? • *How do I know how many cookies I have?*	When I want to know how many, I count.
How do I show how many I have? • *If Mom was making a shopping list, how do I show her how many cookies to buy for the class snack?*	When I write the number, I show how many.
How do I tell if groups have more, less, or are the same? • *If I share my cookies, how do I know that we all have the same amount?*	When I count, I see how groups are the same or different.

Source: Kindergarten RCD Curriculum Design Team, San Diego Unified School District, San Diego, CA

Rigorous Curriculum Design Math Unit Planning Organizer
Grade 1: San Diego Unified School District

Subject(s)	Math
Grade/Course	1st Grade
Unit of Study	Shapely Shapes (Geometry & Fractions)
Pacing	

"UNWRAPPED" Priority Standards ONLY

1.G.2: COMPOSE two-dimensional shapes (rectangles, squares, trapezoids, triangles, half-circles, and quarter-circles) or three-dimensional shapes (cubes, right rectangular prisms, right circular cones, and right circular cylinders) to CREATE a composite shape, and COMPOSE new shapes from the composite shape.

1.G.3: PARTITION circles and rectangles into two and four equal shares, DESCRIBE the shares using words halves, fourths, and quarters, and USE the phrases half of, fourth of, and quarter of. DESCRIBE the whole as two of, or four of the shares. UNDERSTAND for these examples that decomposing into more equal shares creates smaller shares.

"Unwrapped" Concepts (students need to know)	"Unwrapped" Skills (students need to be able to do)	Taxonomy Levels	
		Bloom's / DOK	
1.G.2 2-dimensional shapes • squares • rectangles • trapezoids • triangles • half-circles • quarter circles 3-dimensional shapes • cubes • right rectangular prisms • right circular cones • right circular cylinders new shapes	COMPOSE	6	2
composite shapes (*using 2-dimensional and 3-dimensional shapes*)	to CREATE	6	2
1.G.3 equal shares • whole/parts • circles & rectangles • halves, fourths, quarters	PARTITION (DIVIDE) DESCRIBE and USE phrases	6 1	3 2
more equal shares equals smaller shares	UNDERSTAND	2	3

Essential Questions	Corresponding Big Ideas
How is a trapezoid the same as or different from a square?	When forming standard 2-dimensional and 3-dimensional shapes we must adhere to certain mathematically defined attributes. (teacher) *Shapes are named because of how they are made. (student)*
How can you make a (3-dimensional shape) out of (plane shapes)? (i.e., How can you make a cylinder out of a rectangle and circles?)	There are common 2-dimensional and 3-dimensional shapes that can be put together to make other shapes. (teacher) *Shapes can be put together to make other shapes. (student)*
How could you share a _____ fairly with a friend? Or with four friends?	Equal shares describe the whole and its equal parts using shapes and groups. (teacher) *Shapes and groups can be divided into equal parts called fractions. (student)*

Source: 1st Grade RCD Curriculum Design Team, San Diego Unified School District, San Diego, CA

Rigorous Curriculum Design Math Unit Planning Organizer
Grade 2: San Diego Unified School District

Subject(s)	Math
Grade/Course	2nd Grade
Unit of Study	UNIT 5: EXPANDING OUR WORLD (NUMBERS TO 1,000)
Pacing	
Overview of Unit	In this unit students will use concrete models, drawings, and strategies based on place value to add and subtract numbers within 1000. They will come to understand the Big Ideas that some strategies are more effective when adding and subtracting larger numbers, and that addition and subtraction are inverse operations.

Priority Common Core State Standards
Supporting Standards

2.NBT.7: Add and subtract within 1000, using concrete models or drawings and strategies based on place value, properties of operations, and/or the relationship between addition and subtraction; relate the strategy to a written method. Understand that in adding or subtracting three-digit numbers, one adds or subtracts hundreds and hundreds, tens and tens, ones and ones; and sometimes it is necessary to compose or decompose tens or hundreds.

2.NBT.3: Read and write numbers to 1000 using base-ten numerals, number names, and expanded form.

2.NBT.8: Mentally add 10 or 100 to a given number 100–900, and mentally subtract 10 or 100 from a given number 100–900.

2.NBT.4: Compare two three-digit numbers based on meaning of the hundreds, tens, and ones digits, using >, =, and < to record the results of comparisons.

2.NBT.9: Explain why addition and subtraction strategies work, using place value and the properties of operations.

2.MD.8: Solve word problems involving dollar bills, quarters, dimes, nickels, and pennies, using $ and ¢ symbols appropriately. *Example: If you have 2 dimes and 3 pennies, how many cents do you have?*

"UNWRAPPED" Priority Standards

2.NBT.7: ADD and SUBTRACT within 1000, US(E)ing concrete models or drawings and strategies based on place value, properties of operations, and/or the relationship between addition and subtraction; RELATE the strategy to a written method. UNDERSTAND that in adding or subtracting three-digit numbers, one adds or subtracts hundreds and hundreds, tens and tens, ones and ones; and sometimes it is necessary to COMPOSE or DECOMPOSE tens or hundreds.

2.NBT.9: EXPLAIN WHY addition and subtraction strategies work, US(E)ing place value and the properties of operations.

"Unwrapped" Concepts (students need to know)	"Unwrapped" Skills (students need to be able to do)	Taxonomy Levels	
		Bloom's / DOK	
Numbers within 1000	ADD and SUBTRACT	2	3

Concrete models or drawings and Strategies based on
    Place value
    Properties of operations
    Relationship between addition and
        subtraction
	USE	3	3

Strategies to a written method	RELATE	4	3
Hundreds and hundreds, tens and tens, ones and ones	UNDERSTAND	4	2
Tens or hundreds	COMPOSE and DECOMPOSE	4	3

Addition and subtraction strategies
    Place value and properties of
        operations
	EXPLAIN/USE	4	3

Essential Questions	Corresponding Big Ideas
Which strategy works best for me to add and subtract big numbers? Why?	T: Some strategies are faster or more efficient for adding and subtracting big numbers. S: Some strategies for adding and subtracting big numbers are easier or faster for me.
How are addition and subtraction related?	T: Addition and subtraction are inverse operations. S: Addition and subtraction undo each other. OR I can use addition to check subtraction or subtraction to check addition.

Source: 2nd Grade RCD Curriculum Design Team, San Diego Unified School District, San Diego, CA

McMinnville School District—Kindergarten

UNIT NUMBER 5	Addition & Subtraction		
Unit Length	**January 27–March 7, 2013** 25-day unit with 3-day buffer		
"Unwrapped" PRIORITY Standards	**K.OA.2: SOLVE addition and subtraction word problems, and ADD and SUBTRACT within 10, e.g., by using objects or drawings to represent the problem.** **K.CC.2: COUNT forward beginning from a given number within the known sequence (instead of having to begin at 1).**		

"Unwrapped" PRIORITY Standards Graphic Organizer	Concepts	Skills	Bloom's
	Addition Word Problems	SOLVE	4
	Subtraction Word Problems	SOLVE	4
	Within 10	ADD	4
	Within 10	SUBTRACT	4
	Forward beginning from a given number	COUNT	3

Supporting Standards	K.OA.1: Represent addition and subtraction with objects, fingers, mental images, drawings, sounds (e.g., claps), acting out situations, verbal explanations, expressions, or equations. (Drawings need not show details, but should show the mathematics in the problem.)
Essential Questions	• What is addition and subtraction? • What is a story problem? • How do you solve a story problem?
Big Ideas	• Addition is putting together and subtraction is taking groups apart. • A story problem tells a story using words and numbers and then asks a question that the learner must find the answer to. • To solve a story problem you have to start with what you know and figure out what you don't know. You can use different strategies for solving the same problem.

Source: Kindergarten RCD Team, McMinnville School District, McMinnville, Oregon

McMinnville School District—Grade 1

UNIT NUMBER ONE	Number Sense
Unit Length	**September 9–October 16, 2013** 23 days with 3 buffer days
"Unwrapped" PRIORITY Standards	**1.NBT.3: COMPARE** two two-digit numbers based on meanings of the tens and ones digits, **RECORDING** the results of comparisons with the symbols >, =, and <. **1.NBT.2: UNDERSTAND** that the two digits of a two-digit number represent amounts of tens and ones. **UNDERSTAND** the following as special cases: c. The numbers 10, 20, 30, 40, 50, 60, 70, 80, 90 refer to one, two, three, four, five, six, seven, eight, or nine tens (and 0 ones).

	Concepts	Skills	Bloom's
"Unwrapped" PRIORITY Standards Graphic Organizer	Two two-digit numbers based on meanings of the tens and ones digits	COMPARE	4
	Results of comparisons with the symbols >, =, and <	RECORD	1
	That the two digits of a two-digit number represent amounts of tens and ones	UNDERSTAND	2
	The following as special cases: The numbers 10, 20, 30, 40, 50, 60, 70, 80, 90 refer to one, two, three, four, five, six, seven, eight, or nine tens (and 0 ones)	UNDERSTAND	2

Supporting Standards	1.OA.5: Relate counting to addition and subtraction (e.g., by counting on 2 to add 2).
	
	1.OA.7: Understand the meaning of the equal sign, and determine if equations involving addition and subtraction are true or false.
	
	1.NBT.2: Understand that the two digits of a two-digit number represent amounts of tens and ones. Understand the following as special cases:
	    a. 10 can be thought of as a bundle of ten ones—called a "ten."
	    b. The numbers from 11 to 19 are composed of a ten and one, two, three, four, five, six, seven, eight, or nine ones.

Essential Questions	What makes a two-digit number? How do you compare two two-digit numbers?
Big Ideas	A two-digit number is made up of tens and ones. You compare two-digit numbers using >, < and =.

Source: Grade 1 RCD Team, McMinnville School District, McMinnville, Oregon

McMinnville School District—Grade 2

UNIT NUMBER THREE	Time & Money		
Unit Length	**December 2, 2013–January 24, 2013** 26 days with a 3-day buffer		
"Unwrapped" PRIORITY Standards	**2.OA.1:** USE addition and subtraction within 100 to SOLVE one- and two-step word problems involving situations of adding to, taking from, putting together, taking apart, and comparing, with unknowns in all positions, e.g., by US(E)ing drawings and equations with a symbol for the unknown number to represent the problem. PRIORITY **2.MD.7:** TELL and WRITE time from analog and digital clocks to the nearest five minutes, using a.m. and p.m. PRIORITY **2.MD.8:** SOLVE word problems involving dollar bills, quarters, dimes, nickels, and pennies, using $ and ¢ symbols appropriately. PRIORITY		

"Unwrapped" PRIORITY Standards Graphic Organizer	Concepts	Skills	Bloom's
	Addition within 100: one- and two-step word problems: • Adding to, taking from, putting together, taking apart, and comparing, with unknowns in all positions, symbol for the unknown number to represent the problem	SOLVE, USING	3
	Time from analog and digital clocks to nearest five minutes using a.m. and p.m.	TELL and WRITE	2 (3)
	Word problems involving dollar bills, quarters, dimes, nickels, and pennies, using $ and ¢ symbols.	SOLVE	3

Supporting Standards	2. NBT.2: Count within 1000; skip-count by 5s, 10s, and 100s
Essential Questions	1. How are addition and subtraction related? 2. How can you solve problems with dollars and cents? 3. How can you tell time to the nearest 5 minutes and know if it is a.m. or p.m.?
Big Ideas	1. Addition is putting things together and subtraction is taking things apart. They are inverse (opposite) operations. 2. You have to know what each bill and coin is and count the value of each bill and coin. 3. You can use a digital or analog clock to tell time. When using an analog clock you must look at the hour hand to tell the hour and look at the minute hand and count by fives to tell the minutes. If it is between midnight and noon, it is a.m. If it is between noon and midnight, it is p.m.

Source: Grade 2 RCD Team, McMinnville School District, McMinnville, Oregon

West Hartford, Connecticut—Kindergarten:
Unit 2, Geometry Part 1 (2-D and 3-D Shapes)

Pacing Guide: This unit is designed to be implemented over the course of 14 days. Based on the nature of math instruction for the kindergarten learner we acknowledge that all children may not master this content at the end of 14 days. Most children will reach mastery with continued content instruction as determined by the classroom teacher throughout the year.

UNIT OVERVIEW

In this unit, students will build their understanding of shapes. They begin to use formal language in naming shapes, focusing on geometric attributes for the basis of shape identification, rather than on color, size, or orientation. Students will identify 2-dimensional shapes and be exposed to 3-dimensional shapes. They begin to recognize the variation that shapes can have (for example, all triangles do not have equal length sides). Students describe objects in the environment using terms such as above, below, beside, etc., to explain the location of object. In this unit, students will also begin to explore measurement, determining attributes that describe objects and can be measured, such as weight and height, and determining if an object has more or less of this attribute than other objects.

Common Core State Standards
• **K.G.1:** DESCRIBE objects in the environment USING names of shapes and DESCRIBE the relative positions of these objects using terms such as above, below, beside, in front of, behind, and next to.
• **K.G.2:** Correctly name shapes regardless of their orientations or overall size.
• **K.G.3:** Identify shapes as two-dimensional (lying in a plane, "flat") or three-dimensional ("solid").
• **K.MD.1:** Describe measurable attributes of objects, such as length or weight. Describe several measurable attributes of a single object.
• **K.MD.2:** Directly compare two objects with a measurable attribute in common, to see which object has "more of"/"less of" the attribute, and describe the difference. *For example, directly compare the heights of two children and describe one child as taller/shorter.*
<div align="right">**Standards in bold are Priority** Standards that are not in bold are supporting</div>

"UNWRAPPED" STANDARDS		
"Unwrapped" Concepts (students need to know)	"Unwrapped" Skills (students need to be able to do)	Bloom's Taxonomy Level Webb's Depth of Knowledge Level

K.G.1:
• *Objects in environment*
• *Relative position using terms:*
  • **Above**
  • **Below**
  • **Beside**
  • **In front of**
  • **Behind**
  • **Next to**
	DESCRIBE objects in the environment using the relative positions of these objects using terms (above, below, beside, in front of, behind, and next to)	B = 2 (Understand)
		DOK = 1 (Recall and reproduction)

• *Names of shapes*
  • **Squares**
  • **Circles**
  • **Triangles**
  • **Hexagons**
  • **Cubes**
  • **Cones**
  • **Cylinders**
  • **Spheres**
	IDENTIFY shapes (squares, circles, triangles, rectangles, hexagons, cubes, cones, cylinders, and spheres) by name	B = 1, 2 (Remember)
		DOK = 1 (Recall and reproduction)

ESSENTIAL QUESTIONS	BIG IDEAS
1. *What are the names of these shapes? (2D shape focus, with exposure to 3D shapes)*	1. Every shape has a special word name that I can say.
2. *How can I explain where I see shapes?*	2. Shapes are everywhere in the environment.

Source: Kindergarten RCD Curriculum Design Team, West Hartford Public Schools, West Hartford, CT

West Hartford, Connecticut—Grade 1:
Unit 1, Numeracy

Pacing Guide: This unit is designed to be implemented over the course of 10 days. Based on the nature of math instruction for the first grade learner we acknowledge that all children may not master this content at the end of 10 days. These concepts will continue to be integrated throughout the year and most children will reach mastery with continued instruction.

UNIT OVERVIEW

In this unit, students will strengthen early numeracy and counting concepts along the way to more powerful mathematical ideas. Students will build an understanding of number relationships that supports the development of addition and subtraction. Students will show a number that is one or two more than the set they have, or one or two less than the set they have, using objects. They will count, starting from any number, and read and write numerals relating to a set of objects. Students will strengthen their understanding of the numbers 0–20, focusing on the "teens," understanding that these numbers are made of "ten and some more" and will become fluent in building and naming teen numbers and using the language of these numbers. Students will strengthen their understanding of the structures of early numeracy by using 5 and 10 as benchmarks in visual problem solving with five- and ten-frames, and will explore the placement of numbers on the number line and hundreds chart, discovering patterns that support their counting. Students will work with small groups of objects to strengthen their ability to recognize small numbers of one to five objects without counting (subitizing) and to develop the concept of a number containing smaller numbers (part-part-whole), a concept that will support later addition and subtraction concepts. Students will review the counting sequence and will continue working on counting through the year, with the goal of counting to 120.

Common Core State Standards
• **1.NBT.1: COUNT to 120, starting at any number less than 120. In this range, READ and WRITE numerals and REPRESENT a number of objects with the written numeral.**
• **1.OA.5:** Relate counting to addition and subtraction (e.g., by counting on 2 to add 2).
• **1.NBT.2 (b): UNDERSTAND that the numbers from 11 to 19 are composed of a ten and one, two, three, four, five, six, seven, eight, or nine ones.**

Standards in bold are Priority
Standards that are not in bold are supporting

"UNWRAPPED" STANDARDS		
"Unwrapped" Concepts (students need to know)	"Unwrapped" Skills (students need to be able to do)	Bloom's Taxonomy Level Webb's Depth of Knowledge Level
• **1.NBT.1: Count to 120, starting at any number less than 120. In this range, read and write numerals and represent a number of objects with the written numeral.**	**COUNT** (to 120, starting at any number less than 120) **READ** (numerals that represent a group of objects) **WRITE** (numerals to represent a group of objects)	B = 1 (Remember) DOK = 1 (Recall and reproduction)
• **1.NBT.2 (b): Understand that the numbers from 11 to 19 are composed of a ten and one, two, three, four, five, six, seven, eight, or nine ones.**	**UNDERSTAND** (that the numbers from 11 to 19 are composed of a ten and one, two, three, four, five, six, seven, eight, or nine ones.)	B = 2 (understand) DOK = 1 (Recall and reproduction)

ESSENTIAL QUESTIONS	BIG IDEAS
1. *What are the number names and how do I say them, write them to show how many objects I have, and read them?*	1. I say the number names in the same order, starting at any number, and counting to ... (120 by the end of the year). I write the counting number that shows how many objects there are. (1.NBT.1)
2. *How can I make the numbers 11–19?*	2. I can make the numbers 11–19 with ten and some more (one, two, three ... more.) (1.NBT.2 (b))

Source: Grade 1 RCD Curriculum Design Team, West Hartford Public Schools, West Hartford, CT

Other Examples of Essential Questions and Corresponding Big Ideas in Math and English Language Arts

To conclude this chapter, Wintonbury Early Childhood Magnet School and Laurel Elementary School in Bloomfield, Connecticut, contributed various pairs of English language arts and math Essential Questions and Big Ideas. These are derived from several "unwrapped" K–2 Common Core English language arts strands (indicated parenthetically) and two math domains, Counting and Cardinality and Operations and Algebraic Thinking. Even without the corresponding graphic organizers, they offer primary educators further examples of how to word Big Ideas and Essential Questions.

Essential Questions	Corresponding Big Ideas
Reading (RL) *How can my understanding of characters and details make me a better reader of fiction?*	Paying attention to characters and details in fiction texts helps me to understand the story.
Reading Informational Texts (RI) *How can my understanding of the main ideas and details make me a better reader of nonfiction?*	Identifying the main idea and details in nonfiction texts helps me to understand the topic.
Foundational Skills (RF) *How will listening and writing sounds in words help me to become a better reader and writer?*	Knowing each letter and its sound will help me to read and write.
Language *How will learning new words help me to understand my world and to share my ideas?*	Learning new words will help me to understand my world and share my ideas.
Writing *How can I share my ideas and knowledge through writing?*	I can write to tell others what I think and have learned.
Mathematics—Counting and Cardinality *How can you show, count, and write numbers 0 to 20?* *How can you show and compare numbers to 10?*	I can use numbers instead of objects to show how many. Knowing *greater than and less than* will help me to compare two numbers.
Mathematics—Operations and Algebraic Thinking (K.OA) *How can you solve word problems using addition and subtraction?*	Addition and subtraction helps me to solve real-life math problems.

CHAPTER 6

Upper Elementary Grade Examples

One of the most beneficial features of the original *"Unwrapping" the Standards* (2003) book was its inclusion of more than 85 examples of "unwrapped" standards, Big Ideas, and Essential Questions specific to each grade span, K–2, 3–5, 6–8, and 9–12, from numerous content areas. Educators always appreciate seeing examples: especially Big Ideas and Essential Questions. These concrete samples help greatly to convey what the explanatory content describes. For these reasons, I knew it was important to include in this volume similar examples of "unwrapped" Common Core State Standards in English language arts and literacy and in mathematics.

Four school systems that I have worked closely with, two in the eastern United States and two in the West, graciously responded to my request for "unwrapped" Common Core examples created by their educators. The two east coast districts are West Hartford and Bloomfield, both in Connecticut. The two west coast districts are San Diego Unified School District in California and McMinnville School District in Oregon. It was my great privilege over a period of many months to lead their educators and leaders through the Rigorous Curriculum Design framework I created to help educators write new curricula for the Common Core. The four parts of the "unwrapping" process were the first steps they followed in developing their curricular units of study in English language arts and literacy and in math that later included unit-specific formative and summative assessments, authentic performance tasks, instructional resources, and differentiated instructional strategies.

I always encourage educators and curriculum writers to follow the framework of "unwrapping" and curriculum design as prescribed but then to "make the process their own" by customizing the format for their units of study. Reprinted here are the first sections of the Rigorous Curriculum Design Unit Planning Organizer you have seen throughout the previous explanatory chapters. Many grade-level or course-level design teams in the four districts used this template as is; others chose to modify it somewhat. To respect their particular district formatting, I have included the graphic organizers as they were submitted to me. Because you now understand the complete "unwrapping" process, you will be able to understand the content represented in these district examples even when it varies from my original format. Also, note that not every district included both Bloom's *and* DOK cognitive levels on their initial graphic organizers.

I have organized these grade-span examples by district and by content area, rather than interspersing all the examples for each grade level. This will make each district's examples "self-contained" and hopefully easier for you to read and understand.

Rigorous Curriculum Design Unit Planning Organizer

Subject(s)	
Grade/Course	
Unit of Study	
Pacing	

Priority Common Core State Standards (Bolded) Supporting Standards

"UNWRAPPED" Priority Standards

"Unwrapped" Concepts (students need to know)	"Unwrapped" Skills (students need to be able to do)	Taxonomy Levels	
		Bloom's / DOK	

Essential Questions	Corresponding Big Ideas

ELA EXAMPLES

Rigorous Curriculum Design ELA Unit Planning Organizer
Grade 3: San Diego Unified School District

Subject(s)	ELA
Grade/Course	Grade 3
Unit of Study	Unit 6: Comparing Themes in Literature
Pacing	25 days, followed by 2 buffer days

Priority Common Core State Standards
Supporting Standards

RL.3.2: Recount stories, including fables, folktales, and myths from diverse cultures; determine the central message, lesson, or moral and explain how it is conveyed through key details in the text.

RL.3.9: Compare and contrast the themes, settings, and plots of stories written by the same author about the same or similar characters (e.g., in books from a series).

> RL.3.1: Ask and answer questions to demonstrate understanding of a text, referring explicitly to the text as the basis for the answers.

> RL.3.3: Describe characters in a story (e.g., their traits, motivations, or feelings) and explain how their actions contribute to the sequence of events.

W.3.1: Write opinion pieces on topics or texts, supporting a point of view with reasons.

> W.3.1.a: Introduce the topic or text they are writing about, state an opinion, and create an organizational structure that lists reasons.

> W.3.1.b: Provide reasons that support the opinion.

> W.3.1.c: Use linking words and phrases (e.g., *because, therefore, since, for example*) to connect opinion and reasons.

> W.3.1.d: Provide a concluding statement or section.

W.3.3: Write narratives to develop real or imagined experiences or events using effective technique, descriptive details, and clear event sequences.

> W.3.3.a: Establish a situation and introduce a narrator and/or characters; organize an event sequence that unfolds naturally.

> W.3.3.b: Use dialogue and descriptions of actions, thoughts, and feelings to develop experiences and events or show the response of characters to situations.

> W.3.3.c: Use temporal words and phrases to signal event order.

> W.3.3.d: Provide a sense of closure.

W.3.6: With guidance and support from adults, use technology to produce and publish writing (using keyboarding skills) as well as to interact and collaborate with others.

Priority Common Core State Standards *(continued)*
Supporting Standards

L.3.1.a: Explain the function of nouns, pronouns, verbs, adjectives, and adverbs in general and their functions in particular sentences. (Note: Not included on graphic organizer.)

L.3.1.c: Use abstract nouns (e.g., childhood).

L.3.1.i: Produce simple, compound, and complex sentences.

L.3.3.a: Choose words and phrases for effect.

L.3.4.c: Use a known root word as a clue to the meaning of an unknown word with the same root (e.g., company, companion).

L.3.5.c: Distinguish shades of meaning among related words that describe states of mind or degrees of certainty (e.g., knew, believed, suspected, heard, wondered).

SL.3.5: Create engaging audio recordings of stories or poems that demonstrate fluid reading at an understandable pace; add visual displays when appropriate to emphasize or enhance certain facts or details.

"UNWRAPPED" Priority Standards
(Note: Priority language standard bolded above was not "unwrapped" for inclusion here.)

RL.3.2: RECOUNT stories, including fables, folktales, and myths from diverse cultures; DETERMINE the central message, lesson, or moral and EXPLAIN HOW it is conveyed through key details in the text.

RL.3.9: COMPARE and CONTRAST the themes, settings, and plots of stories written by the same author about the same or similar characters (e.g., in books from a series).

W.3.1: WRITE opinion pieces on topics or texts, SUPPORTING a point of view with reasons.

W.3.3: WRITE narratives to DEVELOP real or imagined experiences or events USING effective technique, descriptive details, and clear event sequences.

"Unwrapped" Concepts (students need to know)	"Unwrapped" Skills (students need to be able to do)	Taxonomy Levels Bloom's / DOK	
		Bloom's	DOK
• Central Message, Lesson, Moral	RECOUNT (stories—fables, folktales, myths from diverse cultures)	1	1
	DETERMINE (central message, lesson, moral)	4	3
• Key Details	EXPLAIN HOW (central message, lesson, or moral is conveyed through key details)	2	2
• Themes • Settings • Plots • Characters	COMPARE AND CONTRAST (themes, settings, plots-same author or same/similar characters)	2	2, 4
Opinion Pieces—topics, texts • Point of View with Reasons	WRITE (opinion pieces)	6	2
	SUPPORT (point of view)	5	3
Narratives—real or imagined experiences or events • Techniques • Sequences • Details	WRITE (narratives)	6	2
	DEVELOP (real or imagined experiences or events)	6	2
	USE (techniques, sequences, and details)	3	3

Essential Questions	Corresponding Big Ideas
How can I determine the central message/lesson/moral of a text?	Key details convey central messages, lessons, or morals in fables, folktales, and myths.
What is an opinion? What makes an opinion strong?	A strong opinion is supported with reasons from multiple texts.
How is theme used to compare stories?	There are common themes, settings, plots, or characters across multiple texts.

Source: 3rd Grade RCD Curriculum Design Team, San Diego Unified School District, San Diego, CA

Rigorous Curriculum Design ELA Unit Planning Organizer
Grade 4: San Diego Unified School District

Subject(s)	English Language Arts—Reading: Informational
Grade/Course	4th Grade
Unit of Study	Unit 5: Compare and Contrast First and Secondhand Accounts
Pacing	25 days

Priority Common Core State Standards
Supporting Standards

RI.4.6: Compare and contrast a firsthand and secondhand account of the same event or topic; describe the differences in focus and the information provided.

RI.4.1: Refer to details and examples in a text when explaining what the text says explicitly and when drawing inferences from the text.

RI.4.3: Explain events, procedures, ideas, or concepts in a historical, scientific, or technical text, including what happened and why, based on specific information in the text.

RI.4.5: Describe the overall structure (e.g., chronology, comparison, cause/effect, problem/solution) of events, ideas, concepts, or information in a text or part of a text.

RI.4.8: Explain how an author uses reasons and evidence to support particular points in a text.

W.4.2: Write informative/explanatory texts to examine a topic and convey ideas and information clearly.

   a. Introduce a topic clearly and group related information in paragraphs and sections; include formatting (e.g., headings), illustrations, and multimedia when useful to aiding comprehension.

   b. Develop the topic with facts, definitions, concrete details, quotations, or other information and examples related to the topic.

   c. Link ideas within categories of information using words and phrases (e.g., *another, for example, also, because*).

   d. Use precise language and domain-specific vocabulary to inform about or explain the topic.

   e. Provide a concluding statement or section related to the information or explanation presented.

W.4.6: With some guidance and support from adults, use technology, including the Internet, to produce and publish writing as well as to interact and collaborate with others; demonstrate sufficient command of keyboarding skills to type a minimum of one page in a single sitting.

W.4.7: Conduct short research projects that build knowledge through investigation of different aspects of a topic.

W.4.8: Recall relevant information from experiences or gather relevant information from print and digital sources; take notes, paraphrase, and categorize information, and provide a list of sources.

W.4.9: Draw evidence from literary or informational texts to support analysis, reflection, and research.

L.4.2c: Use a comma before a coordinating conjunction in a compound sentence.

L.4.2a: Use correct capitalization.

L.4.2b: Use commas and quotation marks to mark direct speech and quotations from a text.

L.4.4c: Consult reference materials (e.g., dictionaries, glossaries, thesauruses), both print and digital, to find the pronunciation and determine or clarify the precise meaning of key words and phrases and to identify alternate word choices *in all content areas*.

"UNWRAPPED" Priority Standards
(Note: Priority language standard bolded above was not "unwrapped" for inclusion here.)
RI.4.6: **Compare and contrast** a firsthand and secondhand account of the same event or topic; **describe** the differences in focus and the information provided.
W.4.2: **Write** informative/explanatory texts to **examine** a topic and **convey** ideas and information clearly.

"Unwrapped" Concepts (students need to know)	"Unwrapped" Skills (students need to be able to do)	Taxonomy Levels	
		Bloom's / DOK	

Reading:
• Same event/topic
  • Firsthand (primary source)
  • Secondhand (secondary source)
• Differences
  • Focus
  • Information provided
	COMPARE/CONTRAST (first/second hand account same topic)	5	4

	DESCRIBE (differences in focus and info provided)	4	2
Writing: • Topic • Informative and/or explanatory • Ideas and information	WRITE (informative/explanatory) EXAMINE (a topic)	6 2	3 or 4 2
	CONVEY (ideas and info clearly)	3	3

Essential Questions	Corresponding Big Ideas
Why is it important to use multiple resources with differing points of view?	Reading about something from first- and second-hand accounts (primary/secondary sources) influences our understandings about an event or topic.
How do writers share information about a topic they have studied?	Good writers create informational text to convey what they have learned about a topic.

Source: 4th Grade RCD Curriculum Design Team, San Diego Unified School District, San Diego, CA

Rigorous Curriculum Design ELA Unit Planning Organizer
Grade 5: San Diego Unified School District

Subject(s)	Language Arts: Reading—Informational
Grade/Course	Grade 5
Unit of Study	Unit 5: Nonfiction: UNIT NAME: EXPLORING THE ROLE OF POINT-OF-VIEW IN ARGUMENT
Pacing	Total: 30 days (25 instructional, 5 buffer days)

Priority Common Core State Standards
Supporting Standards

Informational:

(Priority CCSS) RI.5.6:
   Analyze multiple accounts of the same event or topic, noting important similarities and differences in the point of view they represent.

(Supporting Standard) R.I.5.4:
   Determine the meaning of general academic and domain-specific words and phrases in a text relevant to a grade topic or subject area.

(Supporting Standard) RI.5.8:
   Explain how an author uses reasons and evidence to support particular points in a text, identifying which reasons and evidence support which point(s).

Writing (Opinion):

(Priority Standard) W.5.1:
   Write opinion pieces on topics or texts. Support a point of view with reasons and information.

(Priority Standard) W.5.1a:
   Introduce a topic or text clearly, state an opinion, and create an organizational structure in which ideas are logically grouped to support the writer's purpose.

(Priority Standard) W.5.1b:
   Provide logically ordered reasons that are supported by facts and details.

(Priority Standard) W.5.1d:
   Provide a concluding statement or section related to the opinion presented.

(Supporting Standard) W.5.8:
   Recall relevant information from experiences or gather from print and digital sources; summarize or paraphrase information in notes and finished work, and provide a list of sources.

"UNWRAPPED" Priority Standards

Informational:

RI.5.6: ANALYZE multiple accounts of the same event or topic, NOTE important similarities and differences in the point of view they represent.

Writing (Opinion):

W.5.1: WRITE opinion pieces on topics or texts. SUPPORT a point of view with reasons and information.

W.5.1a: INTRODUCE a topic or text clearly, STATE an opinion, and CREATE an organizational structure in which ideas are logically grouped to support the writer's purpose.

W.5.1b: PROVIDE logically ordered reasons that are supported by facts and details.

W.5.1d: PROVIDE a concluding statement or section related to the opinion presented.

"Unwrapped" Concepts (students need to know)	"Unwrapped" Skills (students need to be able to do)	Taxonomy Levels	
		Bloom's / DOK	

• SAME EVENTS/TOPIC
  *Multiple Accounts
• POINT OF VIEW
  *similarities
  *differences
	• ANALYZE (same events/multiple accounts)
	• NOTE (similarities/differences in pts of view)
		4
		
		2
			3
			
			2

• OPINION PIECE	• WRITE (opinion pieces)	6	4
• POINT OF VIEW	• SUPPORT (point of view with reasons and information)	5	3
	• INTRODUCE (topic or text)	2, 3	1
	• STATE (opinion)	2	2
• ORGANIZATIONAL STRUCTURE *with logical grouping of ideas	• CREATE (organizational structure with logical grouping of ideas to support writer's purpose)	6	4
• REASONS *supported by facts/details	• PROVIDE (logically ordered reasons supported by facts/details)	5	3
• CONCLUDING STATEMENT *related to opinion	• PROVIDE (concluding statement related to opinion)	5	3

Essential Questions	Corresponding Big Ideas
Why is it important to understand different points of view?	Analyzing points of view from multiple accounts of an event/topic helps form your own opinion.
How can you write a strong opinion piece that communicates your point of view?	When writing my opinion, it will be stronger with supported reasons and relevant information.
Why is an organizational structure necessary to a writer?	Writing requires an organizational structure so that the author's ideas are presented, supported, and concluded effectively.

Source: 5th Grade RCD Curriculum Design Team, San Diego Unified School District, San Diego, CA

McMinnville School District—Grade 3

UNIT 1	Determining the Main Idea
Unit Length	**September–November**
"Unwrapped" PRIORITY Standards	**RL.3.1:** ASK and ANSWER questions to DEMONSTRATE understanding of a text, REFERRING explicitly to the text as the basis for the answers. **RL.3.2:** RECOUNT stories, including fables, folktales, and myths from diverse cultures; DETERMINE the central message, lesson, or moral and EXPLAIN how it is conveyed through key details in the text. **RI.3.2:** DETERMINE the main idea of a text; RECOUNT the key details and EXPLAIN how they support the main idea.

	Concepts	Skills	Bloom's
"Unwrapped" PRIORITY Standards Graphic Organizer	Main Idea	DETERMINE	4
	Key details	RECOUNT	1/2
	Support the main idea	EXPLAIN	2
	Questions	ASK AND ANSWER	4
	Understanding the text	DEMONSTRATE	2
	Text	REFER	5
	Stories, fables, folktales, myths from diverse cultures	RECOUNT	1/2
	Central message/lesson/moral	DETERMINE	4
	Key details	EXPLAIN	2

Supporting Standards	RL.3.7: Explain how specific aspects of a text's illustrations contribute to what is conveyed by the words in a story (e.g., create mood, emphasize aspects of a character or setting). RL.3.10: By the end of the year, read and comprehend literature, including stories, dramas, and poetry, at the high end of the grades 2–3 text complexity band independently and proficiently.
Essential Questions	1. What is the main idea? 2. How do you know if the main idea is really the main idea? 3. What are key details? Why are they important?
Big Ideas	1. The main idea is what the text is mainly about. 2. Main ideas are supported by key details. 3. Key details support the main idea.

Source: Grade 3 RCD Team, McMinnville School District, McMinnville, Oregon

McMinnville School District—Grade 4

UNIT 4	Effective Communication and Oregon Economics
Unit Length	4 Weeks
"Unwrapped" PRIORITY Standards	**W.4.5:** With guidance and support from peers and adults, DEVELOP and STRENGTHEN writing as needed by PLANNING, REVISING, and EDITING. (Editing for conventions should demonstrate command of Language standards 1–3 up to and including grade 4.) **L.4.1:** DEMONSTRATE command of the conventions of standard English grammar and usage when writing or speaking. **L.4.1a:** USE relative pronouns (*who, whose, whom, which, that*) and relative adverbs (*where, when, why*). **L.4.1f:** PRODUCE complete sentences, RECOGNIZING and CORRECTING inappropriate fragments and run-ons. **L.4.1g:** Correctly USE frequently confused words (e.g., *to, too, two; there, their*). **L.4.2:** DEMONSTRATE command of the conventions of standard English capitalization, punctuation, and spelling when WRITING. **L.4.2b:** USE commas and quotation marks to mark direct speech and quotations from a text. **L.4.2c:** USE a comma before a coordinating conjunction in a compound sentence.

	Concepts	Skills	Bloom's
"Unwrapped" PRIORITY Standards Graphic Organizer	Writing	Develop	3 (apply)
	Writing	Strengthen	4 (analysis)
	Writing	Plan	3 (apply)
	Writing	Revise	4 (analysis)
	Writing	Edit	3 (apply)
	Command of conventions of standard English grammar and usage	Demonstrate	3 (apply)
	Relative pronouns and adverbs	Use	3 (apply)
	Complete sentences	Produce	6 (create)
	Fragments/run-ons	Recognize/correct	2 (understand)
	Frequently confused words (e.g. to, too, two, there, their)	Use	3 (apply)
	Command of conventions, capitalization, punctuation, spelling	Demonstrate/ Write	6 (create)
	Commas, quotation marks to mark direct speech and quotations from text	Use	3 (apply)
	Commas in compound sentences	Use	3 (apply)

UNIT 4	**Effective Communication and Oregon Economics** *(continued)*
Supporting Standards	W.4.2a: Introduce a topic clearly and group related information in paragraphs and sections; include formatting (e.g., headings), illustrations, and multimedia when useful to aiding comprehension. W.4.2b: Develop the topic with facts, definitions, concrete details, quotations, or other information and examples related to the topic. W.4.2c: Link ideas within categories of information using words and phrases (e.g., *another, for example, also, because*). W.4.2d: Use precise language and domain-specific vocabulary to inform about or explain the topic. W.4.2e: Provide a concluding statement or section related to the information or explanation presented. L.4.1b: Form and use the progressive (e.g., *I was walking; I am walking; I will be walking*) verb tenses. L.4.1c: Use modal auxiliaries (e.g., *can, may, must*) to convey various conditions. L.4.1d: Order adjectives within sentences according to conventional patterns (e.g., *a small red bag* rather than *a red small bag*). L.4.1e: Form and use prepositional phrases. L.4.2d: Spell grade-appropriate words correctly, consulting references as needed.
Oregon Sciencce and Social Studies Standards	4.11: Identify conflicts involving use of land, natural resources, economy, and competition for scarce resources, different political views, boundary disputes, and cultural differences within Oregon and between different geographical areas. 4.12: Explain how people in Oregon have modified their environment and how the environment has influenced people's lives. 4.14: Explain the organization and functions of Oregon government. 4.18: Identify key industries of Oregon.
Essential Questions	• **How do you develop your writing?** • **How do you strengthen your writing?** • How do you organize an informative piece of writing? • How do you develop your ideas in an informative text?
Big Ideas	• **You develop your writing by planning and drafting.** • **You strengthen your writing by revising for content and editing for conventions.** • Informative writing has a clear introduction, with information organized into paragraphs or sections. Formatting such as headings, illustrations, and multimedia may also aid in the reader's comprehension. Make sure your conclusion is related to the information you presented. • You can develop your topic using facts, definitions, concrete details, quotations, or other information and examples related to the topic. You need to use precise language and vocabulary including words or phrases that link your ideas together.

Source: Grade 4 RCD Team, McMinnville School District, McMinnville, Oregon

McMinnville School District—Grade 5

UNIT 1	Character and Setting
Unit Length: 5 weeks	In this unit teachers will be using a fictional text of their choice to engage students in comparing and contrasting characters and settings.
"Unwrapped" PRIORITY Standards	**RL.5.3: COMPARE and CONTRAST two or more characters, settings, or events in a story or drama, DRAWING ON specific details in the text (e.g., how characters interact).**

"Unwrapped" PRIORITY Standards Graphic Organizer	Concepts	Skills	Bloom's
	Characters	Compare and contrast	Analyze(4)
	Settings	Compare and contrast	Analyze(4)
	Events	Compare and contrast	Analyze(4)
	Details	Draw on (Use)	Apply (3)

Supporting Standards	RL.5.1: Quote accurately from a text when explaining what the text says explicitly and when drawing inferences from the text.
	RL.5.4: Determine the meaning of words and phrases as they are used in a text, including figurative language such as metaphors and similes.
	RL.5.6: Describe how a narrator's or speaker's point of view influences how events are described.
	SL.5.1: Engage effectively in a range of collaborative discussions (one-on-one, in groups, and teacher-led) with diverse partners on grade 5 topics and texts, building on others' ideas and expressing their own clearly.
Essential Question	How do details help the reader compare and contrast characters and setting in a story?
Big Idea	Details in a story can be used to analyze characters and setting.

Source: Grade 5 RCD Team, McMinnville School District, McMinnville, Oregon

West Hartford Public Schools English/Language Arts: Grade 3

Unit 1: Characters in Action

Pacing Guide: This unit is designed to be implemented over the course of 23 days with 2 buffer days.

UNIT OVERVIEW

In this introductory unit, Characters in Action, third graders will review elements of story and describe characters based on their traits, feelings and motivations by examining what they think, say, and do. Students will then analyze how characters' actions can impact the story events. Students will look at examples of narrative writing and talk about tasks and purposes that lend themselves to the narrative genre. Students will build short narrative pieces by establishing a situation, introducing the narrator and/or characters, organizing a sequence of events, and providing a sense of closure. StoryTown selections will be used to teach the Priority Standards and comprehension skills. Students will also learn the rules for collaborative conversations and practice speaking and listening in both whole and small groups. Additionally, StoryTown will be utilized as the core resource as referenced in the skills section for reading foundational skills and language standards. A series of assured learning experiences are included that ask students to apply and practice their new skills in a structured format.

This unit planner should inform the majority of your direct instruction and influence small-group activities. However, it is not intended to cover the entire scope of daily literacy in your classroom. Small-group reading instruction, including guided reading, should continue to occur regularly as in past years. Additionally, students should read and write independently on a regular basis.

STANDARDS

RL.3.3: Describe characters in a story (e.g., their traits, motivations, or feelings) and explain how their actions contribute to the sequence of events.

RL.3.1: Ask and answer questions to demonstrate understanding of a text, referring explicitly to the text as the basis for the answers.

RL.3.5: Refer to parts of **stories**, dramas, and poems when writing or speaking about a text, using terms such as **chapter**, scene, and stanza; describe how each successive part builds on earlier sections.

RL.3.7: Explain how specific aspects of a text's illustrations contribute to what is conveyed by the words in a story (e.g., create mood, emphasize aspects of a character or setting).

RF.3.3: Know and apply grade-level phonics and word analysis skills in decoding words.

    c. Decode multi-syllable words.

W.3.3: Write narratives to develop real or imagined experiences or events using effective technique, descriptive details, and clear event sequences.

    a. Establish a situation and introduce a narrator and/or characters; organize an event sequence that unfolds naturally.

    b. Use dialogue and descriptions of actions, thoughts, and feelings to develop experiences and events or show the response of characters to situations.

    c. Use temporal words and phrases to signal event order.

    d. Provide a sense of closure.

W.3.4: With guidance and support from adults, produce writing in which the development and organization are appropriate to task and purpose.

    L.3.1: Demonstrate command of the conventions of standard English grammar and usage when writing or speaking.

        a. Explain the function of nouns, pronouns, verbs, adjectives, and adverbs in general and their functions in particular sentences.

        i. Produce simple, compound, and complex sentences.

STANDARDS *(continued)*

L.3.2: *Demonstrate command of the conventions of Standard English capitalization, punctuation, and spelling when writing.*

   e. *Use conventional spelling for high-frequency and other studied words and for adding suffixes to base words (e.g., sitting, smiled, cries, happiness).*

   f. *Use spelling patterns and generalizations (e.g., word families, position-based spellings, syllable patterns, ending rules, meaningful word parts) in writing words.*

   g. *Consult reference materials, including beginning dictionaries, as needed to check and correct spellings.*

L.3.5: *Demonstrate understanding of word relationships and nuances in word meanings.*

   c. *Distinguish shades of meaning among related words that describe states of mind or degrees of certainty (e.g., knew, believed, suspected, heard, wondered).*

SL.3.1: Engage effectively in a range of collaborative discussions (one-on-one, in groups, and teacher-led) with diverse partners on grade 3 topics and texts, building on others' ideas and expressing their own clearly.

   b. Follow agreed-upon rules for discussions (e.g., gaining the floor in respectful ways, listening to others with care, speaking one at a time about the topics and texts under discussion).

SL.3.6: Speak in complete sentences when appropriate to task and situation in order to provide requested detail or clarification.

Priority
Supporting
Skills

"UNWRAPPED" STANDARDS

Standard	"Unwrapped" Concepts (students need to know)	"Unwrapped" Skills (students need to be able to do)	Bloom's/ Webb's DOK
RL.3.3	**Characters in a story (e.g., their traits, motivations, or feelings)**	**DESCRIBE (characters in a story) and EXPLAIN (how their actions contribute to the sequence of events)**	2/2 Understand/ Skills
RL.3.1	Questions to demonstrate understanding of a text	ASK & ANSWER (questions to demonstrate understanding of a text) REFERRING EXPLICITLY (to text)	2/2 Understand/ Skills
RL.3.5	Parts of **stories**	REFER TO (parts of **stories** such as **chapter**) & DESCRIBE (how each successive part builds on earlier sections)	2/2 Understand/ Skills
RL.3.7	Text's illustrations	EXPLAIN HOW (text's illustrations contribute to what is conveyed by the words in a story [e.g., create mood, emphasize aspects of a character or setting])	2/2 Understand/ Skills

"UNWRAPPED" STANDARDS (continued)			
Standard	"Unwrapped" Concepts (students need to know)	"Unwrapped" Skills (students need to be able to do)	Bloom's/ Webb's DOK
W.3.3	Narratives to develop real or imagined experiences or events	WRITE (narratives to develop real or imagined experiences or events) • ESTABLISH (situation) • INTRODUCE (narrator and/or characters) • ORGANIZE (an event sequence that unfolds naturally) • USE (dialogue and descriptions of actions, thoughts, and feelings) to DEVELOP (experiences and events) or SHOW (response of characters to situations) • USE (temporal words and phrases to signal event order) • PROVIDE (sense of closure)	2/3 Understand/ Strategic Thinking
W.3.4	Writing appropriate to task and purpose	PRODUCE (writing appropriate to task and purpose)	4/1 Analyze/Recall
SL.3.1b	Agreed-upon rules for discussions	ENGAGE EFFECTIVELY (in range of collaborative discussions with diverse partners) • FOLLOW (agreed-upon rules for discussions [e.g., gaining the floor in respectful ways, listening to others with care, speaking one at a time about the topics and texts under discussion])	3/3 Apply/Strategic Thinking
SL.3.6	Complete sentences	SPEAK (in complete sentences when appropriate to task and situation) IN ORDER TO PROVIDE (requested detail or clarification)	3/2 Apply/Skills

ESSENTIAL QUESTIONS	BIG IDEAS
How do I describe characters in a story and explain how their actions contribute to the sequence of events?	I can describe characters by analyzing what they think, say, and do to identify their traits, motivations, and feelings and how their actions contribute to the sequence of events.
How do I write a narrative story?	I write a narrative story by introducing the narrator and/or characters and situation, developing the story using an organized sequence of events, and providing a sense of closure.
How do I effectively engage in collaborative discussions?	I effectively engage in collaborative discussions by following the agreed-upon rules.

Source: Grade 3 RCD Curriculum Design Team, West Hartford Public Schools, West Hartford, CT

West Hartford Public Schools English/Language Arts: Grade 4

Unit 6: Mythology

Pacing Guide: This unit is designed to be implemented over the course of 20 days with 2 buffer days.

UNIT OVERVIEW

This unit culminates the study of literature by having students explore traditional literature (folktales) from different cultures as well as myths. Students will reflect on the themes presented as well as the patterns of events (competition, quest, transformation) and compare these aspects across texts. Attention will be paid to figurative language (adages and proverbs), references to characters in mythology, and unknown words. Students will practice strategies for figuring out these language concepts. Students will review the purpose, audience, and tasks associated with the three main genres of writing: narrative, expository/informational, and opinion, and will have opportunities to practice each genre over the course of the unit in RAFT assignments. The culminating project for this unit will allow students to self-select a folktale or myth and reflect on this text in comparison to others they have read. A final product will be created to match the task, purpose, and audience determined and students will present to their peers.

Adage: a traditional saying that is accepted by many as true or partially true

Proverb: a well-known saying that gives good advice or expresses a supposed truth

RAFT is an acronym for Role, Audience, Format, and Topic. In a RAFT, students take on a particular role, develop a product for a specified audience in a particular format and on a topic that gets right at the heart of what matters most in a particular segment of study. At some points, a teacher may want to assign students particular RAFTs and at other points may want the students to make the choice. RAFT assignments are typically of fairly short duration and can be completed at school or at home (Tomlinson, 2003).

STANDARDS

STANDARDS

RL.4.9: Compare and contrast the treatment of similar themes and topics (e.g., opposition of good and evil) and patterns of events (e.g., the quest) in stories, myths, and traditional literature from different cultures.

RL.4.4: Determine the meaning of words and phrases as they are used in a text, including those that allude to significant characters found in mythology (e.g., Herculean).

RL.4.6: Compare and contrast the point of view from which different stories are narrated, including the difference between first- and third-person narrations.

RL.4.7: Make connections between the text of a story or drama and a visual or oral presentation of the text, identifying where each version reflects specific descriptions and directions in the text.

RF.4.3: Know and apply grade-level phonics and word analysis skills in decoding words.

    a. Use combined knowledge of all letter-sound correspondences, syllabication patterns, and morphology (e.g., roots and affixes) to read accurately unfamiliar multisyllabic words in context and out of context.

RF.4.4: Read with sufficient accuracy and fluency to support comprehension.

    b. Read grade-level prose and poetry orally with accuracy, appropriate rate, and expression.

W.4.4: Produce clear and coherent writing in which the development and organization are appropriate to task, purpose, and audience.

W.4.5: With guidance and support from peers and adults, develop and strengthen writing as needed by planning, revising, and editing.

W.4.6: With some guidance and support from adults, use technology, including the Internet, to produce and publish writing as well as to interact and collaborate with others; demonstrate sufficient command of keyboarding skills to type a minimum of one page in a single sitting.

STANDARDS (continued)

W.4.9: Draw evidence from literary or informational texts to support analysis, reflection, and research.
   a. Apply grade 4 Reading standards to literature (e.g., "Describe in depth a character, setting, or event in a story or drama, drawing on specific details in the text [e.g., a character's thoughts, words, or actions].").

L.4.2: Demonstrate command of the conventions of standard English capitalization, punctuation, and spelling when writing.
   d. Spell grade-appropriate words.

L.4.4: Determine or clarify the meaning of unknown and multiple-meaning words and phrases based on grade 4 reading and content, choosing flexibly from a range of strategies.
   b. Use common, grade-appropriate Greek and Latin affixes and roots as clues to the meaning of a word (e.g., telegraph, photograph, autograph).

L.4.5: Demonstrate understanding of figurative language, word relationships, and nuances in word meanings.
   b. Recognize and explain the meaning of common idioms, adages, and proverbs.

SL.4.4: Report on a topic or text, tell a story, or recount an experience in an organized manner, using appropriate facts and relevant, descriptive details to support main ideas or themes; speak clearly at an understandable pace.

SL.4.6: Differentiate between contexts that call for formal English (e.g., presenting ideas) and situations where informal discourse is appropriate (e.g., small-group discussion); use formal English when appropriate to task and situation.

L.4.3: Use knowledge of language and its conventions when writing, speaking, reading, or listening.
   b. Choose punctuation for effect.

Priority
Supporting
Skills

"UNWRAPPED" STANDARDS

Standard	"Unwrapped" Concepts (students need to know)	"Unwrapped" Skills (students need to be able to do)	Bloom's/ Webb's DOK
RL.4.9	**Similar themes and topics and patterns of events**	**COMPARE & CONTRAST (treatment of similar theme and topics [e.g., opposition of good and evil] & patterns of events [e.g., the quest] in stories, myths, and traditional literature from different cultures)**	**4/4 Analyze/ Extended Thinking**
RL.4.4	Meaning of words and phrases as they are used in a text	DETERMINE (meaning of words and phrases as they are used in a text, including those that allude to significant characters found in mythology [e.g., Herculean])	3/2 Apply/Skills & Concepts
RL.4.6	Point of view from which different stories are narrated	COMPARE AND CONTRAST (point of view from which different stories are narrated, including first and third person)	2/3 Understand/ Strategic Thinking
RL.4.7	Connections between the text of a story or drama and visual or oral presentations of the text	MAKE (connections between the text of a story or drama and a visual or oral presentation of the text) and IDENTIFY (where versions reflect specific descriptions and directions in the text)	2/2 Understand/Skills & Concepts

	"UNWRAPPED" STANDARDS *(continued)*		
Standard	**"Unwrapped" Concepts (students need to know)**	**"Unwrapped" Skills (students need to be able to do)**	**Bloom's/ Webb's DOK**
W.4.4		PRODUCE (clear and coherent writing, appropriate to task, purpose, and audience)	
W.4.5		DEVELOP and STRENGTHEN (writing by planning, revising, and editing with support from peers and adults)	3/1 Apply/ Recall & Reproduction
W.4.6		USE (technology including the Internet) to PRODUCE AND PUBLISH (writing) with some adult guidance • INTERACT & COLLABORATE (with others) • TYPE (minimum of one page in a sitting)	3/3 Apply/ Strategic Thinking
W.4.9a	Evidence	DRAW (evidence from literary or informational texts) to SUPPORT analysis, reflection, and research	2/2 Understand/ Skills & Concepts
SL.4.4	**Appropriate facts & relevant, descriptive details to support main idea from topic or text**	**REPORT ON (topic or text) USING (appropriate facts & relevant, descriptive details to support main ideas or themes)** • **SPEAK clearly at an understandable pace.**	**2/2 Understand/ Skills & Concepts**
SL.4.6	Formal English	DIFFERENTIATE (between contexts that call for formal English and situations where informal discourse is appropriate) & USE (formal English when appropriate to task and situation)	3/2 Apply/ Skills & Concepts

ESSENTIAL QUESTIONS	BIG IDEAS
How do I compare and contrast stories, myths, and traditional literature from different cultures?	In order to compare and contrast literature I look at the treatment of the theme and the pattern of events to find similarities and differences.
How do I talk and write about what I have learned so that others understand?	When I talk or write about what I have learned, I need to organize the information so that it matches the task and purpose and can be clearly understood by the audience.
How do I understand figurative language and unknown words or phrases in a text or in a conversation?	I can use strategies such as thinking about the context, looking at parts of the words, and what I know about words to help me understand figurative language and unknown words and phrases.

Source: Grade 4 RCD Curriculum Design Team, West Hartford Public Schools, West Hartford, CT

West Hartford Public Schools English/Language Arts: Grade 5

Unit 1: What's It All About?

Pacing Guide: This unit is designed to be implemented over the course of 23 days with 2 buffer days.

UNIT OVERVIEW

This unit starts off the year with a study of informational texts and allows for science connections with the study of the Moon. Students will revisit how to navigate informational text and summarize the information. Students will also practice identifying main ideas and supporting key details within a text and analyzing authors' craft to see how authors support their points with reasons and evidence. StoryTown selections will be used to teach the Priority Standards and comprehension skills. The study of nonfiction will carry over to writing where students will review the basics of writing in the informative/explanatory genre. In all literacy activities the teacher and students will work on establishing and following rules for collaborative discussions and discuss what roles they can play in a variety of settings and structures. Additionally, StoryTown will be utilized as the core resource as referenced in the skills section for reading foundational skills and language standards. A series of assured learning experiences are included that ask students to apply and practice their new skills in a structured format.

This unit planner should inform the majority of your direct instruction and influence small-group activities. However, it is not intended to cover the entire scope of daily literacy in your classroom. Small-group reading instruction, including guided reading, should continue to occur regularly as in past years. Additionally, students should read and write independently on a regular basis.

STANDARDS
RI.5.2: Determine two or more main ideas of a text and explain how they are supported by key details; summarize the text.
RI.5.8: Explain how an author uses reasons and evidence to support particular points in a text, identifying which reasons and evidence support which point(s).
RI.5.1: Quote accurately from a text when explaining what the text says explicitly and when drawing inferences from the text.
RI.5.4: Determine the meaning of general academic and domain-specific words and phrases in a text relevant to a grade 5 topic or subject area.
RI.5.7: Draw on information from multiple print or digital sources, demonstrating the ability to locate an answer to a question quickly or to solve a problem efficiently.
W.5.9: Draw evidence from literary or informational texts to support analysis, reflection, and research.
b. Apply grade 5 Reading standards to informational texts (e.g., "Explain how an author uses reasons and evidence to support particular points in a text, identifying which reasons and evidence support which point[s]").
RF.5.3: Know and apply grade-level phonics and word analysis skills in decoding words.
a. Use combined knowledge of all letter-sound correspondences, syllabication patterns, and morphology (e.g., roots and affixes) to read accurately unfamiliar multisyllabic words in context and out of context.
W.5.2: Write informative/explanatory texts to examine a topic and convey ideas and information clearly.
a. Introduce a topic clearly, provide a general observation and focus, and group related information logically; include formatting (e.g., headings), illustrations, and multimedia when useful to aiding comprehension.
b. Develop the topic with facts, definitions, concrete details, quotations, or other information and examples related to the topic.
c. Link ideas within and across categories of information using words, phrases, and clauses (e.g., in contrast, especially).
d. Use precise language and domain-specific vocabulary to inform about or explain the topic.
e. Provide a concluding statement or section related to the information or explanation presented.

STANDARDS (continued)

W.5.4: Produce clear and coherent writing in which the development and organization are appropriate to task, purpose, and audience.

L.5.1: Demonstrate command of the conventions of standard English grammar and usage when writing or speaking.
a. Explain the function of conjunctions, prepositions, and interjections in general and their function in particular sentences.

L.5.2: Demonstrate command of the conventions of standard English capitalization, punctuation, and spelling when writing.
c. Use a comma to set off the words yes and no (e.g., Yes, thank you), to set off a tag question from the rest of the sentence (e.g., It's true, isn't it?), and to indicate direct address (e.g., Is that you, Steve?).
e. Spell grade-appropriate words correctly, consulting references as needed.

L.5.4: Determine or clarify the meaning of unknown and multiple-meaning words and phrases based on grade 5 reading and content, choosing flexibly from a range of strategies.
c. Consult reference materials (e.g., dictionaries, glossaries, thesauruses), both print and digital, to find the pronunciation and determine or clarify the precise meaning of key words and phrases.

L.5.5: Demonstrate understanding of figurative language, word relationships, and nuances in word meanings.
a. Interpret figurative language, including similes and metaphors, in context.
b. Recognize and explain the meaning of common idioms, adages, and proverbs.
c. Use the relationship between particular words (e.g., synonyms, antonyms, homographs) to better understand each of the words.

SL.5.1: Engage effectively in a range of collaborative discussions (one-on-one, in groups, and teacher-led) with diverse partners on grade 5 topics and texts, building on others' ideas and expressing their own clearly.
b. Follow agreed-upon rules for discussions and carry out assigned roles.

SL.5.3: Summarize the points a speaker makes and explain how each claim is supported by reasons and evidence.

Priority
Supporting
Skills

"UNWRAPPED" STANDARDS			
Standard	"Unwrapped" Concepts (students need to know)	"Unwrapped" Skills (students need to be able to do)	Bloom's/ Webb's DOK
RI.5.2	Two or more main ideas of a text	DETERMINE (two or more main ideas of a text) & EXPLAIN (how they are supported by key details) SUMMARIZE (text)	2/2 Understand/ Skills & Concepts
RI.5.8	Reasons and evidence to support particular points in a text	EXPLAIN (how author uses reasons and evidence to support particular points in a text) IDENTIFYING (which reasons and evidence support which point[s])	2/3 Understand/ Strategic Thinking
RI.5.1	What the text says explicitly and when drawing inferences	QUOTE ACCURATELY (from a text when explaining what the text says explicitly and when drawing inferences from the text)	2/3 Understand/ Strategic Thinking
RI.5.4	Meaning of general academic and domain-specific words and phrases	DETERMINE (meaning of general academic and domain-specific words and phrases in a text relevant to a grade 5 topic or subject area)	3/2 Apply/ Skills & Concepts
RI.5.7	Information from multiple print or digital sources	DRAW ON (information from multiple print or digital sources) LOCATE (answer to a question quickly or to solve a problem efficiently)	3/2 Apply/ Skills & Concepts

	"UNWRAPPED" STANDARDS *(continued)*		
Standard	**"Unwrapped" Concepts (students need to know)**	**"Unwrapped" Skills (students need to be able to do)**	**Bloom's/ Webb's DOK**
W.5.2	Informative/explanatory texts	WRITE (informative/explanatory texts to examine a topic and convey ideas and information) • **INTRODUCE (topic clearly) by PROVIDING (general observation and focus)** • **GROUP (related information logically**; include formatting (e.g., headings), illustrations, and multimedia when useful to aiding comprehension) • **DEVELOP (topic with facts, definitions, concrete details, quotations, or other information and examples related to the topic)** • LINK (ideas within and across categories of information) USING (words, phrases, and clauses [e.g., in contrast, especially]) • USE (precise language and domain-specific vocabulary to inform about or explain the topic) • **PROVIDE (concluding statement or section related to the information or explanation presented)**	3/3 Apply/ Strategic Thinking
W.5.4	Clear and coherent writing appropriate to task, purpose, and audience.	PRODUCE (clear and coherent writing in which the development and organization are appropriate to task, purpose, and audience)	2/3 Understand/ Strategic Thinking
W.5.9b	Evidence from literary or informational texts	DRAW (evidence from informational texts) to SUPPORT (analysis, reflection, and research)	2/3 Understand/ Strategic Thinking
SL.5.1	**Collaborative discussions (one-on-one, in groups, and teacher-led) with diverse partners on grade 5 topics and texts**	**ENGAGE EFFECTIVELY (in collaborative discussions [one-on-one, in groups, and teacher-led] with diverse partners on grade 5 topics and texts) BUILDING ON (others' ideas) & EXPRESSING (their own clearly)** • **FOLLOW (agreed-upon rules for discussions) & CARRY OUT (assigned roles)**	3/2 Apply/Skills & Concepts
SL.5.3	Points a speaker makes	SUMMARIZE (points a speaker makes) & EXPLAIN (how each claim is supported by reasons and evidence)	2/3 Understand/ Strategic Thinking

ESSENTIAL QUESTIONS	BIG IDEAS
How do I identify the main ideas within an informational text and describe how the author supports each main idea with key details?	I need to determine what the key details are and look for relationships within the information the author provides in order to identify the main ideas in an informational text.
How do I summarize informational text?	I summarize informational text by restating the main ideas and supporting details in my own words and describe why the author thought it was important to share this information.
How do I use what I know about informational texts to write my own informative/explanatory piece?	I introduce a topic clearly, organize and group my supporting information to develop the topic with facts, definitions, concrete details, quotations, or other information and examples, and provide a concluding statement related to the information presented.
How do I engage effectively in collaborative discussions?	In order to engage effectively in collaborative discussions so that I can build on others' ideas and express my own ideas clearly, I follow agreed-upon rules and carry out the role that is assigned to me.

Source: Grade 5 RCD Curriculum Design Team, West Hartford Public Schools, West Hartford, CT

Metacomet Elementary School, Bloomfield, CT
Grade 3 Writing Units 2013/2014

Subject(s)	Writing
Grade/Course	3
Unit of Study	Unit 1: Memoir (Correlates with Unit 1 Writing—Personal Narrative: Character and Author's Message)
Pacing	29 days (25 days instruction; 4 days reteaching/enrichment)

Overarching Standards (OS)—
STANDARDS THAT ARE EMPHASIZED THROUGHOUT THE YEAR IN EVERY UNIT OF STUDY

Writing

W.3.4: With guidance and support from adults, produce writing in which the development and organization are appropriate to task and purpose.

W.3.5: With guidance and support from peers and adults, develop and strengthen writing as needed by planning, revising, and editing.

W.3.6: With guidance and support from adults, use technology to produce and publish writing (using keyboarding skills) as well as to interact and collaborate with others.

W.3.10: Write routinely over extended time frames (time for research, reflection, and revision) and shorter time frames (a single sitting or a day or two) for a range of discipline-specific tasks, purposes, and audiences.

Language

L.3.1: Demonstrate command of the conventions of standard English grammar and usage when writing or speaking.

PRIORITY CCSS

Writing

W.3.3: Write narratives to develop real or imagined experiences or events using effective technique, descriptive details, and clear event sequences.

W.3.3a: Establish a situation and introduce a narrator and/or characters; organize an event sequence that unfolds naturally.

W.3.3c: Use temporal words and phrases to signal event order.

W.3.3d: Provide a sense of closure.

Language

L.3.1a: Explain the function of nouns, pronouns, verbs, adjectives, and adverbs in general and their functions in particular sentences.

L.3.1e: Form and use the simple (e.g., I walked; I walk; I will walk) verb tenses.

L.3.1f: Ensure subject-verb and antecedent agreement.

L.3.1i: Produce simple, compound, and complex sentences.

L.3.2d: Form and use possessives.

L.3.2f: Use spelling patterns and generalizations (e.g., word families, position-based spellings, syllable patterns, ending rules, meaningful word parts) in writing words.

Concepts (What students need to know)	Skills (What students need to be able to do)	DOK Levels
Memoir • Personal memories • Establishing a situation • Narrator • Characters • Event sequence that unfolds naturally	ESTABLISH (a situation in writing with personal memories)	4
	INTRODUCE (a narrator and/or characters in writing)	4
	ORGANIZE (write an event sequence that unfolds naturally)	2
Language Standards • Parts of Speech • Function of nouns, pronouns, verbs, adjectives, and adverbs • Parts of speech in sentences	IDENTIFY (the function of nouns, pronouns, verbs, adjectives, and adverbs)	1
	EXPLAIN (the function of nouns, pronouns, verbs, adjectives, and adverbs in particular sentences)	1
Examining & Producing Sentences • Subject-verb and antecedent agreement • Simple, compound, and complex sentences • Spelling patterns and generalizations (e.g., word families, position-based spellings, syllable patterns, ending rules, meaningful word parts)	ENSURE (subject-verb and antecedent agreement)	1
	PRODUCE (simple, compound, and complex sentences)	1
	APPLY (spelling patterns and generalizations [e.g., word families, position-based spellings, syllable patterns, ending rules, meaningful word parts] in writing.)	2

Essential Questions	Corresponding Big Ideas
1. How do writers tell their personal story?	1. Writers develop memoirs by choosing a time in their lives, and creating a narrator, characters, and events to tell their personal story.
2. How do writers know when to use words?	2. Writers identify the parts of speech to help them understand when to use words.
3. How do writers edit their sentences to be sure that they are clear?	3. Writers edit their sentences for subject-verb agreement and spelling to be sure they can be understood by others.

Source: Grade 3 Curriculum Design Team, Metacomet Elementary School, Bloomfield, CT

Metacomet Elementary School, Bloomfield, CT
Grade 4 Reading Units 2013/2014

Subject(s)	Reading/Language Arts
Grade/Course	4
Unit of Study	Unit 1: How Themes Communicate Different Messages (Correlates with Unit 1 Writing—Personal Narrative: Character and Author's Message)
Pacing	29 days (25 days instruction; 4 days reteaching/enrichment)

Overarching Standards (OS)—
STANDARDS THAT ARE EMPHASIZED THROUGHOUT THE YEAR IN EVERY UNIT OF STUDY

Reading

RL.4.10: By the end of the year, read and comprehend literature, including stories, dramas, and poetry, in the grades 4–5 text complexity band proficiently, with scaffolding as needed at the high end of the range.

RI.4.10: By the end of year, read and comprehend informational texts, including history/social studies, science, and technical texts, in the grades 4–5 text complexity band proficiently, with scaffolding as needed at the high end of the range.

Speaking and Listening

SL.4.1: Engage effectively in a range of collaborative discussions (one-on-one, in groups, and teacher-led) with diverse partners on *grade 4 topics and texts,* building on others' ideas and expressing their own clearly.

Foundational Skills

RF.4.3: Know and apply grade-level phonics and word analysis skills in decoding words.

RF.4.4: Read with sufficient accuracy and fluency to support comprehension.

PRIORITY CCSS
(Note: Concepts and Skills Were Not Underlined and Capitalized; See Graphic Organizer for Targeted Concepts and Skills)

Reading

RL.4.1: Refer to details and examples in a text when explaining what the text says explicitly and when drawing inferences from the text.

RL.4.2: Determine a theme of a story, drama, or poem from details in the text; summarize the text.

RL.4.9: Compare and contrast the treatment of similar themes and topics (e.g., opposition of good and evil) and patterns of events (e.g., the quest) in stories, myths, and traditional literature from different cultures.

Speaking and Listening

SL.4.1a: Come to discussions prepared, having read or studied required material; explicitly draw on that preparation and other information known about the topic to explore ideas under discussion.

SL.4.1b: Follow agreed-upon rules for discussions and carry out assigned roles.

Foundational Skills

RF.4.3a: Use combined knowledge of all letter-sound correspondences, syllabication patterns, and morphology (e.g., roots and affixes) to read accurately unfamiliar multisyllabic words in context and out of context.

RF.4.4c: Use context to confirm or self-correct word recognition and understanding, rereading as necessary.

PRIORITY CCSS (*continued*)

(Note: Concepts and Skills Were Not Underlined and Capitalized; See Graphic Organizer for Targeted Concepts and Skills)

Writing

W.4.9a: Apply *grade 4 Reading standards* to literature (e.g., "Describe in depth a character, setting, or event in a story or drama, drawing on specific details in the text [e.g., a character's thoughts, words, or actions].").

Concepts (What students need to know)	Skills (What students need to be able to do)	DOK Levels
Summary • theme of story, drama, poem • details	DETERMINE (theme and relevant details from text) SUMMARIZE (text)	3 1, 2
Comparing/Contrasting Literature • treatment of similar themes and topics • patterns of events • stories, myths, and traditional literature from different cultures.	COMPARE/CONTRAST (themes, topics, patterns of events)	3
Book Discussions • preparation • information about the topic (background knowledge and studied materials)	EXPLORE (text) DISCUSS (ideas about text) EVALUATE (text)	2 3 4
Read • multisyllabic words	READ	1
Context • word recognition • understanding	USE (context)	2

Essential Questions	Corresponding Big Ideas
1. *How do I figure out the meaning of a text?*	1. Details guide me to understand the meaning of a text.
2. *What tools can readers use to notice similarities and differences?*	2. Story elements help me identify similarities and differences in literature.
3. *How do I prepare for group discussion?*	3. Readers use background knowledge and information learned to participate in group discussions.
4. *What do readers do when reading difficult words?*	4. Readers use a variety of strategies to help them decode and understand meanings of difficult words.

Source: Grade 4 Curriculum Design Team, Metacomet Elementary School, Bloomfield, CT

MATH EXAMPLES

Rigorous Curriculum Design Math Unit Planning Organizer
Grade 3: San Diego Unified School District

Subject(s)	Mathematics
Grade/Course	3rd Grade
Unit of Study	Fractured (Fractions)
Pacing + Buffer	20 days + 5 "Buffer" days

Priority Common Core State Standards
Supporting Standards

3.NF.3: Explain equivalence of fractions in special cases, and compare fractions by reasoning about their size.

> **3.NF.3a: Understand two fractions as equivalent (equal) if they are the same size, or the same point on a number line.**

> **3.NF.3b: Recognize and generate simple equivalent fractions (e.g., 1/2 = 2/4, 4/6 = 2/3). Explain why the fractions are equivalent, e.g., by using a visual fraction model.**

> **3.NF.3c: Express whole numbers as fractions, and recognize fractions that are equivalent to whole numbers. *Examples: Express 3 in the form 3 = 3/1; recognize that 6/1 = 6; locate 4/4 and 1 at the same point of a number line diagram.***

> **3.NF.3d: Compare two fractions with the same numerator or the same denominator by reasoning about their size. Recognize that comparisons are valid only when the two fractions refer to the same whole. Record the results of comparisons with the symbols >, =, or <, and justify the conclusions, e.g., by using a visual fraction model.**

3.NF.1: Understand a fraction 1/*b* as the quantity formed by 1 part when a whole is partitioned into *b* equal parts; understand a fraction *a/b* as the quantity formed by *a* parts of size 1/*b*.

3.NF.2: Understand a fraction as a number on the number line; represent fractions on a number line diagram.

> 3.NF.2a: Represent a fraction 1/*b* on a number line diagram by defining the interval from 0 to 1 as the whole and partitioning it into *b* equal parts. Recognize that each part has size 1/*b* and that the endpoint of the part based at 0 locates the number 1/*b* on the number line.

> 3.NF.2b: Represent a fraction *a/b* on a number line diagram by marking off *a* lengths 1/*b* from 0. Recognize that the resulting interval has size *a/b* and that its endpoint locates the number *a/b* on the number line.

"UNWRAPPED" Priority Standards

3.NF.3a: UNDERSTAND two fractions as equivalent (equal) if they are the same size, or the same point on a number line.

3.NF.3b: RECOGNIZE and GENERATE simple equivalent fractions (e.g., 1/2 = 2/4, 4/6 = 2/3). EXPLAIN why the fractions are equivalent (e.g., by using a visual fraction model).

3.NF.3c: EXPRESS whole numbers as fractions, and RECOGNIZE fractions that are equivalent to whole numbers. *Examples: Express 3 in the form 3 = 3/1; recognize that 6/1 = 6; locate 4/4 and 1 at the same point of a number line diagram.*

3.NF.3d: COMPARE two fractions with the same numerator or the same denominator by REASONING about their size. RECOGNIZE that comparisons are valid only when the two fractions refer to the same whole. RECORD the results of comparisons with the symbols >, =, or <, and JUSTIFY the conclusions, e.g., by using a visual fraction model.

"Unwrapped" Concepts (students need to know)	"Unwrapped" Skills (students need to be able to do)	Taxonomy Levels Blooms/DOK	
Two fractions as equivalent • Same size or same point on number line	UNDERSTAND	2	1
Simple equivalent fractions	RECOGNIZE	1	1
Simple equivalent fractions	GENERATE	3	2
Why fractions are equivalent	EXPLAIN	2	2
Whole numbers as fractions	EXPRESS	2	2
Fractions equivalent to whole numbers	RECOGNIZE	1	1
Two fractions with same numerator or same denominator • Size	COMPARE	2	2
	by REASONING	2	2
Comparisons valid only when two fractions refer to same whole	RECOGNIZE	1	1
Results of comparisons with symbols >, =, or <	RECORD	2	2
Conclusions	JUSTIFY	5	3

Essential Questions	Corresponding Big Ideas
When do the digits 1 and 2 equal each other?	Visual models and a number line can be used to represent, explain, and compare *equivalent fractions*.
Why do some fractions and whole numbers look different but are equal in value?	Visual models and a number line can be used to represent, explain, and compare *whole numbers as fractions*.
Why is his half of a cake bigger than my half?	Visual models and a number line can be used to represent, explain, and compare *fractions with the same numerator or the same denominator*.

Source: 3rd Grade RCD Curriculum Design Team, San Diego Unified School District, San Diego, CA

Rigorous Curriculum Design Math Unit Planning Organizer
Grade 4: San Diego Unified School District

Subject(s)	Mathematics
Grade/Course	4th Grade
Unit of Study	Unit 6: Decimals
Pacing + Buffer	17 days (15 days with 2 buffer days)
Overview of Unit	The standards within this unit serve as a mathematical foundation for students. It is important to ensure student understanding of the big ideas and essential questions within this unit for students' ongoing success.
	This unit presupposes that students have been taught place value of whole numbers and decimals to 100ths, base-ten concepts and notation, fraction concepts (numerator, denominator, equivalent fractions), number lines, and models. This unit will focus on fraction and decimal concepts.
	This unit will prepare students to compare decimals by reasoning about their size, recognize that comparisons are valid when the decimals refer to the same whole, record the results of their comparisons, and justify their conclusions.
Common Core Critical Areas of Focus	Compare two decimals to hundredths.
	Reason about the size of decimals.
	Recognize that comparisons are valid only when the two decimals refer to the same whole.
	Record the results of comparisons with the symbols >, =, or <.
	Justify the conclusions using a variety of models.

Priority Common Core State Standards
Supporting Standards

4.NF.7: COMPARE two decimals to hundredths BY REASONING about their size. RECOGNIZE that comparisons are valid only when the two decimals refer to the same whole. RECORD the results of comparisons with the symbols >, =, or <, and JUSTIFY the conclusions, e.g., by using the number line or another visual model.

4.NF.5: EXPRESS a fraction with denominator 10 as an equivalent fraction with denominator 100, and USE this technique to add two fractions with respective denominators 10 and 100. *For example, express 3/10 as 30/100, and add 3/10 + 4/100 = 34/100.*

4.NF.6: USE decimal notation for fractions with denominators 10 or 100. *For example, rewrite 0.62 as 62/100; describe a length as 0.62 meters; locate 0.62 on a number line diagram.*

"UNWRAPPED" Priority Standards
Supporting Standards

4.NF.7: COMPARE two decimals to hundredths BY REASONING about their size. RECOGNIZE that comparisons are valid only when the two decimals refer to the same whole. RECORD the results of comparisons with the symbols >, =, or <, and JUSTIFY the conclusions, e.g., by using the number line or another visual model.

"Unwrapped" Concepts (students need to know)	"Unwrapped" Skills (students need to be able to do)	Taxonomy Levels Blooms/DOK	
Two decimals to hundredths	COMPARE	2	2
	BY REASONING	5	4
Comparisons are valid only when two decimals refer to the same whole	RECOGNIZE	4	3
Results of comparisons with the symbols >, =, or <	RECORD	1	1
Conclusions using number line or other visual model	JUSTIFY	5	3

Essential Questions	Corresponding Big Ideas
When are two halves not alike?	The whole determines the value of the number.
Can two different numbers have the same value?	When comparing fractions and decimals with the same whole, they can be represented in different ways.

Source: 4th Grade RCD Curriculum Design Team, San Diego Unified School District, San Diego, CA

Rigorous Curriculum Design Math Unit Planning Organizer
Grade 5: San Diego Unified School District

Subject(s)	Mathematics
Grade/Course	5th Grade
Unit of Study	Unit 1: How Do I Express Myself Using Algebraic Reasoning?
Pacing + Buffer	17 days (15 days with 2 buffer days)
Overview of Unit	Students will make function tables and apply them to real-world situations. They will find relationships between two functions. • Parenthesis • Concepts of equality • Write simple expressions • Function tables without variables • Introduce variables in expressions/equations • Introduce variables into function tables • Introduce 1 quadrant coordinate grid • Coordinate grid as a representation to graph a function • Compare rules of two function tables

Priority Common Core State Standards
Supporting Standards

5.OA.3: GENERATE two numerical patterns using two given rules. IDENTIFY apparent relationships between corresponding terms. FORM ordered pairs consisting of corresponding terms from the two patterns, and GRAPH the ordered pairs on a coordinate plane. *For example, given the rule "Add 3" and the starting number 0, and given the rule "Add 6" and the starting number 0, generate terms in the resulting sequences, and observe that the terms in one sequence are twice the corresponding terms in the other sequence. Explain informally why this is so.*

5.OA.1: Use parentheses, brackets, or braces in numerical expressions, and evaluate expressions with these symbols.

5.OA.2: Write simple expressions that record calculations with numbers, and interpret numerical expressions without evaluating them. *For example, express the calculation "add 8 and 7, then multiply by 2" as 2 x (8 + 7). Recognize that 3 x (18932 + 921) is three times as large as 18932 + 921, without having to calculate the indicated sum or product.*

5.G.1: Use a pair of perpendicular number lines, called axes, to define a coordinate system, with the intersection of the lines (the origin) arranged to coincide with the 0 on each line and a given point in the plane located by using an ordered pair of numbers, called its coordinates. Understand that the first number indicates how far to travel from the origin in the direction of one axis, and the second number indicates how far to travel in the direction of the second axis, with the convention that the names of the two axes and the coordinates correspond (e.g., x-axis and x-coordinate, y-axis and y-coordinate).

5.G.2: Represent real-world and mathematical problems by graphing points in the first quadrant of the coordinate plane, and interpret coordinate values of points in the context of the situation.

Number and Operations in Base Ten Major Cluster:

5.NBT.5: Fluently multiply multi-digit whole numbers using the standard algorithm.

5. NBT.7: Add, subtract, multiply, and divide decimals to hundredths, using concrete models or drawings and strategies based on place value, properties of operations, and/or the relationship between additional and subtraction; relate the strategy to a written method and explain the reasoning used.

"Unwrapped" Concepts (students need to know)	"Unwrapped" Skills (students need to be able to do)	Taxonomy Levels Blooms/DOK	
TWO PATTERNS TWO GIVEN RULES	GENERATE USING (USE)	2	2
RELATIONSHIPS BETWEEN CORRESPONDING TERMS	IDENTIFY	2	1
ORDERED PAIRS FROM TWO PATTERNS	FORM	4	3
ORDERED PAIRS	GRAPH	2	2

Essential Questions	Corresponding Big Ideas
Why do I graph ordered pairs and how do I use them?	Graphing ordered pairs helps to predict and compare data.
Why should I make a function table for my rule and how do I apply it to the world?	Visual representations help you understand rules and patterns.
How can I find the connections between rules?	There can be a relationship between two rules.

Source: 5th Grade RCD Curriculum Design Team, San Diego Unified School District, San Diego, CA

McMinnville School District—Grade 3

UNIT 3	Fractions
Unit Length	**February–March**
"Unwrapped" PRIORITY Standards	(Grade 3 expectations in this domain are limited to fractions with denominators 2, 3, 4, 6, and 8.) *3.NF.1: UNDERSTAND a fraction1/b as the quantity formed by 1 part when a whole is partitioned into b equal parts; UNDERSTAND a fraction a/b as the quantity formed by a parts of size 1/b.* *3.NF.3: EXPLAIN equivalence of fractions in special cases, and COMPARE fractions by REASONING about their size.* *A. UNDERSTAND two fractions as equivalent (equal) if they are the same size, or the same point on a number line.* *B. RECOGNIZE and GENERATE simple equivalent fractions. EXPLAIN why the fractions are equivalent, e.g., by USING a visual fraction model.* *C. EXPRESS whole numbers as fractions, and RECOGNIZE fractions that are equivalent to whole numbers.* *D. COMPARE two fractions with the same numerator or the same denominator by REASONING about their size. RECOGNIZE that comparisons are valid only when the two fractions refer to the same whole. RECORD the results of comparisons with the symbols >, =, or <, and JUSTIFY the conclusions, e.g., by USING a visual fraction model.*

	Concepts	Skills	Bloom's
"Unwrapped" PRIORITY Standards Graphic Organizer	a fraction 1/b as the quantity formed by 1 part when a whole is partitioned into b equal parts	UNDERSTAND	2
	a fraction a/b as the quantity formed by a parts of size 1/b	UNDERSTAND	2
	equivalence of fractions in special cases	EXPLAIN	2
	fractions	COMPARE	4
	about their size	REASON	4
	two fractions as equivalent (equal) if they are the same size, or the same point on a number line	UNDERSTAND	2
	simple equivalent fractions	RECOGNIZE	1
	simple equivalent fractions	GENERATE	5
	why fractions are equivalent	EXPLAIN	2
	whole numbers as fractions	EXPRESS	2
	fractions that are equivalent to whole numbers	RECOGNIZE	2
	two fractions with the same numerator or the same denominator	COMPARE	4
	about their size	REASON	4

UNIT 3	Fractions (*continued*)		
	Concepts	**Skills**	**Bloom's**
"Unwrapped" PRIORITY Standards Graphic Organizer	that comparisons are valid only when the two fractions refer to the same whole	RECOGNIZE	2
	the results of comparisons with the symbols >, =, or <	RECORD	6
	the conclusions	JUSTIFY	6
	a visual fraction mode	USE	3
Supporting Standards	3.NF.2: Understand a fraction as a number on the number line; represent fractions on a number line diagram. A. Represent a fraction 1/b on a number line diagram by defining the intervals 0 to 1 as the whole and partitioning it into b equal parts. Recognize that each part has size 1/b and that the part based at 0 locates the number 1/b on the number line. B. Represent a fraction a/b on a number line diagram by marking off a lengths 1/b from 0. Recognize the resulting intervals have size a/b and that its endpoint locates the number a/b on the number line.		
Essential Questions	1. What is a fraction and how do you know? 2. How can you prove that one fraction is greater or less than others? 3. What are equivalent fractions?		
Big Ideas	1. A fraction is a part of a whole or set. 2. To determine the size of a fraction, you must compare the numerator and denominator and/or compare visual models. 3. Equivalent fractions are the same size or at the same point on a number line.		

Source: Grade 3 RCD Team, McMinnville School District, McMinnville, Oregon

McMinnville School District—Grade 4

UNIT 5	Add, Subtract, and Multiply Fractions
Unit Length	**Mid-May to June.** 2 weeks to pilot as much as possible in 2014, but designed as a full unit for 2014/2015
"Unwrapped" PRIORITY Standards	**4.NF.3: Understand a fraction a/b with a>1 as a sum of fractions 1/b** **4.NF.3b: Decompose a fraction into a sum of fractions with the same denominator in more than one way, recording each decomposition by an equation. Justify decompositions, e.g., by using a visual model.** *For example: 3/8 = 1/8 +1/8 + 1/8; 3/8 = 1/8 + 2/8 ; 2 1/8= 1 +1 + 1/8 = 8/8 + 8/8 + 1/8.* **4.NF.3c: Add and subtract mixed numbers with like denominators, e.g., by replacing each mixed number with an equivalent fraction, and/or by using properties of operations and the relationship between addition and subtraction.** **4.NF.3d: Solve word problems involving addition and subtraction of fractions referring to the same whole and having like denominators, e.g., by using visual fraction models and equations to represent the problem.** **4.NF.4 : Apply and extend previous understandings of multiplication to multiply a fraction by a whole number.** **4.NF.4b: Understand a multiple of** *a/b* **as a multiple of 1/***b***, and use this understanding to multiply a fraction by a whole number.** *For example, use a visual fraction model to express 3 x (2/5) as 6 x (1/5), recognizing this product as 6/5. (In general, n x (a/b) = (n x a)/b.)* **4.NF.4c: Solve word problems involving multiplication of a fraction by a whole number, e.g., by using visual fraction models and equations to represent the problem.** *For example, if each person at a party will eat 3/8 of a pound of roast beef, and there will be 5 people at the party, how many pounds of roast beef will be needed? Between what two whole numbers does your answer lie?*

	Concepts	Skills	Bloom's
"Unwrapped" PRIORITY Standards Graphic Organizer	Fractions into a sum of fractions • Same denominator • More than one way • Using equations	DECOMPOSE	3
	Decompositions using a visual fraction model	JUSTIFY	4
	Mixed numbers with like denominators • Replace with an equivalent fraction • Use properties of operations • Use relationship between addition and subtraction	ADD/ SUBTRACT	3
	Word problems with addition and subtraction of fractions • Same whole • Like denominators	SOLVE	4
	Word Problem • Visual fraction models • Equations	REPRESENT	3

UNIT 5	Add, Subtract, and Multiply Fractions (*continued*)		
	Concepts	**Skills**	**Bloom's**
"Unwrapped" PRIORITY Standards Graphic Organizer	A multiple of a/b as a multiple of 1/b • Multiply a fraction by a whole number [e.g., n x (a/b) = (n x a)/b]	UNDERSTAND	3
	Word problems involving multiplication with a fraction and a whole number	SOLVE	4
	Word Problem • Visual fraction models • Equations	REPRESENT	3
Supporting Standards	*4.NF.3a: Understand addition and subtraction of fractions as joining and separating parts referring to the same whole.* *4.NF.4a: Understand a fraction a/b as a multiple of 1/b. For example, use a visual fraction model to represent 5/4 as the product 5 x (1/4), recording the conclusion by the equation 5/4 = 5 x (1/4).*		
Essential Questions	1. Why do we use visual models to represent fractions and equations? 2. Why is it important to understand how to add, subtract, and multiply fractions and whole numbers?		
Big Ideas	1. Using visual models to represent fractions and equations helps create a picture of the meaning in the fractional equation. 2. People need to understand adding, subtracting, and multiplying fractions and whole numbers for everyday tasks like cooking, building/constructing, sewing, and sharing materials with others.		

Source: Grade 4 RCD Team, McMinnville School District, McMinnville, Oregon

McMinnville School District—Grade 5

UNIT NUMBER 2	Add, Subtract, and Multiply and Divide Whole Numbers and Decimals to the Hundredths
Unit Length	To be determined
"Unwrapped" PRIORITY Standards	**5.NBT.6:** FIND whole-number quotients of whole numbers with up to four-digit dividends and two-digit divisors, USING strategies based on place value, the properties of operations, and/or the relationship between multiplication and division. ILLUSTRATE and EXPLAIN the calculation by USING equations, rectangular arrays, and/or area models. **5.NBT.7:** ADD, SUBTRACT, MULTIPLY, and DIVIDE decimals to hundredths, USING concrete models or drawings and strategies based on place value, properties of operations, and/or the relationship between addition and subtraction; RELATE the strategy to a written method and EXPLAIN the reasoning used.

"Unwrapped" PRIORITY Standards Graphic Organizer	Concepts	Skills	Bloom's
	Whole-number quotients of whole numbers up to: • Four-digit dividends • Two-digit divisors	Find	1
	Strategies based on: • Place value • Properties of operations • Relationships based on multiplication and division	Use	3
	Calculations	Illustrate and Explain	2
	• Rectangular arrays • Area models • Equations	Use	1
	Decimals: • Tenths • Hundredths	Add, Subtract, Multiply, Divide	2
	• Models • Drawings • Strategies of place value • Properties of operations • Relationship between addition and subtraction	Use	1
	Written Method	Relate	3
	Materials Used	Explain	2

UNIT NUMBER 2	Add, Subtract, and Multiply and Divide Whole Numbers and Decimals to the Hundredths (*continued*)
Supporting Standards	5.NBT.5: Fluently multiply multi-digit whole numbers using the standard algorithm.
Essential Questions	1. What are strategies I can use to find the quotient of a long division problem? 2. What are strategies I can use to add, subtract, multiply, and divide decimals?
Big Ideas	1. A long division problem can be solved many different ways such as using the standard algorithm, a multiplication menu, a rectangular array, or an area model. 2. There are a variety of strategies that can be used to add, subtract, multiply, and divide decimal numbers and each of these operations can be visualized using concrete models or drawings.

Source: Grade 5 RCD Team, McMinnville School District, McMinnville, Oregon

West Hartford Math: Grade 5

Unit 1: Plotting and "Plane-ing"—Coordinate Planes

Pacing Guide: This unit is designed to be implemented over the course of 10 days with 2 buffer days.

UNIT OVERVIEW

Students will learn how to generate number patterns and graph them on a coordinate plane. This is an important foundational skill for later work with linear functions. In this unit, students will generate number patterns using given rules, form ordered pairs of corresponding terms, graph the pairs, and identify relationships between the terms. *This unit will not teach students about linear equations, but will teach the foundational skills for linear equations.*

Students will learn to identify a location on a coordinate plane as an ordered coordinate pair (x, y), where x and y indicate the distances from the origin in the horizontal and vertical directions, respectively. Students will use the coordinate plane to learn about geometry topics such as parallel and perpendicular lines and to represent real-world contexts such as locations on maps. Students will work in the first quadrant of a coordinate plane in fifth grade. In sixth grade, students will work in all four quadrants.

Key vocabulary:

> axis/axes, coordinate plane, coordinate system, coordinates, coordinate values, corresponding terms, horizontal, intersect, ordered pair, origin, patterns, perpendicular, quadrant, relationships, vertical, x-axis, x-coordinate, y-axis, y-coordinate

Common Core State Standards
5.OA.3: ANALYZE patterns and relationships. GENERATE two numerical patterns USING two given rules. IDENTIFY apparent relationships between corresponding terms. FORM ordered pairs consisting of corresponding terms from the two patterns, and GRAPH the ordered pairs on a coordinate plane. For example, given the rule "Add 3" and the starting number 0, and given the rule "Add 6" and the starting number 0, generate terms in the resulting sequences, and observe that the terms in one sequence are twice the corresponding terms in the other sequence. **EXPLAIN informally why this is so.**
5.G.1: Use a pair of perpendicular number lines, called axes, to define a coordinate system, with the intersection of the lines (the origin) arranged to coincide with the 0 on each line and a given point in the plane located by using an ordered pair of numbers, called its coordinates. Understand that the first number indicates how far to travel from the origin in the direction of the second axis, with the convention that the names of the two axes and the coordinates correspond (e.g., *x-axis* and *y-axis* and *y-coordinate*).
5.G.2: REPRESENT real-world and mathematical problems by GRAPHING points in the first quadrant of the coordinate plane, and INTERPRET coordinate values of points in the context of the situation.

Priority
Supporting

Note: Standard 5.G.1, a *supporting* standard, was "unwrapped" and included in the graphic organizer.

"UNWRAPPED" STANDARDS		
"Unwrapped" Concepts (students need to know)	"Unwrapped" Skills (students need to be able to do)	Bloom's Taxonomy Level Webb's DOK Level
5.OA.3 Ordered Pairs	GENERATE two numerical patterns using two given rules	B = 3 (Apply) DOK = 1 (Recall and Reproduction)
5.OA.3 Ordered Pairs	IDENTIFY apparent relationships between corresponding terms	B = 2 (Understand) DOK = 2 (Skills/Concepts)
5.OA.3 Ordered Pairs	FORM ordered pairs consisting of corresponding terms from two patterns	B = 2 (Understand) DOK = 2 (Skills/Concepts)
5.OA.3 Ordered Pairs	GRAPH ordered pairs consisting of corresponding terms from two patterns	B = 2 (Understand) DOK = 1 (Recall and Reproduction)
5.G.1 Coordinate Points/Coordinate Plane	Use a pair of perpendicular number lines, called axes, to DEFINE a coordinate system, with the intersection of the lines (origin) arranged to coincide with the 0 on each line and a given point in the plane located by using an ordered pair of numbers, called its coordinates.	B = 2 (Understand) DOK = 2 (Skill/Concept)
5.G.1 Coordinate Points/Coordinate Plane	UNDERSTAND that the first number indicates how far to travel from the origin in the direction of one axis, and the second axis, with the convention that the names of the two axes and the coordinates correspond.	B = 2 (Understand) DOK = 1 (Recall and Reproduction)
5.G.2 Coordinate Points/Coordinate Plane	REPRESENT real-world and mathematical problems by graphing points in the first quadrant of the coordinate plane, and interpret coordinate values of points in the context of the situation.	B = 3 (Apply) DOK = 2 (Skills and Concepts)

ESSENTIAL QUESTIONS	BIG IDEAS
1. How can I use mathematical rules to generate a numerical pattern?	1. Ordered pairs can be formed from two patterns. (5.OA.3) (MP 1, 6, 8)
2. How can I represent a numerical pattern?	2. A pattern on a coordinate plane can be represented using ordered pairs. (5.OA.3, 5.G.1, **5.G.2**) (MP 1, 4, 6, 8)
3. How can I use a coordinate plane to solve a real-world problem?	3. A coordinate plane can be used to graph ordered pairs to solve and/or represent a solution to real-world problems. (5.OA.3, 5.G.1, **5.G.2**) (MP 1, 4, 6, 8)

Source: Grade 5 RCD Curriculum Design Team, West Hartford Public Schools, West Hartford, CT

CHAPTER 7

Middle School Examples

One of the most beneficial features of the original *"Unwrapping" the Standards* (2003) book was its inclusion of more than 85 examples of "unwrapped" standards, Big Ideas, and Essential Questions specific to each grade span, K–2, 3–5, 6–8, and 9–12, from numerous content areas. Educators always appreciate seeing examples: especially Big Ideas and Essential Questions. These concrete samples help greatly to convey what the explanatory content describes. For these reasons, I knew it was important to include in this volume similar examples of "unwrapped" Common Core State Standards in English language arts and literacy and in mathematics.

Four school systems that I have worked closely with, two in the eastern United States and two in the West, graciously responded to my request for "unwrapped" Common Core examples created by their educators. The two east coast districts are West Hartford and Bloomfield, both in Connecticut. The two west coast districts are San Diego Unified School District in California and McMinnville School District in Oregon. It was my great privilege over a period of many months to lead their educators and leaders through the Rigorous Curriculum Design framework I created to help educators write new curricula for the Common Core. The four parts of the "unwrapping" process were the first steps they followed in developing their curricular units of study in English language arts and literacy and in math that later included unit-specific formative and summative assessments, authentic performance tasks, instructional resources, and differentiated instructional strategies.

I always encourage educators and curriculum writers to follow the framework of "unwrapping" and curriculum design as prescribed but then to "make the process their own" by customizing the format for their units of study. Reprinted here are the first sections of the Rigorous Curriculum Design Unit Planning Organizer you have seen throughout the previous explanatory chapters. Many grade-level or course-level design teams in the four districts used this template as is; others chose to modify it somewhat. To respect their particular district formatting, I have included the graphic organizers as they were submitted to me. Because you now understand the complete "unwrapping" process, you will be able to understand the content represented in these district examples even when it varies from my original format. Also, note that not every district included both Bloom's *and* DOK cognitive levels on their initial graphic organizers.

I have organized these grade-span examples by district and by content area, rather than interspersing all the examples for each grade level. This will make each district's examples "self-contained" and hopefully easier for you to read and understand.

Rigorous Curriculum Design Unit Planning Organizer

Subject(s)	
Grade/Course	
Unit of Study	
Pacing	

Priority Common Core State Standards (Bolded) Supporting Standards

"UNWRAPPED" Priority Standards

"Unwrapped" Concepts (students need to know)	"Unwrapped" Skills (students need to be able to do)	Taxonomy Levels Bloom's / DOK	

Essential Questions	Corresponding Big Ideas

ELA EXAMPLES

Rigorous Curriculum Design ELA Unit Planning Organizer
Grade 6: San Diego Unified School District

Subject(s)	English
Grade/Course	6

Unit of Study	Unit 3: Analyzing & Comparing Literary Nonfiction
	    Part A—Analyzing Single Texts
	    Part B—Comparing Multiple Texts and Media

Pacing	20 days for Part A, 25 days for Part B, 5 buffer days

Priority Common Core State Standards
Supporting Standards

Part A

RI.6.2: Determine a central idea of a text and how it is conveyed through particular details; provide a summary of the text distinct from personal opinions or judgments.

RI.6.3: Analyze in detail how a key individual, event, or idea is introduced, illustrated, and elaborated in a text (e.g., through examples or anecdotes).

    RI.6.1: Cite textual evidence to support analysis of what the text says explicitly as well as inferences drawn from the text.

    RI.6.4: Determine the meaning of words and phrases as they are used in a text, including figurative, connotative, and technical meanings.

    RI.6.5: Analyze how a particular sentence, paragraph, chapter, or section fits into the overall structure of a text and contributes to the development of the ideas.

    RI.6.6: Determine an author's point of view or purpose in a text and explain how it is conveyed in the text.

W.6.2: Write informative/explanatory texts to examine a topic and convey ideas, concepts, and information through the selection, organization, and analysis of relevant content.

    W.6.2a: Introduce a topic; organize ideas, concepts, and information, using strategies such as definition, classification, comparison/contrast, and cause/effect; include formatting (e.g., headings), graphics (e.g., charts, tables), and multimedia when useful to aiding comprehension.

    W.6.2b: Develop the topic with relevant facts, definitions, concrete details, quotations, or other information and examples.

    W.6.2c: Use appropriate transitions to clarify the relationships among ideas and concepts.

    W.6.2d: Use precise language and domain-specific vocabulary to inform about or explain the topic.

    W.6.2e: Establish and maintain a formal style.

    W.6.2f: Provide a concluding statement or section that follows from the information or explanation presented.

    SL.6.1: Engage effectively in a range of collaborative discussions (one-on-one, in groups, and teacher-led) with diverse partners on grade 6 topics, texts, and issues, building on others' ideas and expressing their own clearly.

Priority Common Core State Standards
Supporting Standards

Part B

RI.6.9: Compare and contrast one author's presentation of events with that of another (e.g., a memoir written by and a biography on the same person).

RI.6.1: Cite textual evidence to support analysis of what the text says explicitly as well as inferences drawn from the text.

RI.6.2: Determine a central idea of a text and how it is conveyed through particular details; provide a summary of the text distinct from personal opinions or judgments.

RI.6.3: Analyze in detail how a key individual, event, or idea is introduced, illustrated, and elaborated in a text (e.g., through examples or anecdotes).

RI.6.4: Determine the meaning of words and phrases as they are used in a text, including figurative, connotative, and technical meanings.

RI.6.7: Integrate information presented in different media or formats (e.g., visually, quantitatively) as well as in words to develop a coherent understanding of a topic or issue.

W.6.2: Write informative/explanatory texts to examine a topic and convey ideas, concepts, and information through the selection, organization, and analysis of relevant content.

W.6.2a: Introduce a topic; organize ideas, concepts, and information, using strategies such as definition, classification, comparison/contrast, and cause/effect; include formatting (e.g., headings), graphics (e.g., charts, tables), and multimedia when useful to aiding comprehension.

W.6.2b: Develop the topic with relevant facts, definitions, concrete details, quotations, or other information and examples.

W.6.2c: Use appropriate transitions to clarify the relationships among ideas and concepts.

W.6.2d: Use precise language and domain-specific vocabulary to inform about or explain the topic.

W.6.2e: Establish and maintain a formal style.

W.6.2f: Provide a concluding statement or section that follows from the information or explanation presented.

W.6.7: Conduct short research projects to answer a question, drawing on several sources and refocusing the inquiry when appropriate.

W.6.8: Gather relevant information from multiple print and digital sources; assess the credibility of each source; and quote or paraphrase the data and conclusions of others while avoiding plagiarism and providing basic bibliographic information for sources.

SL.6.4a: Plan and deliver an informative/explanatory presentation that: develops a topic with relevant facts, definitions, and details; uses appropriate transitions to clarify relationships; uses precise language and domain-specific vocabulary; and provides a strong conclusion.

SL.6.5: Include multimedia components (e.g., graphics, images, music, sound) and visual displays in presentations to clarify information.

SL.6.1: Engage effectively in a range of collaborative discussions (one-on-one, in groups, and teacher-led) with diverse partners on grade 6 topics, texts, and issues, building on others' ideas and expressing their own clarity.

SL.6.2: Interpret information presented in diverse media and formats (e.g., visually, quantitatively, orally) and explain how it contributes to a topic, text, or issue under study.

"UNWRAPPED" Priority Standards

PART A

RI.6.2: DETERMINE a central idea of a text and how it is conveyed through particular details; PROVIDE a summary of the text distinct from personal opinions or judgments.

RI.6.3: ANALYZE in detail how a key individual, event, or idea is introduced, illustrated, and elaborated in a text (e.g., through examples or anecdotes).

W.6.2: WRITE informative/explanatory texts to EXAMINE a topic and CONVEY ideas, concepts, and information through the selection, organization, and analysis of relevant content.

PART B

RI.6.9: COMPARE and CONTRAST one author's presentation of events with that of another (e.g., a memoir written by and a biography on the same person).

W.6.2: WRITE informative/explanatory texts to EXAMINE a topic and CONVEY ideas, concepts, and information through the selection, organization, and analysis of relevant content.

W.6.7: CONDUCT short research projects to answer a question, drawing on several sources and REFOCUSING the inquiry when appropriate.

SL.6.4a: PLAN and DELIVER an informative/explanatory presentation that: DEVELOPS a topic with relevant facts, definitions, and details; USES appropriate transitions to clarify relationships; USES precise language and domain specific vocabulary; and PROVIDES a strong conclusion.

SL.6.5: INCLUDE multimedia components (e.g., graphics, images, music, sound) and visual displays in presentations to clarify information.

"Unwrapped" Concepts (students need to know)	"Unwrapped" Skills (students need to be able to do)	Taxonomy Levels	
		Bloom's / DOK	
PART A	**PART A**		
RI.6.2 Central idea Conveyed through details relevant information	DETERMINE (central ideas *through concepts*)—ANALYZE, EVALUATE	4, 5	3
Summary Without personal opinions Not a retell Facts vs. opinions	PROVIDE (summary of text without personal opinions)	2	2
RI.6.3 How key individual, event, or idea is introduced, illustrated, elaborated	ANALYZE (individual/event/idea)—CITE, DETERMINE, ANALYZE	4	3
W.6.2 Informative writing Explanatory text	WRITE (to inform/explain texts) CONVEY (ideas/concepts/information)—SELECT, ORGANIZE, ANALYZE (*relevant content information*)	6	4

"Unwrapped" Concepts (students need to know)	"Unwrapped" Skills (students need to be able to do)	Taxonomy Levels	
		Bloom's / DOK	
PART B	**PART B**		
RI.6.9 one author's presentation of events with that of another	COMPARE/CONTRAST (one author to another *different genres on same topic*)	3	3
W.6.2 Informative/explanatory texts topic, concepts, information; selection, organization, analysis of relevant content.	WRITE (to inform/explain texts) CONVEY (ideas/concepts/ information)—SELECT, ORGANIZE, ANALYZE (*relevant content information*)	6	4
W.6.7 Short research projects; refocus of inquiry	CONDUCT (short research with multiple sources refocusing when needed)	6	4
SL.6.4a informative/explanatory presentation; relevant facts, definitions, details; appropriate transitions to clarify relationships; precise language; domain, specific vocabulary; strong conclusion.	PLAN (informative/explanatory presentation)—*develops topic with relevant facts, definitions, and details* DELIVER (through multimedia and visual displays)	6	4

Essential Questions	Corresponding Big Ideas
1. *Why do authors write informational texts?*	1. Authors write informational texts to provide background and facts, not their opinions, on a topic, concept, or issue.
2. *How do I read informational texts on unfamiliar topics?*	2. When reading informational text on unfamiliar topics, first preview the text, studying all available text features to figure out the main ideas of the text.
	Next, read the running text, annotating or taking notes on the main ideas. Continue to cross check the main ideas with the information gathered in my text preview.
3. *How do I research a topic for a presentation?*	3. When doing research, I should read and take notes on the main ideas. I should develop research questions and then read more to answer the questions and form my thesis statement.
	Applicable to Parts A *and* B

Source: 6th Grade RCD Curriculum Design Team, San Diego Unified School District, San Diego, CA

Rigorous Curriculum Design ELA Unit Planning Organizer
Grade 7: San Diego Unified School District

Subject(s)	English Language Arts
Grade/Course	Grade 7
Unit of Study	Supporting Your Arguments
Pacing	

"UNWRAPPED" Common Core Priority Standards
(Note: Bolded Priority Language Standards were "unwrapped" and included on Graphic Organizer.)

RI.7.8: TRACE and EVALUATE the argument and specific claims in a text, ASSESSING whether the reasoning is sound, and the evidence is relevant and sufficient to support claims.

RI.7.2: DETERMINE two or more central ideas in a text and ANALYZE their development over the course of the text; PROVIDE an objective summary of the text.

RI.7.9: ANALYZE how two or more authors writing about the same topic shape their presentations of key information by emphasizing different evidence or advancing different interpretations of facts.

W.7.2: WRITE informative/explanatory texts to EXAMINE a topic and convey ideas, concepts, and information through the SELECTION, ORGANIZATION, and ANALYSIS of relevant content.

W.7.7: CONDUCT short research projects to ANSWER a question, DRAWING on several sources and GENERATING additional related, focused questions for further research and investigation.

L.7.1: DEMONSTRATE command of the conventions of standard English grammar and usage when writing or speaking.

L.7.1b: CHOOSE among simple, compound, complex, and compound-complex sentences to signal differing relationships among ideas.

L.7.1c: PLACE phrases and clauses within a sentence, RECOGNIZING and CORRECTING misplaced and dangling modifiers.

L.7.4b: USE common, grade-appropriate Greek or Latin affixes and roots as clues to the meaning of a word (e.g., belligerent, bellicose, rebel).

SL.7.1c: POSE questions that elicit elaboration and RESPOND to others' questions and comments with relevant observations and ideas that bring the discussion back on topic as needed.

SL.7.1d: ACKNOWLEDGE new information expressed by others and, when warranted, modify their own view.

SL.7.2: ANALYZE the main ideas and supporting details presented in diverse media and formats (e.g., visually, quantitatively, orally) and EXPLAIN how the ideas clarify a topic, text, or issue under study.

"Unwrapped" Concepts (students need to know)	"Unwrapped" Skills (students need to be able to do)	Taxonomy Levels Bloom's / DOK	
• Argument • Specific Claims • Evidence • Cite Sources	• TRACE & EVALUATE (argument, claim, evidence, cite sources)	4	3
• Central ideas in two or more texts • Development of central ideas in text	• DETERMINE (central ideas in a text) • ANALYZE (development of central ideas in text)	4 4	4 4

• Objective summary
• Two or more authors' point of view on same topic (derived RI.7.2)
  • Presentation of key information
  • Emphasizing different evidence or advancing different interpretations of facts
	• PROVIDE (*objective* summary of text)
	• ANALYZE (same topic; emphasizing different evidence; advancing different interpretations of facts)
		2
		4
			2
			4

• Explanatory/informative texts
  • Topic
    • Ideas
    • Concepts
    • Information
    • Relevancy
	• WRITE (explanatory/informative text)
	• EXAMINE (topic)
	• CONVEY (ideas, concepts and information)
		6
		4
		6
			4
			3
			3

	• SELECT (relevant content) • ORGANIZE (relevant content) • ANALYZE (relevant content)	4 6 4	3 4 4

• Short research projects to answer a question
  • Several cited sources
  • Focused questions for further research
	• CONDUCT (short research projects to answer a question)
	• DRAW (on several sources)
	• GENERATE (focused questions for further research and investigation)
		3
		
		3
		5, 6
			2
			
			4
			2

• Writing and speaking conventions
  • Grammar
  • Usage
	• DEMONSTRATE (conventions)	3	1

• Kinds of sentences to signal different relationships among ideas
  • Simple
  • Compound
  • Complex
  • Compound-complex
	• CHOOSE (among simple, compound, complex, and compound-complex sentences; signal differing relationships among ideas)	3	2

• Phrases • Clauses	• PLACE (phrases and clauses)	3	2

• Modifiers
  • dangling
  • misplaced
	• RECOGNIZE & CORRECT (misplaced and dangling modifiers)	3	2

• Greek and Latin affixes and roots • Clues to meanings of words	• USE (common, grade-appropriate Greek and Latin affixes and roots as clues to meaning)	2	1

• Questioning skills
  • Eliciting elaboration
  • Relevant observations
  • Relevant ideas
	• POSE (questions that elicit elaboration)
	• RESPOND (to others' questions and comments with relevant observations that bring the discussion back to the topic)
		6
		4
			3
			3

• Collegial discussion	• ACKNOWLEDGE (new information expressed by others, collegial discussion) • MODIFY (own view)	2 5	3 3
• Claims and findings in multimedia components and formats	• ANALYZE (main ideas; supporting details in media and a variety of formats) • EXPLAIN (how multimedia and a variety of formats clarify topic, text, or issue)	4 5, 6	3 3

Essential Questions	Corresponding Big Ideas
How can I develop an informed understanding of a topic or event?	Reading/Listening: In order to truly understand a topic or event, it's necessary to analyze multiple sources and points of view (reading skills).
How can I communicate (orally and through writing) an informed point of view on a given topic or event?	Writing/Speaking: An effective, informative/ expository text communicates a topic by conveying concepts and information through the use of relevant content. OR An effective informative/explanatory text communicates a topic by conveying information based on relevant evidence.
How does reading, viewing, and analyzing multiple sources build depth of knowledge of a topic?	The same event can be viewed from different perspectives. OR Understanding different points of view helps us shape our own ideas. OR Understanding different points of view expands knowledge on a topic.

Source: 7th Grade RCD Curriculum Design Team, San Diego Unified School District, San Diego, CA

Rigorous Curriculum Design ELA Unit Planning Organizer
Grade 8: San Diego Unified School District

Subject(s)	ELA
Grade/Course	Grade 8
Unit of Study	How Do Authors Choose to Represent History?
Pacing	

"UNWRAPPED" Priority Standards
(Note: Speaking and Listening Standards concepts/skills added to Graphic Organizer.)

RI.8.2: DETERMINE a central idea of a text and ANALYZE its development over the course of the text, including its relationship to supporting ideas; PROVIDE an objective summary of the text.

RI.8.3: ANALYZE how a text makes connections among and distinctions between individuals, ideas, or events (e.g., through comparisons, analogies, or categories).

RI.8.6: DETERMINE an author's point of view or purpose in a text and ANALYZE how the author acknowledges and responds to conflicting evidence or viewpoints.

W.8.1: WRITE arguments to support claims with clear reasons and relevant evidence.

W.8.2: Write informative/explanatory texts to EXAMINE a topic and CONVEY ideas, concepts, and information through the selection, organization, and analysis of relevant content.

"Unwrapped" Concepts (students need to know)	"Unwrapped" Skills (students need to be able to do)	Taxonomy Levels	
		Bloom's	DOK
RI.8.2: Central idea of a text; development over the course of the text; including relationship to supporting ideas; objective summary of text	DETERMINE (central idea) ANALYZE (development) PROVIDE	4 4	3 3
RI.8.3: Connections among and distinctions between individuals, ideas, events	ANALYZE (CONNECTIONS & DISTINCTIONS)	4	3
RI.8.6: Author's point of view or purpose; Author acknowledges/responds to conflicting evidence or viewpoints	DETERMINE (author's POV) ANALYZE	4	3
W.8.1: Arguments, claims, reasons, and relevant evidence	WRITE TO SUPPORT (arguments, claims, relevant evidence)	4	3
W.8.2: Informative/explanatory texts	EXAMINE (a topic) CONVEY (ideas, concepts, and information) SELECT, ORGANIZE, ANALYZE (relevant content to a topic)	5 6	3, 4 4
SL.8.1: Range of collaborative discussions	ENGAGE (collaborative discussions)	4, 5	3, 4

Essential Questions	Corresponding Big Ideas
How do authors choose to represent history? What is the relationship between an author's experiences and the topic or event an author chooses to write about?	• An author's perspective and historical context of a text affects how and what information is presented on a topic or of an event.
Why read multiple texts on the same topic or event?	• Critical readers read multiple texts on a topic or event to be able to form and share their own ideas. • Providing support from the reading of multiple texts allows for powerful, convincing writing on a given topic or of an event.
What does an informative and convincing written piece look like?	• A well-written argument is supported by reasons and evidence.

Source: 8th Grade RCD Curriculum Design Team, San Diego Unified School District, San Diego, CA

McMinnville School District—Grade 6

UNIT 2	Explanatory Introduction
Unit Length	**21 Days with 5-Day Buffer**
"Unwrapped" PRIORITY Standards	**W.6.5:** With some guidance and support from peers and adults, DEVELOP and STRENGTHEN writing as needed by planning, revising, editing, rewriting, or trying a new approach. **W.6.2f:** PROVIDE a concluding statement or section that follows from the information or explanation presented. **RI.6.2:** DETERMINE a central idea of a text and how it is conveyed through particular details; PROVIDE a summary of the text distinct from personal opinions or judgments. **L.6.3:** USE knowledge of language and its conventions when writing, speaking, reading, or listening.

"Unwrapped" PRIORITY Standards Graphic Organizer	Concepts	Skills	Bloom's
	Writing • Planning • Revising • Editing • Rewriting	Develop/ Strengthen	1, 5
	Conventions Spelling Capitalization Punctuation	Demonstrate/ Use	2, 3
	Concluding Statement	Provide	5
	Central Idea conveyed through details	Determine	2
	Summary, free from personal opinions/judgments	Provide	5

Supporting Standards	**W.6.2a:** Introduce a topic; organize ideas, concepts, and information, using strategies such as definition, classification, comparison/contrast, and cause/effect; include formatting (e.g., headings), graphics (e.g., charts, tables), and multimedia when useful to aiding comprehension. **W.6.2b:** Develop the topic with relevant facts, definitions, concrete details, quotations, or other information and examples. **W.6.2c:** Use appropriate transitions to clarify the relationships among ideas and concepts. **L.6.3a:** VARY sentence patterns for meaning, reader/listener interest, and style. **L.6.4c:** Consult reference materials (e.g., dictionaries, glossaries, thesauruses), both print and digital, to find the pronunciation of a word or determine or clarify its precise meaning or its part of speech. **L.6.4d:** Verify the preliminary determination of the meaning of a word or phrase (e.g., by checking the inferred meaning in context or in a dictionary). **W.6.9:** Draw evidence from literary or informational texts to support analysis, reflection, and research.
Essential Question	What is clear communication, and how does one achieve it?
Big Idea	Clear communication must be planned, refined, and should both engage and inform the audience.

Source: Grade 6 RCD Team, McMinnville School District, McMinnville, Oregon

McMinnville School District—Grade 7

UNIT 5	Argumentative
Unit Length	**Five weeks**
"Unwrapped" PRIORITY Standards	**RI.7.1:** **CITE** several pieces of textual evidence to support analysis of what the text says explicitly as well as inferences drawn from the text. **RI.7.6:** **DETERMINE** an author's point of view or purpose in a text and **ANALYZE** how the author distinguishes his or her position from that of others. **W.7.1:** **WRITE** arguments to support claims with clear reasons and relevant evidence. **W.7.1.a:** **INTRODUCE** claim(s), **ACKNOWLEDGE** alternate or opposing claims, and **ORGANIZE** the reasons and evidence logically. **W.7.1.e:** **PROVIDE** a concluding statement or section that follows from and **SUPPORTS** the argument presented. **SL.7.1:** **ENGAGE** effectively in a range of collaborative discussions (one-on-one, in groups, and teacher-led) with diverse partners on *grade 7 topics, texts, and issues*, **BUILDING** on others' ideas and **EXPRESSING** their own clearly. **SL.7.1.c:** **POSE** questions that elicit elaboration and **RESPOND** to others' questions and comments with relevant observations and ideas that bring the discussion back on topic as needed.

"Unwrapped" PRIORITY Standards Graphic Organizer	Concepts	Skills	Bloom's
	• several pieces of textual evidence to support analysis of what the text says; inferences drawn from text	**CITE**	3 Apply
	• author's point of view/purpose	**DETERMINE**	2 Understand
	• how author distinguishes position from others	**ANALYZE**	4 Analyze
	• arguments to support claims with clear reasons and relevant evidence	**WRITE**	6 Create
	• claim(s)	**INTRODUCE**	6 Create
	• alternate or opposing claims	**ACKNOWLEDGE**	6 Create
	• reasons and evidence logically	**ORGANIZE**	
	• a concluding statement or section that follows from argument presented	**PROVIDE / SUPPORTS**	5 Evaluate
	• effectively in a range of collaborative discussions	**ENGAGE**	3 Apply
	• on others' ideas	**BUILD**	4 Analyze
	• own (ideas) clearly	**EXPRESS**	3 Apply
	• questions that elicit elaboration	**POSE**	6 Create
	• to others' questions and comments with relevant observations and ideas	**RESPOND**	5 Evaluate

McMinnville School District—Grade 7

UNIT 5	Argumentative *(continued)*	
Supporting Standards	W.7.1.c:	Use words, phrases, and clauses to create cohesion and clarify the relationships among claim(s), reasons, and evidence.
	W.7.9:	Draw evidence from literary or informational texts to support analysis, reflection, and research.
	W.7.9.b:	Apply *grade 7 Reading standards* to literary nonfiction (e.g.,"Trace and evaluate the argument and specific claims in a text, assessing whether the reasoning is sound and the evidence is relevant and sufficient to support the claims").
	SL.7.1.b:	Follow rules for collegial discussions, track progress toward specific goals and deadlines, and define individual roles as needed.
	SL.7.1.d:	Acknowledge new information expressed by others and, when warranted, modify their own views.
	SL.7.3:	Delineate a speaker's argument and specific claims, evaluating the soundness of the reasoning and the relevance and sufficiency of the evidence.
	SL.7.4:	Present claims and findings, emphasizing salient points in a focused, coherent manner with pertinent descriptions, facts, details, and examples; use appropriate eye contact, adequate volume, and clear pronunciation.
	SL.7.6:	Adapt speech to a variety of contexts and tasks, demonstrating command of formal English when indicated or appropriate. (See grade 7 Language standards 1 and 3 for specific expectations.)
Essential Questions	What is needed in a good argumentative paper?	
	Why is it important to both listen and respond to others' questions and ideas in a discussion?	
Big Ideas	A good argumentative paper includes a clear thesis, reasons and evidence to support your position, acknowledgement of opposing sides without focusing on them, and a precise conclusion that supports your point.	
	By listening and responding to others, it helps to solidify ideas, show other points of view, and allow a change in ideas. Collaboration with others helps to create a better understanding of the topics and concepts.	

Source: Grade 7 RCD Team, McMinnville School District, McMinnville, Oregon

McMinnville School District—Grade 8

UNIT NUMBER 3	Theme and Evidence
Unit Length	**Sept. 30–Oct. 31** **22 + 3-day buffer**
"Unwrapped" PRIORITY Standards	**RL.8.2:** DETERMINE a theme or central idea of a text and ANALYZE its development over the course of the text, including its relationship to the characters, setting, and plot; PROVIDE an objective summary of the text. **L.8.2:** DEMONSTRATE command of the conventions of standard English capitalization, punctuation, and spelling when writing. **W.8.1:** WRITE arguments to SUPPORT claims with clear reasons and relevant evidence.

"Unwrapped" PRIORITY Standards Graphic Organizer	Concepts	Skills	Bloom's
	• a theme or central idea	DETERMINE	4
	• its relationship to the characters, setting, and plot	ANALYZE	4
	• objective summary	PROVIDE	2
	• command of the conventions of standard English capitalization, punctuation, and spelling	DEMONSTRATE	2
	• arguments	WRITE	6
	• claims with clear reasons and relevant evidence	SUPPORT	5

Supporting Standards	**RL.8.1:** Cite the textual evidence that most strongly supports an analysis of what the text says explicitly as well as inferences drawn from the text. **RL.8.7:** Analyze the extent to which a filmed or live production of a story or drama stays faithful to or departs from the text or script, evaluating the choices made by the director or actors. **RL.8.9:** Analyze how a modern work of fiction draws on themes, patterns of events, or character types from myths, traditional stories, or religious works such as the Bible, including describing how the material is rendered new. **RL.8.10:** By the end of the year, read and comprehend literature, including stories, dramas, and poems, at the high end of the grades 6–8 complexity band independently and proficiently. **W.8.1.c:** Use words, phrases, and clauses to create cohesion and clarify the relationships among claim(s), counterclaims, reasons, and evidence. **W.8.9:** Draw evidence from literary or informational texts to support analysis, reflection, and research. **W.8.9.a:** Apply grade 8 Reading standards to literature (e.g., "Analyze how a modern work of fiction draws on themes, patterns of events, or character types from myths, traditional stories, or religious works such as the Bible, including describing how the material is rendered new").
Essential Questions	1. How do the characters, setting, and plot help develop the theme? 2. What is the purpose of summarizing a text? 3. Why is it important to cite evidence when stating an idea about a text?
Big Ideas	1. Characters, setting, and plot help develop the theme by giving the reader essential elements that support the theme. 2. Summarizing a text is important because it allows the reader to focus only on the important details. 3. Citing evidence is important because it supports your ideas about the text.

Source: Grade 8 RCD Team, McMinnville School District, McMinnville, Oregon

English Language Arts Unit of Study for Grade 6
Bloomfield, Connecticut

Subject(s)	English Language Arts
Grade/Course	Grade 6
Unit of Study	Unit 2—Analyzing Craft and Structure
Pacing	20 days (15 instructional days and 5 reteach/enrichment days)

Overarching Standards (OS)—Emphasized in All Units Throughout the Year

Reading Standards for Literature 6–12
RL.6.10: By the end of the year, read and comprehend literature, including stories, dramas, and poems, in the grades 6–8 text complexity band proficiently, with scaffolding as needed at the high end of the range.

Reading Standards for Informational Text 6–12
RI.6.10: By the end of the year, read and comprehend literary nonfiction in the grades 6–8 text complexity band proficiently, with scaffolding as needed at the high end of the range.

Writing Standards 6–12
W.6.10: Write routinely over extended time frames (time for research, reflection, and revision) and shorter time frames (a single sitting or a day or two) for a range of discipline-specific tasks, purposes, and audiences.

Speaking and Listening 6–12
SL.6.6: Adapt speech to a variety of contexts and tasks, demonstrating command of formal English when indicated or appropriate.

Language Standards 6–12
L.6.6: Acquire and use accurately grade-appropriate general academic and domain-specific words and phrases; gather vocabulary knowledge when considering a word or phrase important to comprehension or expression.

Priority and Supporting CCSS

PRIORITY STANDARDS

RL.6.4: DETERMINE the meaning of words and phrases as they are used in a text, including figurative and connotative meanings; ANALYZE the impact of a specific word choice on meaning and tone.

RI.6.5: ANALYZE how a particular sentence, paragraph, chapter, or section fits into the overall structure of a text and contributes to the development of the ideas.

W.6.1c: USE words, phrases, and clauses to clarify the relationships among claim(s) and reasons.

W.6.3b: USE narrative techniques, such as dialogue, pacing, and description, to DEVELOP experiences, events, and/or characters.

L.6.1e: RECOGNIZE variations from standard English in their own and others' writing and speaking, and IDENTIFY and USE strategies to improve expression in conventional language.

L.6.5a: INTERPRET figures of speech (e.g., personification) in context.

Supporting Standards

RL.6.6: Explain how an author develops the point of view of the narrator or speaker in a text.

RI.6.4: Determine the meaning of words and phrases as they are used in a text, including figurative, connotative, and technical meanings.

L.6.1: Demonstrate command of the conventions of standard English grammar and usage when writing or speaking.

L.6.2: Demonstrate command of the conventions of standard English capitalization, punctuation, and spelling when writing.

L.6.2b: Spell correctly.

L.6.3: Use knowledge of language and its conventions when writing, speaking, reading, or listening.

L.6.4: Determine or clarify the meaning of unknown and multiple-meaning words and phrases based on *grade 6 reading and content*, choosing flexibly from a range of strategies.

L.6.4a: Use context (e.g., the overall meaning of a sentence or paragraph; a word's position or function in a sentence) as a clue to the meaning of a word or phrase.

L.6.5: Demonstrate understanding of figurative language, word relationships, and nuances in word meanings.

L.6.5b: Use the relationship between particular words (e.g., cause/effect, part/whole, item/category) to better understand each of the words.

L.6.5c: Distinguish among the connotations (associations) of words with similar denotations (definitions) (e.g., *stingy, scrimping, economical, unwasteful, thrifty*).

Concepts (What students need to know)	Skills (What students need to be able to do)	Bloom's Taxonomy/ DOK Levels
RL.6.4 • Literal meaning	**RL.6.4** DETERMINE (meaning of words and phrases)	B4, D2
• Figurative meaning • Connotative meaning	DETERMINE (figurative and connotative meanings)	B4, D2
• Word choice	ANALYZE (impact of word choice on meaning)	B4, D4
• Tone • Literary devices (alliteration, rhyme, repetition, and dialogue) • Mood	ANALYZE (impact of word choice on tone)	B4, D4
RI.6.5 Structural Elements of Text • Sentence • Paragraph • Chapter • Section	**RI.6.5** ANALYZE (how structural elements fit into the overall structure of a text)	B4, D4
Various Text Features • Cover • Pictures/Illustrations • Captions • Maps/Graphs • Headings • Glossaries Various Text Structures • Process • Sequence • Cause/Effect • Description • Main Idea/Details • Compare/Contrast	ANALYZE (how structural elements contribute to the development of ideas)	B4, D4
W.6.1c • Words • Phrases	**W.6.1c** USE/APPLY (words, phrases, clauses)	B3, D2
• Clauses • Claim(s) • Reasons	CLARIFY (relationships among claim(s) and reasons)	B2, D3
W.6.3b Narrative Techniques (such as): • Dialogue • Pacing • Description	**W.6.3b** USE/APPLY (narrative techniques)	B3, D2
Elaboration of: • Experiences • Events • Characters	DEVELOP (experiences, events, and/or characters)	B6, D3/D4

Concepts (What students need to know)	Skills (What students need to be able to do)	Bloom's Taxonomy/ DOK Levels
L.6.1e Recognize Standard English	**L.6.1e** RECOGNIZE (variations from standard English)	B1, D1
Strategies to Improve Expression	IDENTIFY (strategies to improve expression)	B1, D1
	USE/APPLY (strategies to improve expression)	B3, D2
L.6.5a Figures of Speech • Personification • Metaphor • Simile • Idiom	**L.6.5a** INTERPRET (figures of speech)	B4, D3

Essential Questions	Corresponding Big Ideas
1. Why do we break apart a text and examine its parts?	1. The analysis of the parts of a text leads to understanding the essence of the whole text.
2. How do the words we choose and the language we use impact our writing?	2. Writers keep readers focused and engaged by using effective narrative and expository techniques.

MATH EXAMPLES

Rigorous Curriculum Design Math Unit Planning Organizer
Grade 6: San Diego Unified School District

Subject(s)	Geometry
Grade/Course	6
Unit of Study	Unit 7: Face Value
Pacing	17 days with 5 buffer days for 22 days total
Overview of Unit	This unit focuses on area, surface area, and volume, and presupposes that students have been taught classification of two-dimensional figures and that they can compare and contrast two-dimensional figures by their attributes, and be able to graph in the first quadrant.

Priority Common Core State Standards
Supporting Standards

6.G.4: Represent three-dimensional figures using nets made up of rectangles and triangles, and use the nets to find the surface area of these figures. Apply these techniques in the context of solving real-world and mathematical problems.

6.G.1: Find the area of right triangles, other triangles, special quadrilaterals, and polygons by composing into rectangles or decomposing into triangles and other shapes; apply these techniques in the context of solving real-world and mathematical problems.

6.G.2: Find the volume of a right rectangular prism with fractional edge lengths by packing it with unit cubes of the appropriate unit fraction edge lengths, and show that the volume is the same as would be found by multiplying the edge lengths of the prism. Apply the formulas $V = l\,w\,h$ and $V = b\,h$ to find volumes of right rectangular prisms with fractional edge lengths in the context of solving real-world and mathematical problems.

6.G.3: Draw polygons in the coordinate plane given coordinates for the vertices; use coordinates to find the length of a side joining points with the same first coordinate or the same second coordinate. Apply these techniques in the context of solving real-world and mathematical problems.

6.NS.3: Fluently add, subtract, multiply, and divide multi-digit decimals using the standard algorithm for each operation.

6.NS.8: Solve real-world and mathematical problems by graphing points in all four quadrants of the coordinate plane. Include use of coordinates and absolute value to find distances between points with the same first coordinate or the same second coordinate

"UNWRAPPED" Priority Standards

6.G.4: REPRESENT three-dimensional figures using nets made up of rectangles and triangles, and USE the nets TO FIND the surface area of these figures. APPLY these techniques in the context of SOLVING real-world and mathematical problems.

"Unwrapped" Concepts (students need to know)	"Unwrapped" Skills (students need to be able to do)	Taxonomy Levels	
		Bloom's / DOK	

• Nets
   • Triangles
   • Rectangles
	• REPRESENT (3D figures using nets made up of rectangles and triangles)	2	2

• Three-dimensional figures
   • Pyramids
   • Prisms
	• USE (nets)
	   TO FIND (surface area)
		3	3

• Surface Area
   • Pyramids
   • Prisms
 	
 • Real-World Problems
	• APPLY (techniques)
	   TO SOLVE (real-world and mathematical problems)
		3	2

Essential Questions	Corresponding Big Ideas
What is a net? What is its mathematical function?	A net is a two-dimensional pattern of a three-dimensional figure that can be folded to form the figure. When laid flat, a net helps you determine the total surface area of a 3-D figure.
How does area relate to surface area?	Surface area is the sum of all of the individual areas of each of the parts.

Source: 6th Grade RCD Curriculum Design Team, San Diego Unified School District, San Diego, CA

Rigorous Curriculum Design Math Unit Planning Organizer
Grade 7: San Diego Unified School District

Subject(s)	Mathematics
Grade/Course	Grade 7
Unit of Study	Unit 7: Geometric Figures—"Dimensions of My World"
Pacing	16 Instructional Days + 4 Buffer (Total 20 days)
Overview of Unit	The standards in this unit focus on the critical area of focus, problem solving with area, surface area and volume working with 2- and 3-dimensional shapes. These shapes are composed of triangles, quadrilaterals, polygons, cubes, and right prisms. Students relate 3-dimensional figures to two-dimensional figures by examining cross sections. They solve real-world and mathematical problems involving area, surface area, and volume of 2- & 3-dimensional objects composed of triangles, quadrilaterals, polygons, cubes, and right prisms. Students will explore these concepts through authentic performance tasks and the continual use of the Mathematical Practice Standards leads to the habits of mind critical for success. Throughout this unit, students will engage in authentic performance tasks, which build understanding in response to the unit's Essential Questions.

Priority Common Core State Standards
Supporting Standards

7.G.6: Solve real-world and mathematical problems involving area, volume and surface area of two- and three-dimensional objects composed of triangles, quadrilaterals, polygons, cubes, and right prisms.

  7.G.3: Describe the two-dimensional figures that result from slicing three-dimensional figures, as in plane sections of right rectangular prisms and right rectangular pyramids.

  7.G.4: Know the formulas for the area and circumference of a circle and use them to solve problems; give an informal derivation of the relationship between the circumference and area of a circle.

  7.RP.3: Use proportional relationships to solve multistep ratio and percent problems. *Examples: simple interest, tax, markups and markdowns, gratuities and commissions, fees, percent increase and decrease, percent error.*

"UNWRAPPED" Priority Standards

7.G.6: SOLVE real-world and mathematical problems involving area, volume and surface area of two- and three-dimensional objects composed of triangles, quadrilaterals, polygons, cubes, and right prisms.

"Unwrapped" Concepts (students need to know)	"Unwrapped" Skills (students need to be able to do)	Taxonomy Levels	
		Bloom's / DOK	

• Area of 2-dimensional objects composed of
   • triangles
   • quadrilaterals
   • polygons
 	
• Volume & Surface Area of 3-dimensional objects composed of
   • Cubes
   • Right prisms
 	
• Surface Area of 3-dimensional objects composed of
   • triangles
   • quadrilaterals
   • polygons
	SOLVE (real-world & mathematical problems)	4	3

Essential Questions	Corresponding Big Ideas
How do I find the area of irregular figures? (example: basketball key)	The area of a 2-dimensional shape can be found by finding the areas of triangles, quadrilaterals, polygons and circles.* (conservation of area)
What solid figures are found in an irregular structure in the world around us?	A 3-dimensional real-world object is not always just a right prism. You may have to put 2 or more solids together to make the object.
How do I find the surface area and volume of irregular solids?	It is easier to find the surface area or volume of an object by making an object into simpler shapes.
	*While area of circles is not part of the Priority Standard, it is in a supporting standard for this unit and represents an important mathematical understanding students need to acquire.

Source: 7th Grade RCD Curriculum Design Team, San Diego Unified School District, San Diego, CA

Rigorous Curriculum Design Math Unit Planning Organizer
Grade 7: San Diego Unified School District

Subject(s)	Mathematics
Grade/Course	Grade 7
Unit of Study	Statistics: What Do We Have In Common? (Unit 8)
Pacing	Total: 12 Instruction Days + 3 "Buffer" Days

"UNWRAPPED" Common Core Priority Standards ONLY

7.SP.4: USE measures of center and measures of variability for numerical data from random samples to DRAW informal comparative inferences about two populations. *For example, decide whether the words in a chapter of a seventh-grade science book are generally longer than the words in a chapter of a fourth-grade science book.*

"Unwrapped" Concepts (students need to know)	"Unwrapped" Skills (students need to be able to do)	Taxonomy Levels	
		Bloom's / DOK	
• Measures of center • Measures of variability for numerical data from random samples	USE	2	2
• informal comparison two populations	DRAW (INFER)	4, 5	3

Essential Questions	Corresponding Big Ideas
How can we use the mean, median, mode, and range to describe and compare a set of data?	The same data can be expressed in multiple ways.
Why are certain representations of data more useful than others?	The way data is expressed can help us understand and analyze it.
Why do we use random samples?	Choosing the appropriate data representation will help to compare and analyze the data.

Source: 7th Grade RCD Curriculum Design Team, San Diego Unified School District, San Diego, CA

Rigorous Curriculum Design Math Unit Planning Organizer
Grade 8: San Diego Unified School District

Subject(s)	Mathematics
Grade/Course	8
Unit of Study	Unit 1: Really? Rational or Irrational? (Number Sense)
Pacing	10 days, 5-day buffer

"UNWRAPPED" Priority Standards ONLY

8.NS.2: USE rational approximations of irrational numbers to COMPARE the size of irrational numbers, LOCATE them approximately on a number line diagram, and ESTIMATE the value of expressions (e.g., $\pi 2$). For example, by truncating the decimal expansion of $\sqrt{2}$, show that $\sqrt{2}$ is between 1 and 2, then between 1.4 and 1.5, and explain how to continue on to get better approximations.

"Unwrapped" Concepts (students need to know)	"Unwrapped" Skills (students need to be able to do)	Taxonomy Levels	
		Bloom's / DOK	
Rational approximations of irrational numbers	USE	4	2
The size of irrational numbers	to COMPARE	2	2
Approximations of irrational numbers on a number line	LOCATE	1	1
Value of irrational expressions	ESTIMATE	3	2

Essential Questions	Corresponding Big Ideas
What are the different sets of real numbers? How do you determine which set each number belongs to?	Every number has a decimal expansion and can be categorized as rational or irrational.
Why do I use 3.14 instead of an exact value for π?	Estimating the value of irrational numbers allows for quick comparison to rational numbers.
Why is using a number line as a visual helpful for estimating the value of an irrational number?	The value of every irrational number lies between two consecutive integers.

Source: 8th Grade RCD Curriculum Design Team, San Diego Unified School District, San Diego, CA

McMinnville School District—Grade 6

Subject(s)	Math
Grade/Course	6th Grade
Unit of Study	Fractions
Pacing	1 Month

"UNWRAPPED" Priority Standards

6.NS.1: INTERPRET and COMPUTE quotients of fractions, and SOLVE word problems involving division of fractions by fractions, e.g., by USING visual fraction models and equations to represent the problem. *For example, create a story context for (2/3) ÷ (3/4) and use a visual fraction model to show the quotient; use the relationship between multiplication and division to explain that (2/3) ÷ (3/4) = 8/9 because 3/4 of 8/9 is 2/3. (In general, (a/b) ÷ (c/d) = ad/bc.) How much chocolate will each person get if 3 people share 1/2 lb of chocolate equally? How many 3/4-cup servings are in 2/3 of a cup of yogurt? How wide is a rectangular strip of land with length 3/4 mi and area 1/2 square mi?*

"Unwrapped" Concepts (students need to know)	"Unwrapped" Skills (students need to be able to do)	Bloom's Taxonomy Levels
Quotients of fractions	INTERPRET/COMPUTE	3
Fractions divided by fractions word problems	SOLVE	3
Visual fraction models and equations to represent word problems	USE	3

Essential Questions	Corresponding Big Ideas
How do you divide fractions?	Fractions are divided by using an algorithm (in common terms known as "keep it, switch it, flip it").
How can division of fractions be modeled?	To model the division of fractions, draw the dividend, circle groups the size of the divisor, and count the groups to get the quotient.
What is another way to write a fraction division problem?	Division problems can be represented with equations.

Source: Grade 6 Team, McMinnville School District, McMinnville, OR

McMinnville School District—Grade 7

UNIT NUMBER 7	RP PROP BLOCK 2
Unit Length	**25 instructional days**
"Unwrapped" PRIORITY Standards	**7.RP.2: RECOGNIZE and REPRESENT** proportional relationships between quantities. a. **DECIDE** whether two quantities are in a proportional relationship, e.g., by testing for equivalent ratios in a table or graphing on a coordinate plane and observing whether the graph is a straight line through the origin. b. **IDENTIFY** the constant of proportionality (unit rate) in tables, graphs, equations, diagrams, and verbal descriptions of proportional relationships. c. **REPRESENT** proportional relationships by equations. *For example, if total cost t is proportional to the number n of items purchased at a constant price p, the relationship between the total cost and the number of items can be expressed as t = pn.* **7.G.A.1: SOLVE** problems involving scale drawings of geometric figures, including **COMPUTING** actual lengths and areas from a scale drawing and **REPRODUCING** a scale drawing at a different scale.

"Unwrapped" PRIORITY Standards Graphic Organizer	Concepts	Skills	Bloom's
	7.RP.2		
	• Proportional relationships	RECOGNIZE	2
		REPRESENT	2
	• 2 quantities are in a proportional relationship	DECIDE	2
	• Constant of proportionality	IDENTIFY	4
	• Proportional relationships by equations	REPRESENT	2
	• Scale drawings	SOLVE	3
	• Actual lengths/areas	COMPUTE	3
	• Scale drawing (different scale)	REPRODUCE	5

Supporting Standards	7.RP.1: Compute unit rates associated with ratios of fractions, including ratios of lengths, areas and other quantities measured in like or different units.
Essential Question	How are proportions used to solve real-world problems including those involving scale factors?
Big Idea	Proportions are used to calculate costs, actual lengths and areas of drawings, and different scales.

Source: Grade 7 RCD Team, McMinnville School District, McMinnville, Oregon

McMinnville School District—Grade 8

UNIT NUMBER	LE Block 3
Unit Length	**4 weeks**
"Unwrapped" PRIORITY Standards	**8.EE.5:** GRAPH proportional relationships, INTERPRETING the unit rate as the slope of the graph. COMPARE two different proportional relationships represented in different ways. For example, compare distance-time graph to a distance-time equation to determine which of two moving objects has a greater speed. **8.F.2:** COMPARE properties of two functions each represented in a different way (algebraically, graphically, numerically, and tables, or by verbal descriptions). For example, given a linear function represented by a table of values and a linear function represented by an algebraic expression, determine which function has the greater rate of change. **8.F.3:** INTERPRET the equation y=mx+b as defining a linear function, whose graph is a straight line; GIVE EXAMPLES of functions that are not linear. For example, the function A = s^2 giving the area of a square as a function of its side length is not linear because its graph contains the points (1,1), (2,4) and (3,9), which are not a straight line. **8.F.1:** UNDERSTAND that a function is a rule that assigns to each input exactly one output. The graph of a function is the set of ordered pairs consisting of an input and the corresponding output. (Function notation is not required at grade 8).

	Concepts	Skills	Bloom's
"Unwrapped" PRIORITY Standards Graphic Organizer	Proportional relationships	GRAPH	3–4
	Equation y=mx+b whose graph is a straight line	INTERPRET	4
	Proportional relationships represented in different ways. Functions represented: • Algebraically • Graphically • Numerically • Table • Verbal Descriptions	COMPARE	2
	Functions that are not linear	GIVE EXAMPLES	1
	Function is a rule that assigns each input to exactly one corresponding output	UNDERSTAND	2

UNIT NUMBER	LE Block 3 *(continued)*
Supporting Standards	8.F.4: Construct a function to model a linear relationship between two quantities. Determine the rate of change and initial value of the function from a description of a relationship or from two ordered pairs (x,y) values, including reading these from a table or from a graph. Interpret the rate of change and initial value of a linear function in terms of the situation it models, and in terms of its graph or table of values.
Essential Questions	What are the properties of slope-intercept form? How do I compare linear equations in algebraic, graphic, numeric, verbal, and table form? How do I interpret properties of linear equations in algebraic, graphic, numeric, verbal, and table form? What are functions? What are examples of non-linear functions?
Big Ideas	Slope is the rate of change (vertical change over horizontal change) and y-intercept is where the graph crosses the y-axis. Slope and y-intercept can be interpreted from algebraic, graphic, numeric, verbal, and table form. Functions are rules in math that assign one input to exactly one output. Students will be able to provide examples of non-linear functions (no constant rate of change).

Source: Grade 8 RCD Team, McMinnville School District, McMinnville, Oregon

West Hartford, CT
Middle School Math Design Team

Subject(s)	Math
Grade/Course	Grade 6
Unit of Study	Unit 1: Statistics—Data Distribution
Pacing	20 days (15 instructional days and 5 reteach/enrichment days)

Common Core Priority Standards

6.SP.2: Understand that a set of data collected to answer a statistical question has a distribution, which can be described, by its center, spread, and overall shape.

Summarize and describe distributions:

6.SP.5c: Giving quantitative measures of center (median and/or mean) and variability (inter-quartile range and/or mean absolute deviation), as well as describing any overall pattern and any striking deviations from the overall pattern with reference to the context in which the data were gathered.

6.SP.5d: Relating the choice of measures of center and variability to the shape of the data distribution and the context in which the data were gathered.

Supporting Standards

.SP.1: Recognize a statistical question as one that anticipates variability in the data related to the question and accounts for it in the answers.

6.SP.3: Recognize that a measure of center for a numerical data set summarizes all of its values with a single number, while a measure of variation describes how its values vary with a single number.

6.SP.4: Display numerical data in plots on a number line, including dot plots, histograms, and box plots.

Summarize numerical data sets in relation to their context, such as by:

6.SP.5a: Reporting the number of observations.
6.SP.5b. Describing the nature of the attribute under investigation including how it was measured and its units of measurement.

6.NS.2: Fluently divide multi-digit numbers using the standard algorithm.

6.NS.3: Fluently add, subtract, multiply, and divide multi-digit decimals using the standard algorithm for each operation.

"UNWRAPPED" Priority Standards

6.SP.2: UNDERSTAND that a set of data collected to answer a statistical question has a distribution, which can be DESCRIBED, by its center, spread, and overall shape.

SUMMARIZE and DESCRIBE distributions:

6.SP.5c: GIVING quantitative measures of center (median and/or mean) and variability (inter-quartile range and/or mean absolute deviation), as well as DESCRIBING any overall pattern and any striking deviations from the overall pattern with reference to the context in which the data were gathered.

6.SP.5d: RELATING the choice of measures of center and variability to the shape of the data distribution and the context in which the data were gathered.

"Unwrapped" Concepts (Students need to know)	"Unwrapped" Skills (Students need to be able to do)	Bloom's and DOK Levels
6.SP.2 Distribution of data • Center • Spread • Shape	UNDERSTAND DESCRIBE	(B2, W2) (B2, W2)
6.SP.5c Numerical data • Measures of center (median, mean) • Variability (range, deviation) • Overall pattern • Striking deviation (outlier)	SUMMARIZE • Give (calculate) • Describe (in context) • Describe (with reference to what was being measured)	(B2, W2) (B3, W2) (B4, W4)
6.SP.5d Choice of measures of center and respective variability (median/inter-quartile range or mean/absolute deviation)	RELATING	(B5, W3)

Essential Questions	Corresponding Big Ideas
1. What are data?	1. Data are facts and statistics collected together for reference or analysis of real-world problems.
2. How can data be described and used?	2. Data can be described by their shape and used to summarize and evaluate the information they represent.
3. Which method should you choose to best describe the data?	3. Choosing the appropriate method to summarize and evaluate data depends on the context.

Source: Middle School Math RCD Curriculum Design Team, West Hartford Public Schools, West Hartford, CT

CHAPTER 8

High School Examples

One of the most beneficial features of the original *"Unwrapping" the Standards* (2003) book was its inclusion of more than 85 examples of "unwrapped" standards, Big Ideas, and Essential Questions specific to each grade span, K–2, 3–5, 6–8, and 9–12, from numerous content areas. Educators always appreciate seeing examples: especially Big Ideas and Essential Questions. These concrete samples help greatly to convey what the explanatory content describes. For these reasons, I knew it was important to include in this volume similar examples of "unwrapped" Common Core State Standards in English language arts and literacy and in mathematics.

Four school systems that I have worked closely with, two in the eastern United States and two in the West, graciously responded to my request for "unwrapped" Common Core examples created by their educators. The two east coast districts are West Hartford and Bloomfield, both in Connecticut. The two west coast districts are San Diego Unified School District in California and McMinnville School District in Oregon. It was my great privilege over a period of many months to lead their educators and leaders through the Rigorous Curriculum Design framework I created to help educators write new curricula for the Common Core. The four parts of the "unwrapping" process were the first steps they followed in developing their curricular units of study in English language arts and literacy and in math that later included unit-specific formative and summative assessments, authentic performance tasks, instructional resources, and differentiated instructional strategies.

In addition, Lori Cook, my former colleague from The Leadership and Learning Center also stepped forward to share a high school algebra example she created for her "unwrapping" work with school districts across the country.

I always encourage educators and curriculum writers to follow the framework of "unwrapping" and curriculum design as prescribed but then to "make the process their own" by customizing the format for their units of study. Reprinted here are the first sections of the Rigorous Curriculum Design Unit Planning Organizer you have seen throughout the previous explanatory chapters. Many grade-level or course-level design teams in the four districts used this template as is; others chose to modify it somewhat. To respect their particular district formatting, I have included the graphic organizers as they were submitted to me. Because you now understand the complete "unwrapping" process, you will be able to understand the content represented in these district examples even when it varies from my original format. Also, note that not every district included both Bloom's *and* DOK cognitive levels on their initial graphic organizers.

I have organized these grade-span examples by district and by content area, rather than interspersing all the examples for each grade level. This will make each district's examples "self-contained" and hopefully easier for you to read and understand.

Rigorous Curriculum Design Unit Planning Organizer

Subject(s)	
Grade/Course	
Unit of Study	
Pacing	

Priority Common Core State Standards (Bolded) Supporting Standards

"UNWRAPPED" Priority Standards

"Unwrapped" Concepts (students need to know)	**"Unwrapped" Skills** (students need to be able to do)	**Taxonomy Levels**	
		Bloom's / DOK	

Essential Questions	**Corresponding Big Ideas**

ELA EXAMPLES

Rigorous Curriculum Design ELA Unit Planning Organizer
Grade 9: San Diego Unified School District

Subject(s)	English
Grade/Course	9th Grade
Unit of Study	Unit 2
Pacing	Total Days Instruction + "Buffer": TBD

"UNWRAPPED" Priority Standards

RL.9–10.2 and RI.9–10.2: DETERMINE a theme or central idea of a text and ANALYZE in detail its development over the course of the text, including how it emerges and is shaped and refined by specific details; PROVIDE an objective summary of the text.

RL.9–10.3: ANALYZE how complex characters (e.g., those with multiple or conflicting motivations) develop over the course of a text, interact with other characters, and advance the plot or develop the theme.

RI.9–10.9: ANALYZE seminal U.S. documents of historical and literary significance.

W.9–10.1: WRITE arguments to support claims in an analysis of substantive topics or texts, USING valid reasoning and relevant and sufficient evidence.

L.9–10.1: DEMONSTRATE command of the conventions of standard English Grammar and usage when writing and speaking.

"Unwrapped" Concepts (students need to know)	"Unwrapped" Skills (students need to be able to do)	Taxonomy Levels Bloom's / DOK	
Theme or central idea of a text	DETERMINE—theme or central idea	4	2
Development of text; how it is shaped by specific details	ANALYZE—development of the text with specific detail	4	3
Objective summary of text	PROVIDE—objective summary	2	3
How complex characters develop over the course of a text, interact with characters, and advance the plot or develop the theme	ANALYZE—how complex characters develop over the course of a text, interact with other characters, and advance the plot or develop the theme	4	3
Seminal U.S. documents of historical and literary significance	ANALYZE—documents of historical/literary significance	4	3
Argument and analysis	WRITE—arguments SUPPORT—claims	6 4/5	4 4
Substantive topics or texts Valid, sufficient, and relevant evidence	ANALYZE (substantive topics or texts) • USE (valid reasoning) • USE (relevant and sufficient evidence)	5 4	4 4
Standard English Grammar writing and speaking	DEMONSTRATE—command of the conventions of standard English Grammar and usage when writing and speaking	3	2

Essential Questions	Corresponding Big Ideas
• How does time period affect a text?	• Understanding the political context and time period helps you analyze theme and author's purpose.
• Why do we learn about history when we are reading a novel?	• Understanding history/historical texts creates connections between culture and literature.
• How do I create a solid, credible argument?	• Effective arguments include logical reasoning and proof, in addition to revealing mastery of language.
• Why do character actions matter to a novel?	• Complexity of character advances the plot and develops the theme.

Source: 9th Grade RCD Curriculum Design Team, San Diego Unified School District, San Diego, CA

Rigorous Curriculum Design ELA Unit Planning Organizer
Grade 10: San Diego Unified School District

Subject(s)	English Language Arts
Grade/Course	10th
Unit of Study	Name TBD

"UNWRAPPED" Common Core Priority Standards

RL.9–10.3: ANALYZE how complex characters (e.g., those with multiple or conflicting motivations) develop over the course of a text, interact with other characters, and advance the plot or develop the theme.

RL.9–10.5: ANALYZE an author's choices concerning how to structure a text, order events within it (e.g., parallel plots), and manipulate time (e.g., pacing, flashbacks) to create such effects as mystery, tension, or surprise.

RL.9–10.6: ANALYZE a particular point of view or cultural experience reflected in a work from outside the United States, drawing on a wide reading of World Literature.

RI.9–10.3: ANALYZE how the author unfolds an analysis or series of ideas and events, including the order in which the points are made, how they are introduced and developed, and the connections that are drawn between them.

RI.9–10.6: DETERMINE an author's point of view or purpose in a text and ANALYZE how an author uses rhetoric to advance that point of view or purpose.

W.9–10.1: WRITE arguments to support claims in an analysis of substantive topics or texts, USING valid reasoning and relevant and sufficient evidence.

"Unwrapped" Concepts (students need to know)	"Unwrapped" Skills (students need to be able to do)	Taxonomy Levels	
		Bloom's	DOK

RL.9–10.3: Know Characters
• Their conflicts
• Motivations
• Sequence of events
• Complex verses simple/or prop characters
  1. How they develop
  2. How they interact
  3. How they advance the plot
  4. Develop the theme
	ANALYZE (Complex characters)	4	4

RL.9–10.5: Know text structure • Order of events • Time (flashbacks/sequential sequence) • Emotion	ANALYZE how author manipulates scenes and characters	4	2

"Unwrapped" Concepts (students need to know)	"Unwrapped" Skills (students need to be able to do)	Taxonomy Levels	
		Bloom's / DOK	
RL.9–10.6: Know the cultural experience of Latino authors • Draw on a wide reading of world literature	ANALYZE (point of view)	4	4
RI.9–10.3: Know the ideas • Order • How they are introduced and developed • Connections drawn	ANALYZE (how author presents information)	4	3
RI.9–10.6: Know rhetoric, writing convention, styles • Rhetoric • Presentation • Advancement of point of view • Tone • Inferences	DETERMINE point of view (analyze point of view/ purpose)	5	4
W.9–10.1: • Arguments to support claims • Analysis of substantive topics or texts • Valid reasoning • Relevant and sufficient evidence	WRITE (argumentative essay using valid reasoning and relevant and sufficient evidence)	6	4

Essential Questions	Corresponding Big Ideas
How do narratives help us understand cultures different from our own and the political and social issues of those cultures?	Narratives contextualize and humanize major political/social issues and events, engaging readers in the consideration of cultures, perspectives, and experiences different than their own.
How do political, social, and cultural contexts shape our understanding of characters, conflicts, and themes in a novel?	Understanding the cultural context (position in the world, belief systems, religions, conflicts, cultural norms) in which a novel is set helps readers analyze the themes of a novel.
How does an author's personal experience influence the stories he/she tells?	Authors draw on their personal experiences to reflect the larger cultural issues they want readers to reflect on and to bring about social change.

Source: 10th Grade RCD Curriculum Design Team, San Diego Unified School District, San Diego, CA

Rigorous Curriculum Design ELA Unit Planning Organizer
Grade 11: San Diego Unified School District

Subject(s)	English
Grade/Course	11th Grade American Literature
Unit of Study	Rationalism (Age of Reason)
Pacing	Total Days Instruction + "Buffer": TBD

"UNWRAPPED" Priority Standards

RI.11–12.2: DETERMINE two or more central ideas of a text and ANALYZE their development over the course of the text, including how they interact and build on one another to provide a complex analysis; PROVIDE an objective summary of the text.

RI.11–12.6: DETERMINE an author's point of view or purpose in a text in which the rhetoric is particularly effective, ANALYZING how style and content contribute to the power, persuasiveness, or beauty of the text.

"Unwrapped" Concepts (students need to know)	"Unwrapped" Skills (students need to be able to do)	Taxonomy Levels Bloom's / DOK	
• Central ideas—2 or more	DETERMINE	2	2
• Development over course of a text • How they interact and build on one another	ANALYZE	4	4
• Objective summary of text	PROVIDE	4	2
• Author's point of view or purpose • Effective rhetoric	DETERMINE	2	2

• How style and content contribute to
  • Power
  • Persuasiveness
  • Beauty
	ANALYZE	5	3

Essential Questions	Corresponding Big Ideas
Which themes are unique to the American experience?	The American identity is derived from ideals and values from the Age of Reason. These include natural rights endowed by The Creator (life, liberty, property), and democracy.
How do rhetorical devices help reveal the author's point of view/purpose?	Authors employ effective rhetorical devices and persuasive content to reveal a compelling point of view/purpose.

Source: 11th Grade RCD Curriculum Design Team, San Diego Unified School District, San Diego, CA

McMinnville School District—Grade 9

Subject(s)	Language Arts
Grade/Course	9th Grade
Unit of Study	Unit 3 Style Analysis

"UNWRAPPED" Priority Standards or Learning Outcomes
Supporting Standards/Outcomes

- RL.9–10.4: **DETERMINE** the meaning of words and phrases as they are used in the text, including figurative and connotative meanings; **ANALYZE** the cumulative impact of specific word choices on meaning and tone (e.g., how the language evokes a sense of time and place; how it sets a formal or informal tone).

- W.9–10.2: **WRITE** informative/explanatory texts to **EXAMINE** and **CONVEY** complex ideas, concepts, and information clearly and accurately through the effective selection, organization, and analysis of content.

- W.9–10.4: **PRODUCE** clear and coherent writing in which the development, organization, and style are appropriate to task, purpose, and audience. (Grade-specific expectations for writing types are defined in standards 1–3 above.)

- L.9–10.3: **APPLY** knowledge of language to **UNDERSTAND** how language functions in different contexts, to **MAKE EFFECTIVE CHOICES** for meaning or style, and to **COMPREHEND** more fully when reading or listening.

- L.9–10.5: **DEMONSTRATE** understanding of figurative language, word relationships, and nuances in word meanings.
    - **INTERPRET** figures of speech (e.g., euphemism, oxymoron) in context and **ANALYZE** their role in the text.

"Unwrapped" Concepts (students need to know)	"Unwrapped" Skills (students need to be able to do)	Bloom's Taxonomy Levels
• Meaning of words and phrases	DETERMINE	5
• cumulative impact of specific word choices on meaning and tone	ANALYZE	4
• informative/explanatory texts	WRITE	6
• complex ideas, concepts, and information clearly and accurately	EXAMINE / CONVEY	4
• clear and coherent writing	PRODUCE	6
• knowledge of language	APPLY	3
• language functions	UNDERSTAND	2
• for meaning or style • when reading or listening	MAKE EFFECTIVE CHOICES	2
• figurative language, word relationships, and nuances in word meanings	COMPREHEND DEMONSTRATE	2 3, 4

Essential Questions	Corresponding Big Ideas
1. How does an author develop the tone or attitude in a piece of literature?	1. The author's tone/attitude is created by specific language choices made throughout the piece.
2. Why do authors use figurative language?	2. Figurative language is used to create tone, mood, and atmosphere in a piece of literature. It is what makes literature come to life for the reader.
3. Why is it important to produce a clear and coherent piece of writing?	3. Clear concise writing is essential to getting one's ideas across to their audience.

Source: Grade 9 RCD Team, McMinnville School District, McMinnville, Oregon

McMinnville School District—Grade 9

Subject(s)	Language Arts
Grade/Course	9th Grade
Unit of Study	Literary Elements and the Short Story

"UNWRAPPED" Priority Standards or Learning Outcomes
Supporting Standards/Outcomes

- RL.9–10.1: **Cite** strong and thorough textual evidence to **support** analysis of what the text says explicitly as well as inferences drawn from the text.

- RL.9–10.5: **Analyze** how an author's choices concerning how to structure a text, order events within it (e.g., parallel plots), and manipulate time (e.g., pacing, flashbacks) create such effects as mystery, tension, or surprise.

- W.9–10.2.a: **Introduce** a topic; **organize** complex ideas, concepts, and information to **make** important connections and distinctions; include formatting (e.g., headings), graphics (e.g., figures, tables), and multimedia when useful to aiding comprehension.

"Unwrapped" Concepts (students need to know)	"Unwrapped" Skills (students need to be able to do)	Bloom's Taxonomy Levels
Evidence (explicit and inferred)	CITE	3
Author's Choices—how they create literary effects (mystery, tension, surprise)	ANALYZE	4
A topic	INTRODUCE	2
Complex ideas	ORGANIZE	5
Important connections	MAKE	5

Essential Questions	Corresponding Big Ideas
1. How does an author create suspense or mystery through plot development?	1. An author's choice of how to structure text, order events within a plot, or manipulate time all work to create mystery and/or suspense within a story.
2. What is the purpose of a thesis sentence?	2. A thesis sentence communicates one's perspective about a topic.
3. What is the function of an introductory paragraph?	3. An introductory paragraph acts as a road map for the reader; it gives the reader a set of directions for how to get through the text.

Source: Grade 9 RCD Team, McMinnville School District, McMinnville, Oregon

McMinnville School District—Grade 10

Subject(s)	Social Studies
Grade/Course	Modern History II (10 Grade) and Literacy
Unit of Study	Civil Rights
Pacing	4 Weeks (10 class periods)

Priority Standards
Supporting Standards

History

HS.5: Examine and evaluate the origins of fundamental political debates and how conflict, compromise, and cooperation have shaped national unity and diversity in world, U.S., and Oregon history. (Historical Knowledge Standard)

HS.6: Analyze ideas critical to the understanding of history, including, but not limited to: populism, progressivism, isolationism, imperialism, communism, environmentalism, liberalism, fundamentalism, racism, ageism, classism, conservationism, cultural diversity, feminism, and sustainability. (Historical Knowledge Standard)

HS.57: Define, research, and explain an event, issue, problem, or phenomenon and its significance to society. (Social Science Analysis Standard)

Priority Common Core Literacy Standards (CCSS)

Reading

RH.9–10.3: Analyze in detail a series of events described in text; determine whether earlier events caused later ones or simply preceded them.

RH.9–10.7: Integrate quantitative or technical analysis (charts, research data) with qualitative analysis in print or digital text.

Writing

W.9–10.2.b: Develop the topic with well-chosen, relevant, and sufficient facts, definitions, concrete details, quotations, or other information and examples appropriate to the audience's knowledge of the topic.

W.9–10.4: Produce clear and coherent writing in which the development, organization, and style are appropriate to task, purpose, and audience.

"Unwrapped" Priority Standards

History

HS.5: **Examine** and **evaluate** the origins of fundamental political debates and how conflict, compromise, and cooperation have shaped national unity and diversity in world, U.S., and Oregon history.

HS.6: **Analyze** ideas critical to the understanding of history, including, but not limited to: populism, progressivism, isolationism, imperialism, communism, environmentalism, liberalism, fundamentalism, racism, ageism, classism, conservationism, cultural diversity, feminism, and sustainability.

HS.57: **Define, research,** and **explain** an event, issue, problem, or phenomenon and its significance to society.

Reading

RH.9–10.3: **Analyze** in detail a series of events described in text; **determine** whether earlier events caused later ones or simply preceded them.

RH.9–10.7: **Integrate** quantitative or technical analysis (charts, research data) with qualitative **analysis** in print or digital text.

Writing

W.9–10.2.b: **Develop** the topic with well-chosen, relevant, and sufficient facts, extended definitions, concrete details, quotations, or other information and examples appropriate to the audience's knowledge of the topic.

W.9–10.4: **Produce** clear and coherent writing in which the development, organization, and style are appropriate to task, purpose, and audience.

"Unwrapped" Concepts (students need to know)	"Unwrapped" Skills (students need to be able to do)	Bloom's Taxonomy Levels
History Origins of fundamental political debates	Examine	4
How conflict, compromise, cooperation have shaped national unity and diversity	Evaluate	5
Ideas: Liberalism, racism, ageism, classism, cultural diversity,	Analyze	4
Event, issue, problem, phenomenon Significance to society	Define, Research, Explain	1 1–6 2
Reading Series of events described (whether earlier events caused later ones or just preceded them)	Analyze Determine	4 4
Quantitative or technical analysis Qualitative analysis	Integrate Analysis	4 4
Writing Topic (see standard for details) Clear and coherent writing (see standard for details)	Develop Produce	3 6

Essential Questions	Corresponding Big Ideas
1. How did segregation separate the nation, states, and local communities?	1. The separatists and the integrationists involved in the conflict held conflicting views and aims.
2. What legislation provided protection against discrimination for all citizens?	2. The government had considerable influence over the laws of the land.
3. What economic programs were created by the government to help segregated groups?	3. The government created programs to help improve the social status of segregated groups that still continue today.

Source: Grade 10 RCD Team, McMinnville School District, McMinnville, Oregon

MATH EXAMPLES

Note: McMinnville School District and West Hartford Public Schools are following the *traditional* pathway for high school math courses. San Diego Unified is in the process of transitioning to the *integrated* pathway, as shown in the final math example.

McMinnville School District—Grade 9

Subject(s)	Algebra 1
Grade/Course	Grade 9/Algebra 1
Unit of Study	Unit 1—Linear Equations and One-Variable Inequalities

"UNWRAPPED" Priority Standards or Learning Outcomes Supporting Standards/Outcomes	
N.Q.1	Use units as a way to understand problems and to guide the solution of multi-step problems; choose and interpret units consistently in formulas; choose and interpret the scale and the origin in graphs and data displays.
A-CED.1	Create equations and inequalities in one variable and use them to solve problems. *Include equations arising from linear and quadratic functions, and simple rational and exponential functions.*
A-CED.4	Rearrange formulas to highlight a quantity of interest, using the same reasoning as in solving equations. *For example, rearrange Ohm's law V = IR to highlight resistance R.*
A-REI.1	Explain each step in solving a simple equation as following from the equality of numbers asserted at the previous step, starting from the assumption that the original equation has a solution. Construct a viable argument to justify a solution method.
A-REI.3	Solve linear equations and inequalities in one variable, including equations with coefficients represented by letters.

"Unwrapped" Concepts (students need to know)	"Unwrapped" Skills (students need to be able to do)	Bloom's Taxonomy Levels
N.Q.1—Understanding Units • Multi-Step Problems • Scales and Graphs • Formula	DESCRIBE CHOOSE and INTERPRET	2 3
A.CED.1—Equations and Inequalities • One-Variable • Equations and Inequalities • Linear	CREATE SOLVE	5 3
A.CED.4—Solve for a Variable • Formulas • Reasoning	REARRANGE and SOLVE USE	5, 3 3
A.REI.1—Justification of Steps in Solving Equations • Step • Argument	EXPLAIN CONSTRUCT	2 5
A.REI.3—Solving Linear Equations and Inequalities	SOLVE	3

Essential Questions	Corresponding Big Ideas
Why are units and scale important?	Units and scale are used to understand and interpret data and solutions.
How do you represent one-variable problems?	Equations and inequalities can be used to represent one-variable problems.
How do you solve a formula for an identified variable?	Formulas can be rearranged to highlight a specific variable.
How do you show your process for solving a one-variable problem?	Every step in solving an equation can be justified using algebraic properties.
How do you solve a linear equation or inequality?	Algebraic properties are used to solve linear equations and inequalities.

Source: Algebra RCD Team, McMinnville School District, McMinnville, Oregon

Rigorous Curriculum Design Unit Planning Organizer
Algebra 1: West Hartford, Connecticut

Subject(s)	Mathematics
Grade/Course	Algebra I
Unit of Study	Unit 3: Functions; Defining Our World
Pacing	17 (+3) Days

Priority Common Core Standards (Bolded)
Supporting Standards

(S) F.IF.1; **(P) F.IF.2;** (S) F.BF.4A

(S) F.LE.1B; (S) F.LE.1C; (S) F.LE.3; (S) F.BF.1A; **(P) F.LE.5**

(P) F.BF.2; (S) F.IF.2; **(P) F.LE.1A;**

(P) F.LE.2

"Unwrapped" Concepts (students need to know)	"Unwrapped" Skills (students need to be able to do)	Bloom's Taxonomy Webb's DOK
Function Notation	USE (Function Notation)	(3, 3)
Functions for Inputs in Domains	EVALUATE (Functions for Inputs in Domains)	(3, 1)
Function Notation Statements in Context	INTERPRET (Function Notation Statements in Context)	(3, 3)
Linear and Exponential Function Growth Over Time	PROVE (How Functions Grow Over Time)	(5, 3)
Parameters in Context Linear & Exponential Function	INTERPRET (Parameters in terms of a context)	(4, 3)
Recursive and Explicit Sequences Arithmetic & Geometric	WRITE (Sequences recursively and with an explicit formula)	(4, 2)
Sequences to model situations and translate between forms Arithmetic & Geometric	USE (Sequences to model situations and TRANSLATE between the two forms)	(4, 3)
Function, given a graph, description of a relationship, or two input-output pairs, reading from a table Linear & exponential, including arithmetic & geometric sequences	CONSTRUCT (functions, given a graph, description of a relationship, or two input-output pairs, reading from a table)	(3, 2)

Essential Questions	Corresponding Big Ideas
1. What are functions and how can we use them to mathematically model real-world situations?	1. Functions are used to mathematically describe relationships where every input (domain) has one and only one output (range), regardless of whether the data is discrete or continuous.
2. What effects do the parameters have on linear, quadratic, and exponential families of functions?	2. Interpreting the parameters of a function (linear, quadratic, exponential) within a context helps to visualize the graph and model the relationship algebraically.
3. How do linear and exponential functions grow over time?	3. There are similarities and differences between the growth rates of linear and exponential functions.

Source: West Hartford High School Math Team, West Hartford, Connecticut

High School, Algebra 1

F.LE.2: CONSTRUCT linear and exponential functions, including arithmetic and geometric sequences, given a graph, a description of a relationship, or two input-output pairs (include reading these from a table).

"Unwrapped" Concepts (students need to know)	"Unwrapped" Skills (students need to be able to do)	Bloom's Taxonomy Level
Linear Functions } arithmetic & geometric sequences Exponential Functions Graph Description of a relationship Two input-output pairs (including reading from a table)	**CONSTRUCT** ↓ GIVEN	**4–6** (to analyze— to create)
Webb's Depth of Knowledge: 1, 2		

Essential Questions	Corresponding Big Ideas
1. Why do we use functions? How can linear functions represent real-world situations?	1. Functions are used to describe situations where a change in one quantity (independent) causes change in another (dependent).
2. What information is included on a table for a function?	2. A table for a function requires independent/dependent variables that produce ordered pairs, which form the graph of the function.
3. How do linear functions grow?	3. A linear function grows at a constant rate (straight line).

Source: Lori Cook, The Leadership and Learning Center

Rigorous Curriculum Design Math Unit Planning Organizer
Integrated Math: San Diego Unified School District

Subject(s)	Mathematics
Grade/Course	Integrated Math I
Unit of Study	Unit 6: Systems of Equations and Inequalities
Pacing	5 weeks (4 weeks + 1-week buffer)

Priority Common Core State Standards
Supporting Standards

A.REI.5: PROVE that, given a system of two equations in two variables, REPLACING one equation by the sum of that equation and a multiple of the other PRODUCES a system with the same solutions. (Linear Combinations/Elimination)

A.REI.11: EXPLAIN why the x-coordinates of the points where the graphs of the equation $y = f(x)$ and $y = g(x)$ intersect are the solutions of the equation $f(x) = g(x)$; FIND the solutions approximately, e.g., USING technology to GRAPH the functions, MAKE tables of values, or FIND successive approximations. Include cases where $f(x)$ and/or $g(x)$ are linear, polynomial, rational, absolute value, exponential, and logarithmic functions. (Note: the emphasis in this unit is only on the first (bolded) part of the standard.)

> A.REI.6: Solve systems of linear equations exactly and approximately (graphs), focusing on pairs of linear equations in two variables

A.REI.12: GRAPH the solutions to a linear inequality in two variables as a half-plane (excluding the boundary in the case of a strict inequality), and GRAPH the solution set to a system of linear inequalities in two variables as the intersection of the corresponding half-planes.

> A.CED.2: Create equations in two or more variables to represent relationships between quantities; graph equations on coordinate axes with labels and scales

A.CED.3: REPRESENT constraints by equations or inequalities, and by systems of equations and/or inequalities, and INTERPRET solutions as viable or nonviable options in a MODELING context.

"UNWRAPPED" Priority Standards ONLY

A.REI.5: PROVE that, given a system of two equations in two variables, REPLACING one equation by the sum of that equation and a multiple of the other PRODUCES a system with the same solutions. (Linear Combinations/Elimination)

A.REI.11: EXPLAIN why the x-coordinates of the points where the graphs of the equation $y = f(x)$ and $y = g(x)$ intersect are the solutions of the equation $f(x) = g(x)$; FIND the solutions approximately, e.g., USING technology to GRAPH the functions, MAKE tables of values, or FIND successive approximations. Include cases where $f(x)$ and/or $g(x)$ are linear, polynomial, rational, absolute value, exponential, and logarithmic functions. (Note: the emphasis in this unit is only on the first (bolded) part of the standard.)

A.REI.12: GRAPH the solutions to a linear inequality in two variables as a half-plane (excluding the boundary in the case of a strict inequality), and GRAPH the solution set to a system of linear inequalities in two variables as the intersection of the corresponding half-planes.

A.CED.3: REPRESENT constraints by equations or inequalities, and by systems of equations and/or inequalities, and INTERPRET solutions as viable or nonviable options in a MODELING context.

"Unwrapped" Concepts (students need to be able to do)	"Unwrapped" Skills (students need to know)	Taxonomy Levels	
		Bloom's / DOK	
A.REI.5			
Prove	Linear combination/Elimination	5	4
Replace	sum of equation and multiple of another	3	1
Produce	same solution	3	1
A.REI.11			
Explain	why x-coordinates where the graphs intersect are solutions	4	3
Find	approximate solutions (via graphing)	2	1
Use	Technology to	3	1
Graph	Functions	3	1
Make	Tables	3	1
Find	Approximations	3	1
A.REI.12			
Graph	solutions to a linear inequality	3	2
Graph	solution set to a system of linear inequalities	3	2
A.CED.3			
Represent	constraints by equations or inequalities, and by systems of equations and/or inequalities	4	2
Interpret	solutions as viable or nonviable in a modeling context	5	3

Essential Questions	Corresponding Big Ideas
Given a real-world situation, how can I create a system of linear equations and/or inequalities and find the solution(s) by using multiple representations?	Writing systems of linear equations and inequalities in two variables allows us to model a real-world situation.
	Solving systems of linear equations and inequalities in two variables enables us to find solutions to difficult life problems.
How are the multiple representations of a solution(s) related to each other?	We can represent solutions algebraically and graphically.
What does the solution(s) to the system of linear equations represent in context?	We can interpret the solution(s) in real-life context.
What does the solution(s) to the system of linear inequalities represent in context?	We can see how multiple representations (Table, Graphically, Word Problem, Algebraically) of a system of equations are interrelated.

Source: High School Math RCD Curriculum Design Team, San Diego Unified School District, San Diego, CA

PART 3

The Big Picture
Connections

CHAPTER 9

Connecting "Unwrapping" the Standards to the "Big Picture"

Rigorous Curriculum Design: How to Create Curricular Units of Study that Align Standards, Instruction, and Assessment (Ainsworth, 2010) was written in response to the emerging need across the nation for school districts to revamp their existing curricula to address the increase in rigor of the Common Core.

Since the units of study curriculum designers create will be based on the foundation of a solid set of vertically aligned Priority Standards and supporting standards, it is absolutely essential to invest the time, energy, and resources needed to establish this standards foundation first.

After the Priority Standards are selected, curriculum design teams of educators will be ready to begin the next foundational step: naming the instructional units of study. These units will "house" both the Priority Standards and the supporting standards.

Following is an overview of the Rigorous Curriculum Design road map and its intentionally sequenced set of steps. To promote shared ownership and in-depth understanding of each of these interconnected steps, it is important that all of them be done *collaboratively* by teams of professional educators with as much involvement as possible by school and district leaders. Note—both in Figure 9.1 and in the section "Design the Curricular Units, From Start to Finish (12 Steps)"—the central role "unwrapping" plays in the entire process of unit design.

Rigorous Curriculum Design Model—An Overview

Part One of the Rigorous Curriculum Design model, "Seeing the Big Picture Connections First," presents a "big picture" diagram (Figure 9.1) that shows the deliberate connections between professional practices that educators have been using successfully for years: Priority Standards, "unwrapping" the standards, common formative assessments, Data Teams, effective teaching strategies, authentic performance tasks, scoring guides, and others. Together, these practices create a cohesive system that educators are implementing over time to improve students' learning— in the classroom and in their corresponding performance on standardized tests.

Parts Two and Three of the Rigorous Curriculum Design model outline the specific steps educators follow to create units of study aligned to the Common Core. They are: "Building a Strong Curricular Foundation" and "Designing the Curricular Units of Study," respectively. Part Four explains how to implement each unit of study. Each step of the entire process is explained in detail with examples in its corresponding chapter of *Rigorous Curriculum Design* (Ainsworth, 2010).

Build a Strong Curricular Foundation (5 Steps)

Before constructing the curricular units of study, it is necessary to first build a strong foundation. Otherwise, curriculum design teams are erecting a superstructure upon an uncertain base. Following is a brief description of each of the five foundational steps:

1. **Prioritize the Standards.** Prioritize and vertically align from grade to grade and course to course the academic content standards (grade- or course-specific CCSS and/or state standards) for selected content areas. These represent the "assured competencies" that students are to know and be able to do by the end of each academic school year so they are prepared to enter the next level of learning.

2. **Name the Units of Study.** Name all of the specific units of study for each grade level and course in the selected content areas. Through these units of study, implemented during the year or course, students will learn and be assessed upon their understanding and application of the particular standards in focus.

3. **Assign Priority Standards and Supporting Standards.** Assign Priority Standards and supporting standards to each unit of study, taking into account "learning

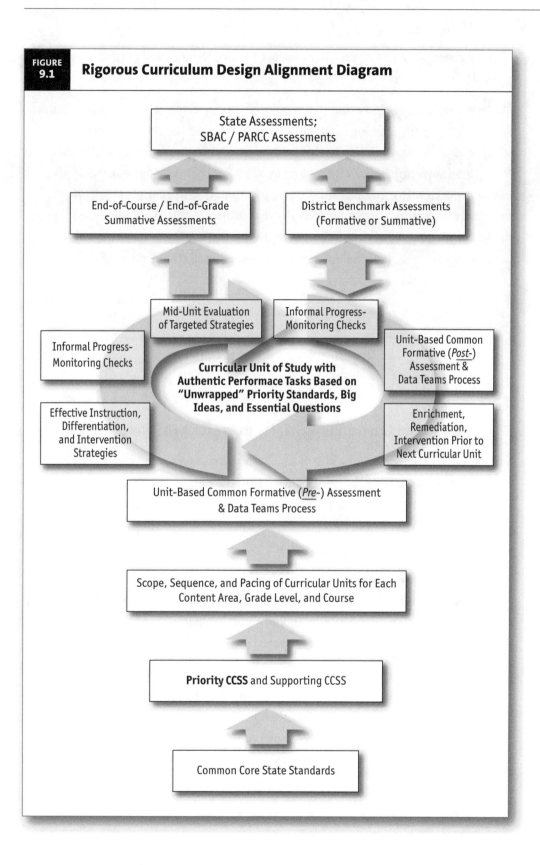

FIGURE 9.1

Rigorous Curriculum Design Alignment Diagram

State Assessments;
SBAC / PARCC Assessments

End-of-Course / End-of-Grade
Summative Assessments

District Benchmark Assessments
(Formative or Summative)

Mid-Unit Evaluation
of Targeted Strategies

Informal Progress-
Monitoring Checks

Informal Progress-
Monitoring Checks

Unit-Based Common
Formative (*Post*-)
Assessment &
Data Teams Process

Curricular Unit of Study with
Authentic Performace Tasks Based on
"Unwrapped" Priority Standards, Big
Ideas, and Essential Questions

Effective Instruction,
Differentiation,
and Intervention
Strategies

Enrichment,
Remediation,
Intervention Prior to
Next Curricular Unit

Unit-Based Common Formative (*Pre*-) Assessment
& Data Teams Process

Scope, Sequence, and Pacing of Curricular Units for Each
Content Area, Grade Level, and Course

Priority CCSS and Supporting CCSS

Common Core State Standards

progressions"—those building blocks of concepts and skills that students need to learn before they can learn other ones.

4. **Prepare a Pacing Calendar.** Referring to the school district master calendar, create a curriculum pacing calendar for implementing the units of study to ensure that all Priority Standards will be taught, assessed, retaught, and reassessed throughout the school year. Factor in a "buffer" (two or more days, up to five) between units for the purpose of reteaching and reassessing close-to-proficient students, intervening and reassessing far-from-proficient students, and enriching proficient and above students. Adjust the length and/or duration of each unit of study so that all of the units can be implemented before the end of the school year.

5. **Construct the Unit Planning Organizer.** Brainstorm a list of elements to include on a unit planning organizer that will be used to create each unit of study. Draft a sample template that includes all of these elements. Revise the template as needed while designing the curricular units.

Design the Curricular Units, From Start to Finish (12 Steps)

With the standards foundation in place, design each curricular unit of study, from start to finish. Here is a synopsis of each of the 12 sequential steps for doing so. Be sure all of these elements (except the weekly and daily planners) appear on the agreed-upon unit planning organizer. Note the critical positioning of the "unwrapping" process as the first three steps in the unit design sequence.

1. **"Unwrap" the Unit Priority Standards.** "Unwrap" the assigned Priority Standards within each individual unit of study to determine the specific, teachable concepts and skills (what students need to know and be able to do) in those standards.

2. **Create a Graphic Organizer.** Create a graphic organizer (outline, bulleted list, concept map, or chart) as a visual display of the "unwrapped" concepts and skills, organized into two parts: one that lists related concepts under headings and the other that lists each skill, related concept, and approximate levels of the revised Bloom's Taxonomy and Webb's Depth of Knowledge. Matching each skill and related concept with the thinking skill levels reveals the skill's degree of rigor.

3. **Decide the Big Ideas and Essential Questions.** Decide the topical Big Ideas (key understandings, student "aha's") derived from the "unwrapped" concepts and

skills for that unit of study. Write Essential Questions that will engage students to discover for themselves the related Big Ideas and state them in their own words by the end of the unit.

4. **Create the End-of-Unit Assessment.** Create the end-of-unit assessment (either individual classroom or common formative post-assessment) directly aligned to the "unwrapped" Priority Standards and their levels of rigor. Align the concepts, skills, and format of the end-of-unit assessment with district or school benchmark assessments (K–8) or midterms and finals/end-of-course exams (9–12).

5. **Create the Unit Pre-Assessment.** Create the pre-assessment aligned or "mirrored" to the post-assessment. "Aligned" means the questions are directly matched to those on the post-assessment but may be fewer in number. "Mirrored" means the pre-assessment will be the exact replica of the number and types of questions that will appear on the post-assessment.

6. **Identify Additional Vocabulary Terms, Interdisciplinary Connections, and 21st-Century Learning Skills.** In addition to the vocabulary of the "unwrapped" Priority Standards concepts, identify other specific academic or technical vocabulary from the supporting standards and text materials that students will need to learn during the unit. Identify any interdisciplinary connections and 21st-century learning skills to emphasize when planning engaging learning experiences and related instruction.

7. **Plan Engaging Learning Experiences.** Design meaningful learning activities directly based upon the "unwrapped" concepts and skills, additional vocabulary terms, interdisciplinary connections, and 21st-century learning skills. Plan engaging learning experiences—authentic performance tasks with real-world applications—that challenge students to utilize deep thought, investigation, and communication. Create accompanying scoring guides (rubrics) as the means for obtaining objective evidence of student learning relative to the standards in focus. Confirm that the planned learning experiences will give students the conceptual and procedural understanding of the "unwrapped" concepts, skills, and levels of rigor they will need to be successful on the end-of-unit post-assessment. These carefully planned learning tasks should be designed to "deliver" students to the Big Ideas of the unit.

8. **Gather Resource Materials.** Gather print materials and seek out technology resources that support the planned learning experiences for the unit. Select the most appropriate instructional resources and materials available that will assist students in learning and applying the "unwrapped" concepts and skills and discovering the Big Ideas.

9. **Select High-Impact Instructional Strategies.** Select high-impact instructional strategies (research-based, differentiation, enrichment, intervention, special education, English language learner, others) that teachers can use during instruction and related learning activities with the whole class, with small groups, and with individual students who have specific learning needs.

10. **Detail the Unit Planning Organizer.** Determine what additional details are needed to supplement the generally worded information on the unit planning organizer. For example, an instructional pacing and sequence of the "unwrapped" concepts and skills based on "learning progressions" (the sequence of concepts and skills students need to know and be able to do as prerequisites for learning the next set of concepts and skills); a listing of specific instructional strategies for specific students based on their learning needs (advanced students, at-risk students, special education students, English language learners) along with suggestions for how to use them.

11. **Create Informal Progress-Monitoring Checks.** Find, design, or suggest quick, informal checks for student understanding (exit slips, short-answer questions, thumbs up/down, etc.)—aligned to the end-of-unit assessment and administered in conjunction with "learning progressions"—for educators to use during the unit of study in order to gauge student understanding and adjust instruction accordingly.

12. **Write the Weekly Plan; Design the Daily Lessons.** Write the weekly lesson plan to implement the unit of study in weekly "installments," using it to guide and focus instruction of the targeted "unwrapped" concepts and skills and engage students in the planned learning experiences and assessments. Design the daily lessons to align with the related weekly plan. (Note: This final step, in particular, is to be completed by classroom educators—not the curriculum design teams.)

How to Implement Each Unit of Study (14 Steps)

When the unit planning organizers are completed and ready to use, implement each of the units according to the scheduled pacing calendars. Here is a brief description of the 14 steps for doing so:

1. **Introduce the Unit of Study to Students.** Present the unit's Essential Questions to students and explain that they will be able to respond to these questions in their own words by the end of the unit. Preview for students the "unwrapped" concepts and other academic vocabulary terms they will be learning and applying.

2. **Administer the Unit Pre-Assessment.** Set the stage by first explaining to students the purpose of a pre-assessment (not for a grade, but to find out what they already know and don't know about the upcoming unit of study so that the teacher can plan instruction accordingly). Then administer the common formative pre-assessment (or individual classroom or program pre-assessment, if not part of a collaborative team).

3. **Score and Analyze Student Data.** Score and analyze student pre-assessments individually or with colleagues in grade-level or course-specific instructional Data Teams to diagnose student learning needs.

4. **Decide How to Differentiate Instruction.** Referring to the unit details provided with the unit planning organizer, decide how to differentiate instruction for specific students based on pre-assessment evidence—including the enrichment of any students who are already proficient prior to unit instruction.

5. **Begin Teaching the Unit.** Begin teaching the planned unit of study, flexibly grouping students according to their learning needs and using identified instructional strategies.

6. **Administer Progress-Monitoring Checks.** Administer frequent, informal progress-monitoring checks aligned to the end-of-unit assessment—that coincide with the building-block progression of "unwrapped" concepts and skills—in order to make accurate inferences regarding students' understanding. These informal checks will assist individual educators and instructional Data Teams in monitoring the effectiveness of their targeted teaching strategies for the unit.

7. **Differentiate Instruction Based on Progress-Monitoring Checks.** Modify and adjust instruction for individual students, small groups, and/or the entire class based on the results of the informal checks for understanding.

8. **Schedule Mid-Unit Evaluation of Instructional Strategies.** Schedule a mid-unit evaluation of the targeted teaching and differentiation strategies to determine their effectiveness. During this meeting, participating teachers will share effective use of the targeted strategies and may decide to change any strategies that are not accomplishing their intended purpose. Individual educators who are not part of an instructional Data Team will reflect on the effectiveness of their own selected strategies and make any needed changes.

9. **Continue Teaching the Unit.** During the remaining weeks of the unit, continue teaching the "unwrapped" concepts and skills in the predetermined "learning progressions" sequence for specific learning activities and engaging learning experiences (authentic performance tasks). Continue using the targeted instructional strategies with all students, different groups of students, and individual students as planned.

10. **Continue Modifying and Adjusting Instruction.** Continue modifying and adjusting instruction as needed for individual students, small groups, and/or the entire class based on evidence derived from ongoing progress-monitoring checks.

11. **Administer the End-of-Unit Assessment.** Administer the common formative post-assessment (or individual end-of-unit assessment if not part of a collaborative team).

12. **Score and Analyze Student Data.** Score and analyze student data individually or with colleagues in grade-level or course-specific instructional Data Teams. Celebrate successes! Plan how to address students' identified learning needs during the "buffer" days/week.

13. **Enrich, Remediate, and Intervene.** During the "buffer" days/week scheduled between the unit of study just completed and the next one scheduled, reteach differently those students who are still not proficient; use Tier 2 and 3 intervention strategies and other appropriate strategies for at-risk students. Reassess all non-proficient students. Enrich those students who are proficient and advanced.

14. Reflect and Begin Again. When the unit is officially completed, reflect individually and/or with colleagues about what worked well and what, if anything, should be changed the next time the unit is implemented. Take a deep breath, redirect your focus, and then repeat the process with the next unit of study.

"Unwrapping" Success

The "unwrapping" process provides a simple way to make sense of complicated standards. As foundational as the practice is to designing a rigorous curriculum and assessments directly aligned to the Priority Standards for each unit of study, "unwrapping" the standards can pave the way to improved instruction and increased success for all students. Here's hoping this process will become a valuable aid to doing so, for you and your colleagues. Wishing you all the best!

REFERENCES

Ainsworth, L. (2003). *"Unwrapping" the standards: A simple process to make standards manageable.* Englewood, CO: Advanced Learning Press.

Ainsworth, L. (2010). *Planning for rigorous curriculum design training manual.* Englewood, CO: Lead + Learn Press.

Ainsworth, L. (2010). *Rigorous curriculum design: How to create curricular units of study that align standards, instruction, and assessment.* Englewood, CO: Lead + Learn Press.

Ainsworth, L. (2011). Connecting common core state standards with common formative assessments. In Book four, *Navigating assessment and collaboration with the common core state standards.* Englewood, CO: Lead + Learn Press.

Ainsworth, L. (2013). *Prioritizing the common core: Identifying specific standards to emphasize the most.* Englewood, CO: Lead + Learn Press.

Ainsworth, L., & Viegut, D. (2006). *Common formative assessments: How to connect standards-based instruction and assessment.* Thousand Oaks, CA: Corwin.

Anderson, L. W., & Krathwohl, D. R. (Eds.). (2001). *A taxonomy for learning, teaching, and assessing: A revision of Bloom's taxonomy of educational objectives.* New York, NY: Longman.

Bloom, B. S., et al. (1956). *The taxonomy of educational objectives: Handbook I, cognitive domain.* New York, NY: David McKay.

Brady, M. (2000, May). The standards juggernaut. *Phi Delta Kappan, 81*(9), 649–651.

Brualdi, A. C. (1998). Classroom questions: ERIC/AE Digest (ERIC Publications ERIC Digests in Full Text No. EDO-TM-98-02 RR93002002). Washington, DC: ERIC Clearinghouse on Assessment and Evaluation.

Carmichael, S. B., Martino, G., Porter-Magee, K., & Wilson, W. S. (2010, July). The state of state standards—and the common core—in 2010. Washington, DC: Thomas Fordham Institute. Retrieved from http://www.edexcellence.net/publications/the-state-of-state-of-standards-and-the-common-core-in-2010.html

Erickson, H. L. (2000). *Concept-based curriculum and instruction: Teaching beyond the facts.* Thousand Oaks, CA: Corwin Press.

Hattie, J. A. (2009). *Visible learning: A synthesis of over 800 meta-analyses relating to achievement.* New York, NY: Routledge.

Hattie, J. (2012). *Visible learning for teachers: Maximizing impact on learning.* New York, NY: Routledge.

Hess, K. K. (2004–2012). Center for Assessment, National Center for the Improvement of Educational Assessment, Inc. [papers posted and available] www.nciea.org

Hess, K. K. (2011). *Learning progressions frameworks designed for use with the common core state standards in English language arts & literacy K–12* (PDF document). Retrieved from http://www.naacpartners.org/publications/ELA_LPF_12.2011_final.pdf

Hess, K. K. (2013). *A guide for using Webb's depth of knowledge with common core state standards.* Washington, DC: Common Core Institute. Retrieved from http://cliu21cng.wikispaces.com/file/view/WebsDepthofKnowledgeFlipChart.pdf/457670878/WebsDepthofKnowledgeFLIPChart.pdf

Mayer, R. E. (2004). Should there be a three-strikes rule against pure discovery learning? The case for guided methods of instruction. *American Psychologist, 59,* 14–19.

Mayer, R. E. (2009). Constructivism as a theory of learning versus constructivism as a prescription for instruction. In S. Tobias and T. M. Duffy (Eds.), *Constructivist theory applied to instruction: Success or failure?* (pp. 184–200). New York, NY: Taylor & Francis.

Mayer, R. E., Stull, A., DeLeeuw, K., Almeroth, K., Bimber, B., Chun, D., Bulger, M., Campbell, J., Knight, A., & Zhang, H. (2009). Clickers in college classrooms: Fostering learning with questioning methods in large lecture classes. *Contemporary Educational Psychology, 34*(1), 51–57.

Sato, E., Lagunoff, R., & Worth, P. (2011, March). Smarter Balanced Assessment Consortium common core state standards analysis: Eligible content for the summative assessment: Final report. WestEd. Retrieved from http://www.smarterbalanced.org/wordpress/wp-content/uploads/2011/12/Smarter-Balanced-CCSS-Eligible-Content-Final-Report.pdf

Tomlinson, C. A. (2003). *Fulfilling the promise of the differentiated classroom: Strategies and tools for responsive teaching.* Alexandria, VA: ASCD.

Traver, R. (1998, March). What is a good guiding question? *Educational Leadership, 55*(6), 70–73.

Webb, N. (1997). Research Monograph Number 6: Criteria for alignment of expectations and assessments on mathematics and science education. Washington, DC: Council of Chief State School Officers.

Wiggins, G., & McTighe, J. (1998). *Understanding by design.* Alexandria, VA: Association for Supervision and Curriculum Development.

Wiggins, G., & McTighe, J. (2005). *Understanding by design* (2nd ed.). Alexandria, VA: Association for Supervision and Curriculum Development.

Wiggs, M. D. (2011). Gaining a deeper understanding of the common core state standards: The big picture. In D. B. Reeves, et al., *Navigating implementation of the common core state standards.* Englewood, CO: Lead + Learn Press.

INDEX